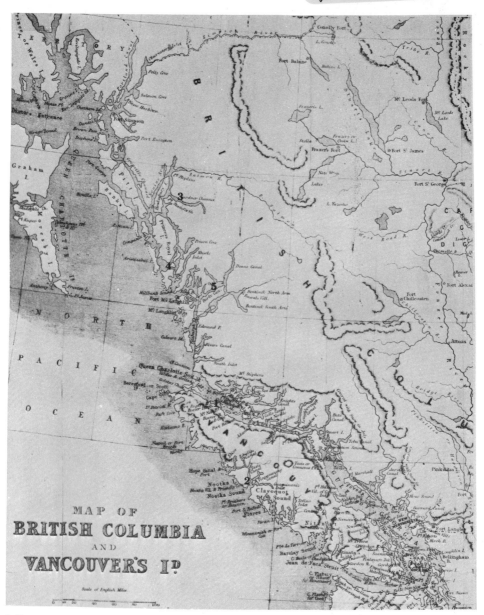

MAP OF
BRITISH COLUMBIA
AND
VANCOUVER'S I.D

Scale of English Miles

1. Fort Rupert Kwakiutl
2. Nootka
3. Haisla
4. Heiltsuq
5. Bella Coola

GOLDMAN, Irving. The mouth of heaven; an introduction to Kwakiutl religious thought. Wiley-Interscience, 1975. 265p map bibl 75-8742. 13.50. ISBN 0-471-31140-5. C.I.P.

Using George Hunt's original translations of his vast corpus of Kwakiutl texts as well as Franz Boas's edited versions, Goldman reinterprets Kwakiutl Indian religion and through it the main features of Kwakiutl culture. Descent, marriage, rank, the winter ceremonial, the potlatch, and warfare all become something different from what Boas, Codere, and others have found. This is likely to be an influential and controversial book. It will appeal especially to those who, inspired by Lévi-Strauss, are discovering new meanings in myths and rituals and relating them to social structures. But it has serious faults: Goldman does not explain his methods and so we cannot know whether he has systematically sifted through the Hunt-Boas corpus or simply dipped in here and there and come up with supporting statements. And it is painfully clear that Goldman is utterly naive about the Kwakiutl language; e.g., he simplifies Boas's spellings so that words pronounced differently look alike and then on the basis of these false likenesses he constructs false etymologies to support hypotheses about conceptual linkages. Still, his hypotheses are stimulating and should

send many readers back to the source. Recommended for upper-division and graduate programs, especially if the Kwakiutl texts are also available.

THE MOUTH
OF HEAVEN

IRVING GOLDMAN is a Professor of Anthropology at Sarah Lawrence College, Bronxville, New York. He holds a Ph.D. in anthropology from Columbia University. He has received honors and grants from the Bollingen Foundation Fellowship, the Social Science Research Council Fellowship, the American Philosophical Society, and has conducted field research in Northwest Canada and the Northwest Amazon. He is also author of *The Cubes: Indians of the Northwest Amazon* and *Ancient Polynesian Society.*

The mouth of heaven, the great face of a
man's mask which is looking right down upon our
lower world; the mouth of heaven at the place
where the sun and moon are walking. As soon,
it is said, as the sun comes near the mouth
of heaven, the mouth of heaven takes the sun in
its mouth and swallows it.

A NAKWAXDAX INDIAN, Boas 1930:179

The Mouth of Heaven

AN INTRODUCTION
TO
KWAKIUTL RELIGIOUS THOUGHT

IRVING GOLDMAN

A WILEY-INTERSCIENCE PUBLICATION

JOHN WILEY & SONS, New York ● London ● Sydney ● Toronto

Library of Congress Cataloging in Publication Data:

Goldman, Irving, 1911-
    The mouth of heaven.

    Continues Ancient Polynesian society.
    "A Wiley-Interscience publication."
    Bibliography: p.
    Includes index.
    1. Kwakiutl Indians—Religion and mythology.
2. Kwakiutl Indians—Social life and customs.
I. Title.
E99.K9G64   299'.7   75-8742
ISBN 0-471-31140-5

Printed in the United States of America

10 9 8 7 6 5 4 3 2 1

To Hannah

PREFACE

Tlogwe is a gift of special powers, an ultimate treasure that spirits give to those Kwakiutl who have dared to enter their secret realms. The recipient, first to be benefited and elevated by the gift, is then allowed the privilege of becoming a benefactor of his community.

In this way, too, through the work of Franz Boas and George Hunt—one the distinguished product of the European academic tradition, the other the gifted son of a Tlingit Indian mother and a Scottish tradesman—we have become the beneficiaries of the treasure of ethnographic knowledge they brought out from the hidden world of Kwakiutl culture. Perhaps the Kwakiutl Indians understood in some way the continuity between their religious mission and the scientific mission of our culture. Hunt surely valued his role as "mediator" between the alien worlds of the Indian and the "Western" scholar.

The alliance between Boas and Hunt made possible the acquisition for posterity and for all mankind of what is probably the greatest single ethnographic treasure. It is not its size alone that gives the Kwakiutl ethnography its prodigious value; it is its authenticity. Unlike many modern field studies that exhibit the writer's methods and theoretical allegiances more than they do their subject, the Boas and Hunt ethnography is in the words and imagery of the Kwakiutl. By freeing ethnography from its confused and labyrinthine entanglement with the alien psyche and intellectual predilections of the ethnographer, Boas and Hunt created the foundations for a genuine ethnology.

And like one of the great *tlogwe*, those magical boxes of the Kwakiutl with their inexhaustible treasure of food and wealth, the Kwakiutl ethnography should nourish the theoretical interests of the profession for generations to come. No matter how scholars may choose to theorize about Kwakiutl, the primary sources will always be there for verification. What all field workers must dread most—that their misconceptions and misunderstandings may remain forever engraved as "truth" because they have not allowed the native to speak for himself—does not apply to the Kwakiutl ethnography. Boas never claimed to "understand" Kwakiutl culture. Some of his interpretative observations are clearly mistaken, but error based on misunderstanding is part of the texture of science, and surely it is no mortal sin. Of the mortal sin of science, the cover-up, Boas is wholly innocent, for every statement made by him about the Kwakiutl can be verified or refuted by the full ethnographic record he made available.

From the presence of so solid a primary source as the Kwakiutl ethnography, "armchair anthropologists" draw the freedom to theorize, to analyze, to interpret, to speculate. They are in no danger of "putting anything over," because refutation is immediately at hand.

The presence of this rich textual source makes me bold and in addition I claim a certain natural connection with the material on Kwakiutl. I was a student of Boas, I worked for him as an assistant on Northwest Coast problems, and I did field work among neighboring Indians. My first teaching was a course on Indians of the Northwest Coast, and I contributed the chapter on Kwakiutl to Mead's work on *Cooperation and Competition Among Primitive Peoples* (1937). Boas gave Kwakiutl and the Northwest Coast a commanding place in the intellectual development of his graduate students at Columbia, as did Ruth Benedict.

Even when I went on to do field work in the South American tropical forest and to work for several years in nonacademic anthropology, the Kwakiutl, or rather the enigma of Kwakiutl culture, remained a haunting presence. Ruth Benedict seemed gifted with a poet's vision of Kwakiutl, but Boas did not hide his bafflement. Like generations of students before me, I waited for the definitive and comprehensive synthesis that would translate the raw ethnography into systematic exposition. The anticipated exposition never came. Boas had evidently decided on the limits of his contribution. He had completed the first and by far the most important phase of Kwakiutl studies. Like a Moses he had brought us to the margins of the promised land. The rest was up to the new generations.

The Boas and Hunt ethnographies have been worked over by many. Most scholars were attracted to the "potlach"; some to the apparent oddities of social stratification, including slavery among "primitive hunters", some to the oddity of descent groups which were neither matrilineal, patrilineal, bilateral, nor exogamous, some to the arts, which are among the most highly developed in North America. It is a curious reflection on the state of ethnological maturity in English-speaking anthropology that the subject on which the corpus of Kwakiutl ethnography was most complete, namely, Kwakiutl religious thought, has been virtually ignored. Boas's original aim to reveal to the outside world the character of Kwakiutl thought was achieved only insofar as the new data were set in print. The only attempt at a thoroughgoing understanding of Kwakiutl religious thought has been that of Müller (1955), a work practically unknown in the English-speaking world. Locher's interesting study (1932) of the serpent theme in Kwakiutl religion was devastated by Boas's review (1933) and never gained credence.

For the most part, scholars seem to have behaved like scavengers, tearing from the flesh of Kwakiutl culture whatever juicy morsel tempted them, ignoring the shape of the being. For this reason the hermeneutical writings on Kwakiutl suffer the same defect. They assume one can understand the part without reference to the whole. Ruth Benedict's classic integrative essay (1934) is selective rather than comprehensive. Nonetheless, it does seek to create a context for specific institutions. Mauss had an approach that recognized the necessity of studying exchange as a "total phenomenon," but did little to carry it out.

Why anthropological scholars have ignored the very rich data on Kwakiutl religious thought that Boas and Hunt so painstakingly assembled is a subject for the intellectual historian to pursue. It seems almost embarrassingly obvious to have to say that without a reasonable understanding of the religious conceptions of a traditional tribal society one cannot understand anything of their secular conceptions. Only a backward sociological tradition dares postulate general theory from only partial examination of available data.

The proverbial committee of blind men could not conjure up the shape of a real elephant. Thus scholars who have examined only portions of the Kwakiutl cultural anatomy have inevitably produced a bizare image. They have projected Kwakiutl character as pathological. They have seen in distribution and exchange archaic forms of welfare and old age insurance, or primitive banking complete with investments earning very high rates of interest. They have seen distressing forms of materialism together with distasteful manifestations of aggressive invidiousness and status climbing. Some have had to defend the Kwakiutl by pointing to examples of an "amiable side." By and large, however, the Kwakiutl "image" has been harshly drawn by writers who have viewed the parts rather than the whole. Without question, the harshest judgment has come from Edward Curtis, who followed Boas among the Kwakiutl between 1910 and 1914. He was stirred by them to write:

> . . . one is impelled to question their knowledge of any such thing as spiritual exaltation or mental pleasure, except as such may be aroused by the gratification of savage passions or purely physical instincts. Chastity, genuine, self-sacrificing friendship, even the inviolability of a guest—a cardinal principle among most Indian tribes—are unknown. It is scarcely exaggeration to say that no single noble trait redeems the Kwakiutl character. (1915:4)

My own effort to bring out main principles of Kwakiutl religious thought lays no claim to completeness either. The totality of available data is well beyond the scope of a single volume, and perhaps beyond the professional lifetime of one scholar. I have sought only to set forth a concept of completeness by filling in a major void in Kwakiutl studies, so that seemingly secular subjects such as economy, rank, lineage, and marriage as well as more arcane subjects such as Kwakiutl cultural character and psyche can be seen in the more genuine context of a religious perspective. When that perspective has been overlooked or maladroitly converted into sociological syllogism, the Kwakiutl image is distorted.

The basic principles of Kwakiutl religious thought are not overly esoteric. The religious ideas, however, are elaborated and repeated in almost endless variation throughout a richly developed body of myth, ritual, and graphic art. A full study of this variety of religious reflection and expression would significantly enrich our comprehension of Kwakiutl. That task remains for a later work or for others who may wish to pursue the subject.

Even though I have not ventured too deeply into symbolic and structural analysis of the system of religious thought, I have tried to be true to Kwakiutl standards of concreteness. The substance of analysis and interpretation has been drawn almost exclusively from the Kwakiutl texts, from both the published and manuscript versions. I have also drawn on Boas's invaluable materials on grammar and vocabulary, and on his summaries of religious concepts and mythological themes. I have been attentive to Boas's personal interpretations of Kwakiutl, and always in keeping with his teaching, have taken the texts themselves as the final guides to interpretation. The texts reveal the lines of thought and the characteristic chains of symbolic associations.

The focus of the work is squarely on Kwakiutl religious thought. I assume, nevertheless, that general observations on Kwakiutl are pertinent to general anthropological theory in several directions. Those general observations that I have drawn seem to me to have particular bearing on theories of exchange, alliance, marriage, descent, chiefship, rank, social stratification (primitive aristocracy), ritual, and religion.

I acknowledge with gratitude the research assistance of my former student, Miss Sidney Schuler. Christopher Boehm, a colleague, read most of the manuscript in early stages and was more than generous with counsel and criticism. I owe special thanks to Professor Alfonso Ortiz for his critical appraisal of a final draft of the manuscript. And Eric Valentine, my editor, I thank warmly for patient and tactful encouragement. I owe thanks to the Columbia University Libraries for making available the Boas and Hunt manuscript materials, and to the Research Libraries of the New York Public Library for an early map of Vancouver Island.

My ultimate acknowledgment is to Boas and Hunt. Boas's position is secure among the immortals of anthropology. Intellectual history owes a special place among the ranks to George Hunt, a full-fledged ethnographer on his own, and second to none in the demanding discipline of authentic collection and description. His personal genius is a reflection of the intellectual caliber of his civilization.

The design motif appearing at the beginnings of chapters is taken from Audrey Hawthorn, *Art of the Kwakiutl and Other Northwest Coast Tribes*, University of Washington Press, Seattle, Washington, 1967, by permission of the publisher.

May 1975

NOTE ON ORTHOGRAPHY

Since this is not a linguistic study, I have taken the liberty of simplifying the Boas and Hunt orthography by omitting all diacritical markings, and by substituting conventional letters for the phonetic symbols used in their manuscripts and published texts. Linguists and specialists have available in the published texts the precise phonetics as set down by Boas. His posthumous work on suffixes (1947) is his final and definitive rendering. I use the term *numema* for lineage as a compromise between Hunt's *numemot* and Boas's *numaym* and *numayma*.

CONTENTS

CONTENTS

THE MOUTH
OF HEAVEN

I

INTRODUCTION

This book is a sequel to my *Ancient Polynesian Society*; it carries the examination of "primitive aristocracies" from the Pacific Islands to the forested shores of the Northwest Coast of North America. For reasons that remain to be discovered, the Indian tribes of this area share formal principles of rank, lineage, and kinship with Pacific islanders. At the same time, each of these civilizations has its distinctive culture. The Kwakiutl, especially, seem very close to what I have designated as the "traditional" Polynesian society. They share with Polynesians a status system of graded hereditary ranking of individuals and of lineages; a social class system of chiefs ("nobles"), commoners, and slaves; concepts of primogeniture and seniority of descent lines; a concept of abstract supernatural powers as special attributes of chiefs; and a lineage system that leans toward patriliny, but acknowledges the maternal lines as well. Finally, Kwakiutl and eastern Polynesians, especially, associate ambiguity of lineage membership with "Hawaiian" type kinship, a fully classificatory system that does not distinguish between maternal and paternal sides, or between siblings and cousins.

Similarities in social systems are countered by major contrasts in economy and ritual pattern. Polynesia has the most meager mammalian life, and must depend heavily on horticulture, arborculture, and deep sea fishing. Kwakiutl combine river and sea fishing with vigorous hunting of land and sea mammals. Polynesian economy is an offshoot of Southeast Asia, that of Kwakiutl, of Eskimo-Aleut and maritime Northeastern Siberia. In short, Polynesian aristocracy is associated with farming, which historians of culture consider to be a progressive force.

In its associations with arctic and subarctic hunting traditions, Kwakiutl aristocracy draws upon a distinctive, highly productive economy, but one specialized in another direction, and with more limited capacity for food storage. Taking into account the even more important ideological concomitants of habitat and economy, these distinctions may help explain why Polynesian aristocracies eventually created states—though on a relatively small scale—and why the Kwakiutl and other tribes of the Northwest Coast never achieved a genuine political consciousness. In Polynesia, aristocratic forms and concepts evolved in political directions. And on the Northwest Coast, as in Polynesia, rank differences generally provoked animated status rivalry. But the setting of antagonistic rivalries remained essentially ritualistic, and nowhere on the Northwest Coast did chiefs command the political powers of their Polynesian counterparts.

Perhaps the most important distinction between Polynesian and Kwakiutl concepts of generalized powers is in attribution to person. *Mana* is a direct attribute of the Polynesian chief. The power, having come down the lineage, resides as a sacred force within the body of the chief, and separates him physically from his community. Even indirect contact with him is dangerous. Tahitian chiefs were carried about so as not to endanger the soil with their sanctity. Their personal sanctity could touch all men and all produce. *Mana* radiated supernatural power and carried political potency in its wake.

Kwakiutl *nawalak* is a self-contained power. It is possessed, but not as a direct attribute of the person. The Kwakiutl chief held sacred powers, but was not personally *tapu*. The *mana* of the Polynesian chief was always present; *nawalak* was to be exhibited, but only on special occasions. In exhibiting his powers the Kwakiutl chief depersonalized himself to impersonate the supernatural being from whom the power had been originally acquired. If politics is the practice of personal persuasions and influences, neither the Polynesian nor the Kwakiutl chiefs could be considered true political leaders. *Mana* moved the Polynesians toward the political, however; *nawalak* immersed their Kwakiutl counterpart more deeply within the world of myth.

The religious imagery of the farmer is generally speaking cooler, less intense, than that of the hunter. Both build around the inevitable theme of renewal of life. Indeed primitive peoples, even as they distinguish hunting from farming as symbolic activities, are careful to preserve the sense of unity of all forms of life, animal and vegetable. Pueblo Indian farmers, for example, associate crops, obviously enough, with summer and with rain ritual, and hunting with winter. They also associate crops with ritual attitudes of benevolence and nonaggression, and the winter hunting season with warfare, illness, and ritual attitudes of antagonism.

The unifying idea is of plants and animals as sentient and responsive to human sentiments toward them. The specific relationships between men and plants and between men and animals are significantly distinctive. Plants may require generalized respect, but because of their closeness to the human species, animals make demands comparable to those of humans. To give life to men the animal must yield his own life, an action regarded among Kwakiutl as among Eskimo as supreme sacrifice. Especially because of their kinship with men the animals' self-sacrifice introduces an extraordinary and intensely personal note into the hunting economy. Whether he acts out of guilt or out of an ethic of equity (in which guilt may or may not be involved), the Kwakiutl hunter cannot free himself from his primordial links with the animal world. Whichever way his aspirations turn he is involved with the animals who grant him his life. Polynesians have no such personally intense connections with their crops, nor with fish.

The religious logic of the hunter, especially its Kwakiutl version, creates the natural ambience for the shaman. The logic of the hunter is brutally concise: life demands deaths. From this binary opposition rooted in the nature of all organic life and understood by all mankind, the Kwakiutl have drawn a variety of logical extensions. For them as hunters the issue of life reemerging from death has a special urgency, the urgency of meeting obligations of reciprocity. Between human beings reciprocity need be little more than a simple action of mutual respect. Between men and the animals they hunt, reciprocity expands into cosmic proportions. At the cosmic level, reciprocity is the reply to the logical possibility of entropy. What is given must be returned. The life yielded is the life returned, and the species are never exhausted.

From a Judaeo-Christian standpoint shamans are mystics. From the point of view of Siberian tribes, Eskimo, and North American Indians, they are the designated transformers within the life cycle. The shaman's personal mission is to enter the "vale of death" and by returning to demonstrate empirically that reversal is possible. The shamanic "technique of ecstasy," in Eliade's apt phrasing, is appropriate to the mission of reversing the life cycle by going outside the normal boundaries of life.

Among Kwakiutl the chiefs, or the so-called "nobility," are equated with shamans. A chief is not necessarily a curing shaman, and a curing shaman need not be a chief. In their major ritual roles, however, the chiefs are addressed as *paxala* (shaman) and behave as shamans. The supernatural powers of chiefs are akin to those of curing shamans, the "medicine men." Thus there is both a parallel with and a distinction between Kwakiutl and Polynesian chiefs. Both have the sanctity of *mana* as well as the sacred powers that pertain to divine ancestry, but are not necessarily identical with the powers of the tribes' professional priests. The priest need not submit himself to the ecstatic experience; the shaman must. Even though priest-chiefs and shaman-chiefs are alike in the very broad sense, seen close up within cultural-historical perspective they diverge. The shaman-chief tradition does not readily evolve in a political direction. Among Kwakiutl, especially, where shamanism, rank, and chiefship have formed an unusual configuration of leadership, shamans are only partly of the human world. For the rest they are locked in with animal and other spirit beings who also govern their actions. Men could not have advanced politically until they had emancipated themselves from religious identification with the animal world, and with its shamanic accessories.

The animal world imposes itself on concepts of property, or more broadly, on wealth. Kwakiutl wealth is largely in the form of mammalian skins or items such as boxes, canoes, or shield-shaped copper plaques ("coppers") that have animal associations. The skins represent the mammals directly, as the unconsumed and durable manifestation of the gift they make of themselves. The exchange of animal skins involves the human community with the animal world. Polynesian wealth is, by contrast, largely in crop, an animate albeit remote and impersonal product. Because of the relative abstractness of crops the Polynesian economy is readily expandable. The Kwakiutl economy—seen for the moment only in its ideological aspect—can only expand markedly at the risk of

[4]

overkill, a brutal offense against nature. More directly, overkill would be an offense against animal kin who have given freely of themselves with the explicit understanding that they would be preserved and respected. Since the evolution of the political community must be accompanied by economic expansion, the Kwakiutl, in this respect, faced both moral and technical limitations, whereas Polynesians were at least freed of the moral restraints.

It was with a view toward exploring the role of religious thought in the course of development of the aristocratic system that I chose the Kwakiutl as a sequel to Polynesia. Kwakiutl exemplify aristocratic ideas in their most intensely religious form, or, conversely, in their least political form.

The basic idea of an elite, especially of an hereditary elite, is in tribal society a religious idea. How elites arose in the beginning we do not know. What we do know is that wherever elites exist in tribal society they are believed to possess special and supernatural powers. Supernatural powers mark them as superior and they are recognized as leaders. Even if elites had arisen because of notable achievements as warriors or as hunters their superior position would not have been stabilized without the religious idea of the concentration of supernatural powers among a few.

The aristocratic idea takes firm hold when people conceive of the line of descent rather than of the person as the conveyor of supernatural powers. In the "real" world of tribal society, descent is not a sociological abstraction, nor a diagram of a bureaucratic table of organization. Descent is itself a conception of supernatural powers or more simply of the natural powers that govern the continuity of species. As genetic lines in nature differ, some strong and durable, others weak and transient, so, men could imagine, do descent lines. The strongest and most durable lines are so, in the religious conception of descent, because they possess supernatural powers, and hence greater vitality. The person is transient, the line is durable. Accordingly, it is a stable and convincing vehicle for transmitting powers.

There is, of course, no inevitable association between religious superiority and a concept of lines of descent. Eskimo shamans, for example, are a religious elite, but the office need not be inherited. The specific office of curing shaman is not hereditary among Kwakiutl either. Rather, the Kwakiutl descent lines control and transmit a highly abstracted version of shamanism. In this regard, the student of shamanism should find in Kwakiutl religion some important clues on transformation of the doctrine from personalized to more general conceptions. For the student of aristocracy, Kwakiutl illustrates still a broader pattern of transformation. The aristocratic idea takes hold of shamanism and converts it to a broader and more general doctrine. Simultaneously, shamanistic doctrines just as forcefully impose their own religious content on aristocracy.

The religious content of shamanistic doctrines develops within a particular cultural environment, within a particular physical habitat, and within a particular historical tradition. I should not, of course, venture to derive Kwakiutl religion from shamanism exclusively. Religion is foremost a product of human imagination, and imagination is free to improvise and to soar, even while it also pursues its naturalistic tracks. Having been fully exposed to the powerful shamanistic traditions of northeastern Siberia, of the Aleutian Islands, of Eskimo and of adjacent interior Athabascan and even more distant Algonquian, the tribes of the Northwest Coast easily fell under shamanic influence.

If the Kwakiutl are typical, one can argue from the extraordinarily rich information on them that shamanistic doctrines form the core around which the religions of the entire region evolved. That core comprises a constellation of connected ideas: (1) persons endowed with granted powers can overcome death; (2) powers are granted to a human elite by animal and other supernatural beings; (3) having received powers, persons are bound into a permanent alliance with their donors. Growing out of and also meshing with the elementary shamanistic core are elaborations, and sympathetic adhesions from other systems of religious thought. The final product is, certainly in the case of Kwakiutl, an imposing synthesis, a truly integrated system of thought on the one commanding human issue, the continuity of species.

I have said enough in anticipation of the chapters that follow to reveal my point of view. To state this viewpoint more directly, religious ideas and the religious life are at the center from the start, and remain at the center of Kwakiutl aristocracy up to the period of active contacts with Christian missionaries and white traders. The exposition of Kwakiutl aristocracy is, in fact, closely synonymous with the exposition of principles of Kwakiutl religion. Accordingly, the main principles of Kwakiutl culture, those that govern lineage, rank, marriage, the distribution and exchange of property, and rivalries and antagonisms among chiefs are also so closely identified with religion as to be conceived of as religious expressions.

Insofar as religion represents the systematic thought of a people on the major issues of their existence it serves as the integrative model for their culture. If a culture can be said to exist as a coherent system of thought, the source of coherence is in its religion. Yet to assert that religion or systematic religious thought is the source of cultural integration is simple tautology. In the primitive world, generally, religion and culture are identical at their core, if not also at their edges. However, the tautology is in this case tolerable because the identity is not often recognized. The subject of religion is usuallly treated in a single or several chapters in a book, as one of several departments of a culture.

In a phenomenon as hypothetical as "culture," perspective is crucial. Perspective on culture presumes an hypothesis on what is central and what is peripheral; it is a point of view about what things belong together, and may thus be a code word for culture theory. The religious perspective should have the highest scientific value for several reasons. Most important, it is real; it represents the genuine view from within. Second, it is tangible; it is in the words and images of the people. The final synthesis of the religious principles of a nonliterate people is, of necessity, hypothesis. But the meanings of symbols, of symbolic behavior, of religious ceremonies are usually self-explicatory, through tangible chains of association. For example, the Kwakiutl themselves explicate the meaning of copper shields (commonly misunderstood as high value currency) when they identify them as red, as salmon, as light, as capable of death and resurrection, as pertaining to the sky and to the sea, and so on. Third, the religious perspective is close to total, it embraces the whole society. No one who had never known it as part of a whole body could understand an eyeball. Similarly, no one can understand a "potlatch" without seeing it within its whole framework—the total culture. Finally, religion as an integrative system of thought identifies all fundamental concepts. The religious structure arises out of natural observations, out of comprehension of natural principles. Ultimately, then, it is perceived natural principles that integrate a society and govern its structure.

At issue is a definition of religion. All definitions are at best partial and unsatisfactory. Epigrammatic statements can not encompass systems of thought that aim at nothing less than comprehensive explanation of the essentials of life and detailed formulation of how to live by them.

It is sound anthropology that to understand a religion one must seek knowledge from its believers, and not from the alien precincts of other religions or from antireligions. The procedural axiom is most pertinent for "primitive" religions, which always have total control of their community. Contemporary religions contend with the competition of sects, as well as with the more fundamental antagonism of scientific and materialistic thought. Competition alone compels them to yield territory. Against the more powerful competition from scientific materialism, traditional religions either specialize in cult or retreat to the more general areas of morality and ethics.

In tribal societies religion has no competitors. It is in full command of the whole range of philosophic synthesis. It engages at the same time in the most determined empirical observations of nature and in the imaginative reconstruction of reality. All varieties of intellectual endeavor contribute to the formulation of religious systems. There is no school from within to draw the lines, saying, "This is science, that is religion!" Tribal societies have terms for the sacred, but not for religion. They have terms for special powers, but no demarcation between the natural and the supernatural. Our difficulty in defining religion for tribal societies is that *we* have an oppositional vocabulary to separate religious from nonreligious, natural from supernatural; *they* do not. The Kwakiutl distinguish oppositions that we may translate as "sacred-secular." Their concept of what we call sacred, does not, however, encompass their religion. It refers only to the presence of powers and spirits that require appropriate human response.

Periodically our science must refresh itself by dipping again into the ethnographic data. For anthropology, as Boas had wisely insisted, the decisive data are those revealing systematic patterns of native thought. It might also be wise to put aside conventional definitions and try to follow the actual lines of that thought through its own distinctive channels. It may be shortsighted or altogether misleading to reason, for example, that marriage is an alliance phenomenon, so that all the many things the native has to say about marriage rituals and bride and groom symbolism may be dismissed either as not relevant or as mere "superstructure" to the sociology of social linkages. There may be deeper issues in alliance than a sociology of utilitarian linkages. The Kwakiutl are best known for their system of ritual exchanges and distributions of property, the so-called "potlatch." It takes little "deep" analysis to discover that "potlatches," even as they deal in "property," even as they bind outsiders into formal exchanges, even as they reflect on the prestige of chiefs, are basically and decidedly religious actions.

To ignore Kwakiutl meanings in favor of consensus sociological reconstructions is to ignore reality. Surely, no science can claim that deeper realities are reached by bypassing the actual phenomenon. Kwakiutl religious thought on such matters as "potlatches," and marriage, and lineage and rank, and property, in fact, defines their basic reality for the anthropologist. In the cultures of tribal societies, the deeper meanings lie not at the sociological or economic but at the religious levels. As Lévi-Strauss has demonstrated, perhaps once and for all, the "savage mind" is no product of a second-rate intelligence. It has a powerful view of its own on the natural order. Nor can primitive religions, which inevitably draw upon the entire natural order, be dismissed as illusion, or as metaphor for sociological reality. Religious thought has grown around serious reflection and around acute observation on conditions of existence. We are not asked to agree with its formulations, only to take it seriously, to become accustomed to its strange imagery. After we have translated these images into the scholarly idiom of mechanical and inanimate concepts, we may find that they are not so strange after all.

Boas, a dedicated and sophisticated scientist, recognized at the start of his career in anthropology that to understand an alien culture in depth would be a liberating experience. Helen Codere's perceptive introduction to his *Kwakiutl Ethnography* cites in German what Boas had written about anthropology as a liberating science. I translate a portion:

> The only means that will set us free is to sink into a new life, into an understanding of a thought, of a feeling, of a form of behavior that has not grown from the soil of our civilization, but rather has had its sources in another cultural tradition. (Boas 1966: xii)

Codere then goes on to portray Boas's intense scientific interest in revealing to the literate world the precise character of Kwakiutl life and thought. Boas was a scholar in whom the scientific and social conscience were wedded for life. He had in mind liberation both from social and academic dogma.

Boas's great work on the southern Kwakiutl tribes unreservedly merits the acclaim given to the monumental. It began in 1885; was continued through personal visits and through correspondence with George Hunt, his Indian collaborator; and ended only at his death in 1942. He made 12 trips to the Northwest Coast and spent a total of 28.5 months in the field (Boas 1966:xxxi).

Boas, of course, was an accurate and industrious observer on his own. Nevertheless, his most felicitous accomplishment was to train George

Hunt, a half-blood Indian born among the Kwakiutl at Fort Rupert, to write his language phonetically and to serve as informant and field worker. Hunt included with his reports literal interlinear translations that allowed Boas to follow the exact line of Kwakiutl thought and meaning. For publication, Boas corrected the texts according to his own understanding of Kwakiutl phonetics and edited Hunt's translations for greater intelligibility, though sometimes sacrificing in the process a certain amount of the exact Kwakiutl flavor. For example, in recording a family history Hunt wrote, "Now I will sing the stories." Boas translates, "Now I will tell the stories" (Boas 1921:836). It is not a big point. Still, singing a genealogy is unquestionably a religious act, since singing (along with dancing) is the appropriate mode of communication with spirits. To tell a story might be taken as a secular activity. Hunt often translated proper names; Boas, unconvinced, usually left them untranslated, a rather disturbing decision since Kwakiutl names are no mere tags but genuine epithets.

One of the more curious and also misleading examples of translation editing refers to the name of a great spirit, the dominant figure in the very important winter dance festival. This spirit known as Baxbakualanuxsiwae is translated by Hunt as Man Eater at the Mouth of the River, and by Boas as Cannibal-at-North-End-of-World. The literal translation by Hunt is the more significant for two reasons. Since the spirit who devours men is not himself human he is not a "cannibal." He is literally a man-eater, in religious thought. That is a most important distinction. The expression "mouth of the river" has metaphoric significance in unifying the images of a spirit who swallows men and of the mouth of a river, which swallows salmon. Boas's translation is sophisticated, since it takes into account the fact that men who impersonate the Man Eater are also men-eaters and hence cannibals. As for "North-End-of-the-World," Boas explains that the Kwakiutl think of the ocean as a river; like all rivers it flows from the north from whence dangerous powers also come (1897:394). Boas has a case for his translation. Scholars would have been served better, however, by having Hunt's translation accompanied by Boas's alternatives. The most disturbing example of editing was to introduce the foreign word "potlatch" into the texts as a substitution for Hunt's more direct translations. I comment on the consequences of this unfortunate substitution in Chapter 7.

I bring out these few examples not to undermine confidence in Boas's editing of Hunt's translations, for by and large Boas has hewed very close to Hunt, but out of fidelity to Boas's intent. Boas assumed scholars would study both the Kwakiutl and the English texts to catch precise internal meanings. Unfortunately, the texts were not published in interlinear format. In *Ethnology of the Kwakiutl,* the English texts are printed on the upper half of the page, the Kwakiutl on the lower half. In *Contributions to the Ethnology of the Kwakiutl* the two texts are on facing pages. In *Religion of the Kwakiutl Indians* they are in different volumes. Even though keyed by numbered sentences the texts are not easy to match. Hence Boas's expectation that future scholars of Kwakiutl would work closely with the texts was not fulfilled. The unpublished interlinear texts, which are easy to use, did not become reasonably available until they were deposited after Boas's death in the libraries of Columbia University and of the American Philosophical Society in Philadelphia. The original texts in the hand of George Hunt and translated into basic English without the blurring effect of a grander generalizing vocabulary are very close to the original meanings, somewhat closer than the edited and published versions. The manuscripts, together with the published texts, constitute an archival treasure of unique value. They are a virtually inexhaustible source of information on Kwakiutl life and thought. Needless to say, I do not represent my work as revealing all the riches they contain.

The information recorded by Hunt, who carried out much of the field work, does not fall into familiar categories. It does not follow directly the questions a sociologically-oriented anthropology was asking. Yet his procedures meet the highest standards of accurate field work—that is, the text is seldom slanted to the Western sensibility. Most of the texts are long narratives that follow the Kwakiutl lines of interest and are in the Kwakiutl literary style. The Boas-Hunt texts are unique in the anthropological literature for their scope and depth, and, above all, for directness of access to the real data. They are in the setting of a Kwakiutl discussing his culture with another Kwakiutl. They bypass the serious problem of communicating with the Western anthropologist, who is either illiterate or clumsy in the native tongue. No anthropologist needs to be reminded of the inadequacy of our understanding of the inner meanings of an alien culture. The problem of understanding the Kwakiutl texts is still present, but then so are the texts. As the discipline of anthropology gains ground in this direction, it will eventually enter more deeply into the cultural recesses of at least this one tribe.

The character of the field data baffled Boas as it has later scholars.

He wrote only one descriptive general work on the Indians. *The Social Organization and Secret Societies of the Kwakiutl* was completed well before the basic data from the Hunt texts were gathered, and so is incomplete. It is, nevertheless, one of the truly remarkable monographs in the anthropological literature. Its merit is not so much in elucidation of principles of Kwakiutl culture, but in description that is so richly detailed that one is seized by the extraordinary and special character of the Indians. Since the time of Boas, and under the driving influence of the sociological tradition, ethnography has veered to the general, dissolving the unique qualities that are the life of a people into a standard formula that kills the culture as surely as a chemical dye kills a laboratory specimen. The "trouble" with Boas's own work and with the Hunt texts was that the profession could not devise the means to kill the Kwakiutl. Because he brought forth a body of information so genuine and refractory it would not easily dissolve, Boas was chided for having held back the development of anthropological theory.

Boas was the first to concede he did not have the "key" to Kwakiutl; he would not yield to simplifications. Perhaps no other field worker was more respectful of the profundity and complexity of native thought, or more zealous in sustaining the scientific principle of total coherence. If a culture is not first grasped as a whole, one cannot understand its parts. Boas sought total descriptions of all phenomena pertaining to Kwakiutl thought. He published fully on myth and religion. His observations in the field on the Winter Ceremonial and on transfers of copper shields are supplemented and corroborated by repeated accounts in the texts, and in the real context of family histories. He published a Kwakiutl grammar and prepared a supplementary grammatical study (published posthumously in 1947). He wrote on the graphic arts and on cooking. Although incomplete, his presentation of social structure is nonetheless powerful and challenging precisely because he would not compromise the integrity of the material to conventional sociological generalizations.

The difficulty Boas and others had with Kwakiutl social structure was due partly to the ravages of history. When Boas began his field work in 1885 the Indian population had already declined precipitously. Disease had been brought in by fur traders and other aliens, and several communities had moved to Fort Rupert where the Hudson's Bay Company had established its post in 1849. Traditional forms of residence and succession had been disrupted enough to obscure the original principles and norms. Christianity, cash economy, and general commercialism had already blanketed traditional exchanges and ritual relationships with a new pragmatic ethic. A Kwakiutl culture was still evident, but it was shaken and twisted, and was struggling desperately to find a firm footing in a slippery situation.

No field situation is more treacherous to the conscientious observer than this—a society in active disequilibrium. In this situation, Boas's empiricism could mislead him, unless he could establish once and for all what was old Kwakiutl and what was new. Inexplicably, because he had all the necessary data in hand, Boas never corrected his early misconstruction of the "potlatch," which he observed only in its new and commercialized setting. But his knowledge of Northwest Coast societies did help him to reconstruct shrewdly the earlier conditions of Kwakiutl lineages and tribes.

Although Boas's empiricism compelled him to record only what he saw and heard, it did not distract him from his central task, which was to record the traditional patterns of Kwakiutl thought. All field work among Kwakiutl after Boas, except for that of Curtis, describes mainly a new or postclassic Kwakiutl. Boas's information reaches back to the precontact period through the memories of old survivors, and through traditional family histories. One such history, that of a Gwasela tribe's chiefly lines, covers 23 generations, a span of almost 400 years (Boas 1921:836–884). Like the Polynesian, the Kwakiutl family histories are regarded by the Indians as authentic genealogical records. The narrator of this history, for example, remarks accurately on the founding of Fort Rupert as a fur trading post. In her ensuing narrative, woolen blankets begin to replace the traditional animal skins in ritual exchange. This momentous cultural shift to store-bought commodities is accurately recorded in the family histories.

It is not unusual for a culture to go underground in the memories of its survivors, at least for some time. Boas's field work, which began 35 years after the founding of Fort Rupert and 100 years after the fur trade had begun among the Kwakiutl, tapped the memory veins to the past. Yet it also recorded in amazing detail the vigorous beat of a culture that was still living. The texts remain authentically Kwakiutl. They convey the Kwakiutl tradition even when they narrate postcontact events.

In drawing upon this archival treasure I have tried to be faithful to the texts, that is, to the Kwakiutl mind. There has been a great deal of scholarly analysis of Kwakiutl institutions, for the most part devoted to the "potlatch" and always from the perspective of the outsider seeking to fit the facts into the framework of established general theory. Modern anthropology has become interested more in the hypothetical "model" of a society, and less in the way the people actually think about their own culture and institutions. A social model is a mental construct of the scholar, who draws first upon his knowledge of how societies are believed to work in general, and then upon selected items of information from the ethnographic data. The authors of a recent work on Indians of the Northwest Coast state the current viewpoint in these words: "The question of whether such models exist in the mind of the native informant, either consciously or unconsciously, is irrelevant in our approach to structure" (Rosman and Rubel 1971:4). From this representative viewpoint, the "potlatch," to take but one example, would be not what the Indians think it is, but what the anthropologist thinks it is.

I start from the Boasian position that we should know first how the native thinks. As scientists we should be able to say: Here are the mental constructs of the native peoples. This is how *they* think about the "potlatch," marriage, kinship and rank, and so on. Here is Kwakiutl culture as the Kwakiutl know it. Then, and later, we can say if we wish: This is how the culture and its institutions would appear in the perspective of current theory. The differences might be instructive.

Kwakiutl Society.   Kwakiutl culture is a somewhat specialized branch of a broader tradition which has come to be known as the Northwest Coast Culture Area. The region was identified by Boas (1895) as stretching from Yakutat Bay in Alaska to the Juan de Fuca Strait. It is a maritime region of bays, islands, and straits, and with streams reaching through mountain passes into the interior. Most Indian communities occupy the narrow and pebbled beaches pressed against the sea by forested mountains.

All observers agree that the Indians were expert fishermen but only adequate inland hunters. Ecologically, this stretch of North Pacific coast may be considered an extension into more temperate climates of the Northwest Eskimo and Aleut habitats. Indians, Eskimo, and Aleutian islanders were part of the same ancient maritime tradition, which included the hunting of sea mammals (seal, sea otter, and whale,), deep sea and coastal fishing, and river fishing during the seasons of the salmon run. The great economic difference was with respect to inland hunting, which for the Eskimo involved the group chase of fleet tundra herds, and for the Indians the more diversified game of the interior forests—deer, elk, black and grizzly bear, beaver, otter, marten, and mountain goat.

The region as a whole offered abundant food, furs for clothing, and timber for housing, canoes, and utensils. One can think of it as a western arctic maritime economy with more opulent possibilities. The factor of ecological continuity with Eskimo and Aleut is significant in connection with certain cultural continuities, especially with respect to relations with animals. The factor of ecological diversity opened for the Indians new prospects for cultural specialization and improvisation upon which all tribes capitalized.

Kroeber's early appraisal of the area as standing apart from all other North American Indian cultures seems generally valid, though one might question his rather extreme view of its isolation. He thought that the Northwest Coast shared with other Indians only the old and universal traits derived from Asia, and that its specific traits were special developments on the spot of late Old World intrusions (1923:7). Although this is not the place to go into matters of such historical complexity, it is actually the total configurations that appear unique, along with such specialized cultural features as art and woodworking. Any systematic analysis of traits would show wide-ranging connections with the entire North American continent. Such traits as the spiritual significance of names, shamanistic societies, and shamanistic combats are well established among Northern Algonquian-speaking peoples. Concepts of a guardian spirit, of a vision quest, of animal protectors, of ritualized warfare, of graded medicine societies, not to mention folklore plots and themes, are widespread. Boas had noticed, for example, that Kwakiutl and Plains Indians shared the identical custom of tethering warriors by skewers through the flesh. In both regions, this form of tethering had celestial meanings. On the Plains the warrior was tethered to a pole dedicated to the sun, among Kwakiutl to the roof beam represented as the Milky Way.

When the "potlatch" is stripped of its extreme traits (some of which are the product of inaccurate description) it does not appear so out of place with ritual property distributions and exchanges among California Indians, northern Algonquian and Plains Indians, and of course Alaskan Eskimo. Sapir observed, also too exuberantly, that "nowhere north of Mexico is the distinction between those of high and those of low birth so sharply drawn as in the West Coast tribes" (1915:359). One can think of the southeastern cultures as historic examples. Conceivably the prehistoric Mississipian Mound Builders were of a similar cultural type. In any case, some form of graded rank is not unusual among North American Indians, when we consider military ranks on the Plains and shamanistic ranks in the Ojibwa medicine societies as variant forms of religious aristocracy.

The impression of Northwest Coast cultural isolation held also by contemporary students of the area (e.g., McFeat 1966) may be exaggerated, but the distinctiveness of the cultures is not. Taking Kwakiutl as one example, one cannot escape the impression of a powerful religious and technical imagination actively and even rapidly evolving new ritual forms and symbols. Cultural interchange among the coast tribes was on a massive scale. Even as one can document fine cultural distinctions among all the tribes, the overall impression is of a common cultural tradition. Cultural interchange is no automatic process of diffusion, but a conscious disposition to take from others and to incorporate it as one's own. Although they spoke different dialects and languages, the many tribes had a common religious outlook and a consensus of common values.

Anthropology has yet to explore in depth the concepts of unity that hold a culture area together. There are hints, however, of the segmentary character of a greater cultural tradition in the primitive world. Within a larger cultural tradition each tribal segment may consider itself an incomplete part of the whole. Each then jealously guards its original uniqueness as it seeks, at the same time, to acquire valuables from the others and is honored that the others have borrowed from it. During my field work among northern Athabascan I listened to awed accounts of the remarkable powers of the neighboring Bella Coola. The Carrier Indians married into Bella Coola families, just as Kwakiutl marry into other tribes to acquire for themselves at least a connection with the treasures of another world. For their part the rich Bella Coola, the undeniable cultural superiors, were not unwilling to export their qualities as a people to the alien inlanders (Goldman 1940).

The Kwakiutl in dealing with culturally equivalent tribes were eager to "borrow" myth, art motifs, and whole ritual themes. The cannibalistic motif, for example, was introduced rather late among the southern Kwakiutl from their northern congeners, the Heiltsuq (Bella Bella). What

I am suggesting is that a culture area is not an aggregate of tribes gradually becoming alike through an osmosis of borrowing, but constitutes, in fact, a superculture with a definite structure of formal similarities and differences. Is it mere chance that the tribes of the Northwest Coast share a ritual and an aesthetic order, but at the same time sustain linguistic differences and differing concepts of descent? Language and descent are related systems that serve to identify the unique origins of a people. They are the fixed and continuous structures.

Rituals and related concepts of supernatural powers establish the capacity of a people to acquire valuable properties from outside sources. Thus they constitute expansive structures. Religious ideas enmesh otherwise separate cultures; the principles of language and social structure sustain their original integrity. The result is a supercommunity whose members speak the same metalanguage, that is, the language of myth, symbol, and ritual, but do not yield up their sense of separate origins.

The main neighboring tribes of the Northwest Coast can be traced from north to south: the Tlingit and Haida, whose separate languages are believed to be distantly related to Athabascan; the Tsimshian who speak a Penutian language; and the Bella Coola who belong to the Salishan linguistic family, which extends from below Vancouver Island to the Columbia River. The name "Kwakiutl" has been applied to the tribes occupying the northern and northerly shores of Vancouver Island and the shores of the opposite mainland. The Kwakiutl language family belongs to the Wakashan stock, which some linguists consider to be a distant branch of Salishan (Spencer, Jennings, et al.: 171). Nootkan tribes, another branch of Wakashan, occupy the western coastline of Vancouver Island. Finally, the southern part of the island and the entire opposite coastal mainland southward to Juan de Fuca Strait are occupied by Salishan-speaking tribes.

From north to south the tribes follow a gradient of matrilineal to patrilineal descent, and of exogamic clans to lineages and more amorphous groupings. Tlingit, Tsimshian, Haida, and the northern Kwakiutl-speaking Haisla form a group that follows matrilineal descent within a system of totemic exogamic clans. The southern Salishan tribes are patrilineal, and the central tribes have either bilateral or dual descent, within a lineage system. Among the central tribes of the coast, the southern Kwakiutl, who are the specific subjects of this book, have in effect a mixed or dual descent. One class of names and ritual properties comes from the father's side, another from the mother's. Since residence is patrilocal (virilocal) and basic rank comes from the father, one may speak of a patrilineal preference. Boas thought of southern Kwakiutl mixed descent as a consequence of opposing influences from northern matrilineal and from southern patrilineal tribes (1897:334). Sapir (1915) held the somewhat different view that the matrilineal clan system was the oldest, having become modified among central groups. There seems to be little historical evidence for either position.

Judging by degree of divergence from parental linguistic stocks, the tribes speaking Athabascan, Tsimshian, Wakashan, and Salishan were very ancient settlers along the coast, a conclusion also put forth by Willey (1966:407) and Borden (1951) on archaeological grounds. We cannot be sure of how many other cultural influences were drawn upon in creating the final configurations. Captain James Cook, fresh from Oceania, was struck by resemblances to New Zealand garments, houses, and woodcrafts (Beaglehole 1955–1967:1098). Resemblances in formal systems of descent and rank with Oceania are also striking, but may be attributed more readily to convergence, since social systems repeat themselves around the world. Now that culture historians are more respectful of Oceanic maritime skills, the possibility of early overseas influences need not be considered remote.

Of relatively recent Oceanic and Asiatic connections that might have influenced the course of Northwest Coast cultures there is far less doubt. Marius Barbeau, an eminent authority on this area, believed that the coastal cultures known to us are rather recent forms, products of relations with the Asian mainland and with Russian traders and explorers (see Duff 1964). Quimby, summarizing published records of visits by foreigners to the Northwest Coast starting in the middle of the eighteenth century, mentions Chinese, Hawaiians, Filipinos, and African Negroes. Meares, he notes, established a community at Nootka in 1788 that included many Chinese, some of whom have intermarried and been assimilated. A Nootka Indian lived in China during that period and visited the Hawaiian Islands before returning home. Hawaiians came directly to the Northwest Coast with Cook and Vancouver (1948).

The Kwakiutl do in fact reveal specific Polynesian traits in respect to rank and kinship. The title *ate,* translated as "lord" (Boas 1921:887), seems cognate with Polynesian *ati* with a similar meaning; Kwakiutl have a talking chief (*elk*) who corresponds in function to the Polynesian counterpart. Kwakiutl kinship has the common Polynesian usages of a single term for siblings of opposite sex, and of differentiating by relative seniority siblings of same sex but not those of opposite sex. Also, with respect to kinship, Kwakiutl and Polynesian societies have similar terms (*-tsaya, -taina*) for younger siblings of the same sex.

There is reason enough to suspect complex origins for Northwest Coast cultures. It is even feasible to imagine the possibility of Kwakiutl as a fusion of Polynesian and North American Indian. But if such fusion had indeed occurred, the hybrid nevertheless attained its own fully integrated cultural character.

We turn now to the Kwakiutl Indians. The designation "Kwakiutl," which probably means Smoke of the World (Boas 1897:553) has come to refer to various groups and tribal aggregations of Indians who are of the Wakashan stock. In the broadest sense it has become the name of a language within Wakashan, which is spoken by many tribes. It has also become the name of a group of closely associated tribes at Fort Rupert. Finally, "great" Kwakiutl is the name one tribe at Fort Rupert has given itself. The Kwakiutl language itself consists of three major branches, Haisla, Heiltsuq, and a third called Kwakiutl. The third branch is spoken by Indians who occupy a territory on the east coast of Vancouver Island and adjacent mainland and who are referred to as Southern Kwakiutl.

The Kwakiutl language falls into three dialects, Koskimo, Newettee, and Kwakiutl. Indians speaking the latter were the main subjects of Boas's and Hunt's studies. This is the group I refer to as the Kwakiutl in this book. Kwakiutl as a subdialect is spoken by 13 tribes who evidently bear a common designation among themselves as the Kwakwakewak (Boas 1897:329) indicative of a substantial sense of common interest.

Among these 13 tribes, one group of four tribes, the Kwakiutl, had left previous settlements to reside at Fort Rupert, where they formed a confederation. The four tribes composing the Fort Rupert Kwakiutl were close enough in common interest for Boas to consider them as one tribe that comprised four subtribes or "septs." In the texts, however, each is considered by the Kwakiutl as a full tribe, and that is how I refer to them. Each of the four has a tradition of separate origin, a normal condition for a tribe. In the gathering of tribes each of the four is equated with the other tribes. Boas, having defined "tribe" as a local group occupying a single village, took common residence as the determining criterion. But taking account of Kwakiutl usage, it is perhaps less confusing to refer to Fort Rupert as a postcontact four-tribe village.

Since in succeeding chapters I discuss the organization of Kwakiutl society from the point of view of religious thought, I offer here a skeletal outline of that organization along more conventional lines. The first concern in reconstructing a social organization is the determination of its outer limits. The broadest social dimension should encompass the entire cultural community within which there is active interchange of ideas and of institutions. This would be an intertribal community. From the Kwakiutl perspective, the entire Northwest Coast is an interconnected community. Within this community, languages and systems of marriage and descent differ, but the main religious ideas and ritual organizations are alike even to the sharing of nomenclature.

The enlarged supercultural community has sociological significance not by virtue of some passive diffusion of traits, but because it was bound together in the past by active intercoastal trade in slaves and animal pelts, and in copper shields, masks, boxes, and other artifacts. However, for all the Indians of the region these artifacts had special meaning as supernatural treasures, whose value, like that of necklaces and armbands in the *kula* trade of Melanesia, depended on a common ritual language. The rapid diffusion of complex ceremonies from tribe to tribe is indicative of a sentiment of commonality among them all. One example may illustrate such commonality. It is believed by Kwakiutl that the killer of a victim seized the latter's names and ritual treasures so they could not descend in the victim's family (Boas 1897:335).[1] We do not know whether this rule was adhered to, but it does imply a concept of community comparable to that of marriage, which formalizes the rules of transmissions of rights.

This broad and vast intertribal community is a more nebulous structure than, say, the European community, but it does have an underlying structure in the interchanges and common ritual language already mentioned, and in the preservation of language and descent differences as indicators of separate origins.

Propinquity intensifies interchange among neighbors, setting up a fluctuating interface among tribal groups who actively intermarry and attend one another's ceremonies. Among Kwakiutl, as I shall shortly demonstrate, there is a stable group of tribes who habitually intermarry and invite one another to their celebrations. Less frequently they draw outside tribes into the marriage and ritual network. Neighbors outside the stable confederation of tribes are more likely to be at war with each other. However, they fight according to common rules allowing them to seize ritual privileges. In this respect intertribal warfare is cognate with marriage.

An inner community is formed by the 13 tribes, who speak of themselves as the Kwakwakewak. They are in no sense a political community. Their bonds are those of regularized intermarriage and of regularized ritual association. The tribes are ranked; the chief of the highest-ranking tribe has ritual precedence, but no powers or authority outside the ritual precincts. All 13 tribes occupy a continuous territory.

Each tribe is a local group occupying a compact village of a dozen or more large, multifamily houses. The genealogical traditions ascribe to each tribe a founding ancestor, who claimed a beach site as soon as he arrived on earth. The principle of tribe hence combined genealogical unity with territory. Practice is another matter, for Boas found that the constituent lineages of each tribe were of two types, branches of the original founder's line, and alien adherents.

It is not difficult to imagine pristine conditions when tribes were maximal lineages whose members affiliated mainly by patrilineal descent. The lineages are ranked, and the chief of the first lineage having ritual precedence and authority is recognized as chief of the tribe. When does a ritual authority become political? If the chief can morally obligate all other lineage heads to support his intertribal feasts and property distributions he can be said to impose his will on the economy of the village. The tribes face each other ritually, but they are also mindful of their pride and sensitive about ascendancy. These are political sentiments that the chief guides and nurtures. In these respects the tribal chief is also a political leader. Myth portrays tribal chiefs as saviors of the tribe in famine and war, and as feared for their supernatural powers. Thus a political concept, though undeveloped, is not lacking.

Although the lineage is also concerned heavily in ritual it has a more substantial economic character than the village tribe. Lineages occupy several houses of the winter village, one of which is its center for feasts and ceremonies and the residence of its chief. The village site is in the name of the tribe; its economic resources, shore and offshore fishing, berry and root gathering grounds, rivers, and inland hunting are in the name of the lineage. The lineage head is a true headman. He is first in ritual and leader of the economy and general adviser, but not a magistrate. Each lineage is basically a common descent group, drawing its membership through paternal descent in the main, but allowing maternal kinsmen to affiliate as well.

[21]

Each lineage recognizes individual families who occupy partitioned sections of a lineage house. In summer fishing, each family owns its own river fishing station. As a rule, men bring their brides to their own homes to form a new household. When the heir to lineage chiefship marries he usually builds a new house and arranges for his kinsmen to share it with him.

Neither tribe nor lineage adheres to rules of exogamy out of consideration of incest prohibition. Exogamy is a social preference of chiefs, who seek to add to their stature by acquiring names and properties. Incest regulations evidently covered only the nuclear family, for there are records of marriage with a half sister. In one family tradition, even the marriage of a man to his mother provoked no comment (Boas and Hunt 1905:164).

To say of the Kwakiutl that they were deeply religious is to say no more than what is true of all American Indians and probably of all primitive peoples, for whom religion means involvement in a consubstantial nature. Scientific materialism postulates the consubstantiality of matter, primitive religions that of life and the powers of life. In their ritual setting the Kwakiutl are in daily touch with forms of life and with sources of power to which they should respond if they are prudent and energetic. There are rivers and ponds whose waters are the "water of life," of which they should drink. They need the good will of all animals upon whom they feed. They ask permission of trees for their planks, of the sun for its general help. They will not hunt or fish without preparing themselves ritually for the encounter. From a materialistic point of view that recognizes only the utility of killing, the ritual of hunting and fishing preparations is for success. From the Indians' point of view, the ritual serves to prepare men to enter the foreign realm of the animals by making them acceptable to the animals.

In what are commonly and crudely called the "crisis rites'" of birth, growth, coming of age, marriage, and death the Kwakiutl (as do all primitive peoples) associate the natural events in their life with corresponding events in other realms of nature. The conception of primitive men as fearfully warding off the perils of the life cycle is but a shallow projection of modern hypochondria upon a less neurotic world. The rituals of the life cycles of men and women represent individual religious rhythms, as do the rituals of hunting and gathering. Illness, a disorder of vital forces and hence of interest to the entire community, initiates another set of individual religious rhythms involving shamanistic rituals.

The individual religious rhythms fill the everyday life of the Kwakiutl. They represent the regular small rhythms (like the tides) of religious sentiment. The Winter Ceremonial introduces the grand religious rhythm, a rhythm literally like that of the seasons themselves. All other forms of ritual activity are generated by specific events in the lives of individuals. The Winter Ceremonial is essentially collective and essentially regulated by impersonal season.

The Ceremonial is an aggregate of many rituals and ritual themes, all under a metaphysical covering wide enough to shelter almost infinite variations and additions. This metaphysical umbrella already has the apt caption of World Renewal Rites, a theme that encompasses the somewhat narrower Kwakiutl conception of transforming death into life. It is essentially a shamanistic rite.

With the beginning of the winter season in November, the entire Kwakiutl community is transformed from a human to a spirit conclave. The tribal and lineage organization is put aside, and a new set of personal names corresponding to the spirit state is assumed. The break with the profane summer season is more or less complete. The lineage houses become ceremonial centers, the entire "nobility," all the holders of honored names, become shamans. The commoners, those who have not inherited honored names, occupy the passive role of spectator. Each village then exists as though it were in a realm dominated by spirits.

The nobility then form two categories of ritual activists. One group, the Seals, are those actively consorting with spirits; the other, the Sparrows, having finished with that experience are now concerned with the overall management of the ceremonial. Among the Kwakiutl more than 50 spirits representing the animal world as well as generalized supernatural beings are impersonated by the Seals. Some are being initiated and "disappear," the others remain in the ceremonial house acting out by mask, song, and dance their impersonations. The most prominent and most important spirits are those of the Man Eater monster and his associates. The privilege of impersonation is normally acquired in marriage or by murder of a privilege holder from an alien tribe and then transmitted as a birthright. Consequently, the religious value of a spirit coordinates more or less with the gradations of human rank; the highest ranks hold the privilege of the Man Eater spirit, a privilege that transforms them into ritual cannibals.

The spirit impersonations are only loosely orchestrated thematically. When the season begins the noble families agree to initiate their children. One family challenges another, one lineage another, and one tribe another. In the course of the season, the ritual action shifts from one lineage house to another. Winter Ceremonials observed by Boas were intertribal. No matter how varied the content, the ritual themes they convey remain the same. The impersonation memorializes a mythical encounter, when the animals or supernatural beings gave powers to a human ancestor. The present impersonator is custodian of those powers, which are generally over life and property. The cannibalistic theme as the most awesome and, in Kwakiutl symbolism, the most far-reaching and all-encompassing, is ritually most demanding; the impersonator-to-be of the Man Eater "goes through," as the Kwakiutl say. Symbolically, he leaves the human world to meet Man Eater and to receive his powers. It is up to the shamans to bring him back safely and to restore him to a normal human state. The novice goes into the woods where he lives alone for four months. He returns emaciated, and with a wild and demonic craving for human flesh, of which he is to be cured.

The events of the Winter Ceremonial have given some scholars an impression of Kwakiutl as a people driven by Dionysian ecstasy and overweening pretensions to personal grandeur. The question then is, do religious themes reveal the personal psyche? Needless to say the answer is not simple.

I have left mention of the "potlatch" to the end of this introduction and include it under religious configuration. The "potlatch" is a religious phenomenon, a complex ritual involving human relations with other realms of life, in particular animals and trees. The explanation of this view cannot be summarized briefly at this point, but is attempted throughout the book. In treating the "potlatch" as a religious phenomenon I am in apparent disagreement with many serious scholars of the subject, who have drawn upon modern Kwakiutl and their modern ideas about wealth. Our disagreement perhaps would not be so decided if we were all dealing with a common historical frame of reference. Mine is of the traditional Kwakiutl before they had become Christianized and commercialized.

II

LINEAGE

Two great interests dominate Kwakiutl social thought and guide the organization of the social community. They are lineage and rank, closely related and, indeed, fully interdependent ideas. The idea of lineage is perhaps foremost, for it expresses essential religious convictions about the nature of connections between contemporary communities and their mythological founders. Such connections, viewed ideally as unbroken, are like a tree growing from ancestral roots; they have religious significance for the Kwakiutl because they are more than pedigrees. They are the transmission lines that convey the original ancestral properties down the generations.

These properties are not mere names, titles, and privileges. They are spiritual goods, representing essential spiritual qualities of founders and ultimately of all ancestors. In the sense that such spiritual qualities or essences of the ancestors are considered vital to the well-being of all descendants, specifically guaranteeing the continued life and above all the vigor of the line, they are fundamental supernatural powers.

The powers of the line derive from the ancestral founders, each of whom is apparently considered as reincarnated in the life of the contemporary bearer of his name. Thus each new generation reconstitutes on earth that primordial state when the founders were just moving out of their nonhuman and nonearthly realms. This primordial state, like that of birth, invokes the great powers of emergence, of transformation, and of initiation. To be connected through lineage with the Beginnings is to be in touch with the generative powers of birth, more fundamentally with the original sources of human creation. Thus the inheritance of names of a lineage is no mere social transmission of membership, it is rather a ritual process—very much like the totemic rituals of Australia—that serves to maintain and periodically to strengthen the links between present generations and their earlier formative state.

The inheritance of a name has the religious significance of a spiritual transposition. The ancestral being leaves one human carrier to be reincarnated in another; this is not a casual emergence, but rather a new birth. Like the biological, or sexual reproduction of the generations, the chain is unbroken and specific. The new bearer matches his biological pedigree with that of his ancestral incarnate. The Kwakiutl visualize two chains of transmission. One, moving by spiritual replication, perpetuates an ancestor; the other, moving biologically, produces human bearers who are qualified to carry the ancestor down the generations. As a rule, it is seniority that ensures the worthiness of the bearer. There seems to be a specific rule that only the first four children of a nuclear family are qualified bearers. All others are in the religious sense superfluous beings.

A bearer's name stands for the incarnation of an ancestral being, and thus represents primary sources of power. Associated with named beings are secondary powers. These are known as *tlogwe*, meaning "coming down to the beach" (Boas 1935b:99), a reference to their having come down from the myth or primordial world in the manner of the ancestral beings. The *tlogwe*, usually translated by Hunt as "treasures," are the gifts of powers that had been obtained by ancestors from supernatural beings, anthropomorphic or zoomorphic. They may be objects, such as poles, house posts, masks, and dishes, or ritual privileges, and are commonly but not inevitably linked with, that is, inherited with, the ancestral name.

Sociologically, lineages are visualized as organized around personal pedigrees. The religious perspective reveals a more complex structure, however. In the Kwakiutl case there are three elements to consider:

names (ancestral beings), treasures or *tlogwe* (the acquired powers of ancestors), and personal pedigrees. Names and *tlogwe* form a linked pair of supernatural powers and are in that respect a single unit vis-à-vis the descent lines of persons. I discuss the separate character of names and *tlogwe* and of persons later in this chapter. We shall then see that names, the incarnations of ancestors, have indeed their own separate but dependent existence apart from persons.

Among Kwakiutl, the concept of lineage has developed around the constant relationship, perhaps on the model of body and soul, between persons and the spirits of their ancestors. Both are vitally interconnected, like the ancient Mayan days and their divine carriers. The day would not move unless conveyed by its god; the god would have no vital mission unless he had a day assigned to him. In the Kwakiutl conception there is a similar human obligation to transmit the ancestral spirits down the corridors of time without evident interruption, which would be a serious break in the flow of life (see Boas 1920:364). Interruptions are not irreparable, though they are definitely calamitous. When defunct names are revived after a generation or so, they are assigned to lesser human carriers (Boas 1921:967). As a rule, only sudden and unexpected death prevents the transmission of the name, of the ancestral spirit, from its present bearer to the assigned heir while both are still alive and vital. The senile bearer would be as unworthy as would be a person of low pedigree.

As Tocqueville observed, it is the democrat who is the generalist. The aristocrat is drawn to the particular. Hence, it is the lineage of all descent groups that epitomizes the specifics of pedigree. It sets apart the founder and all of his special attributes, and it places each of his notable descendants in a precise and particular genealogical spot. Within the genealogical community no two individuals, providing both hold aristocratic pedigree, are alike or precisely comparable. When, because of intermarriages, lineages intersect, each interconnection is precise and particular. All connections are through specific persons. Since each notable person is always in some respect an embodiment of a mythological founder, the entire genealogical network of a community is always a living representation of the beings who existed, or who preexisted in mythological times. In other words, the particularity of the lineage is in harmony with the religious requirement for perpetuating the founders and all their particular attributes.

The founders of lineages were set into an order of rank arbitrarily.

According to one tradition, the Creator had ranked them before they came down to earth as human beings (Boas 1897:339). According to another, they were ranked on earth by a human ancestor who was the first to feast them and to distribute animal skins among them. Neither version implies a principle of immanence, such as seniority. Boas believed that Kwakiutl ranking had grown out of the consistent application of rules of primogeniture and of descent by seniority (1920:360). In Kwakiutl belief, however, primogeniture and seniority of descent only perpetuated a preconceived system. Even then, only primogeniture was the mandatory principle; how the second, third, and fourth children fared in succession was often left to chance.

In Polynesia, a comparable system of ranked lineages developed around a concept of immanence that integrated *mana* and order of birth. Descendants of senior lines held the highest rank and headed the highest-ranking lineages; their juniors held the lower ranks and headed subordinate and lower-ranking lineages. Central was the notion of *mana* as a power that could be apportioned by order of birth and degree of connection to the original founder.

The Kwakiutl system lacked such integration. What was inherited was not a quantity of power, but the right to represent an ancestral or supernatural being whose qualities could be graded on the most general scale.

I discuss principles of rank in the next chapter. Our immediate interest is in the effects of ranking on the organization of lineages. In contrast to clans that generalize memberships, lineages emphasize the specifics of genealogy. Ranking may be understood as still another mode of differentiating the membership of a community, whether it has been formed organically by kinship or by historical circumstances. Rank overcomes what is for Kwakiutl, as well as for Polynesians, the demerit of generality. Through ranking, each person acquires the essential attribute of having a unique place. In this respect, the principle of ranking is analogous to that of totemism, which converts an otherwise generalized human community into specialized entities comparable to natural species (cf. Lévi-Strauss 1963c). Whereas totemism differentiates through the model of natural species, ranking differentiates through the model of natural processes, such as order of birth. Kwakiutl invoke an additional natural process—the order in which animals eat (Boas 1921:784).

Therefore, in another respect, ranking, though differentiating, unifies by applying natural principles of process to the human community. Within a stable system of rank, lineages that may be connected only by historical association achieve a quasi-organic solidarity comparable to that of kinship. Kwakiutl traditions do not portray the original founders of all the lineages as having been kinsmen. However, by perpetuating a fixed order of original rank the Kwakiutl have imposed an additional organic order.

Conceptually, though not by actual structure, the 13 Kwakiutl tribes that come within the primordial system of preset rank constitute a kind of superlineage. The concept of lineage, as I have already explained, asserts an unbroken line or lines of connection between present and first ancestors. Underlying the idea of continuity is the religious conviction that the present reconstitutes the original condition. Actual structure, which is a product of historical contingency, as well as of inherent principles, only approximates the religious concept. The idea of common descent through lines of fixed ranks and names that had been established from the beginning is, however, fundamentally that of lineage. Conventional definitions of lineage are, of course, different. Among Kwakiutl, not even the *numema* are lineages by conventional usage, which insists at the very least on unilineal sex line descent (matriliny or patriliny), not to mention exogamy, as essential criteria (Fortes 1953). But the conventional definitions are far too limited and rigid in ignoring other modes of linearity, for example, social status as in Polynesia (see Goldman 1970).

Among Kwakiutl, similar status qualifications also regulate linearity. In fundamental respects—even though the dimensions are greater—the group of 13 Kwakiutl tribes is like the *waka,* the original canoe load of founders of the New Zealand Maori, that formed the source of connection for the so-called "maximal lineage." Among Kwakiutl, the linear connections are equally well-defined since only one person in each generation represents an original ancestor. Each generation, therefore, reconstitutes the original population of founders.

The point at issue is whether the Kwakiutl social structure, inclusive of the 13 tribes, is represented by a single or by multiple principles of organization. As I understand their system, a broad concept of lineage is indeed central, and all Kwakiutl descent groups reflect varying social expressions of that concept. All cohere within a consistent structure. The 13 tribes are not a mere federation; the tribe is not simply a village within which family lines have gathered. While this coherent structure does not follow exactly the models of segmentary lineages as described by Fortes (1953) and Evans-Pritchard (1940), it is still within that framework. Accepting the original ancestral community as an organic body analogous to an organic kinship body, we might represent it as a "maximal" lineage. The "tribes" are then subsidiary segments or "major" lineages, and the subdivisions of the tribes become "minor" lineages. The basis of the Kwakiutl version of a segmentary lineage model is essentially the original unity, by way of ranking, of the 13 tribes.

To recast Kwakiutl social structure from its present disconnected appearance in the published literature to a segmentary lineage model might be faithful to Kwakiutl thinking, but at the same time disturbing to sociological orthodoxy. Apart from lack of evidence that the members of the founding community were kinsmen (although kinship bilaterality, as we shall see does unite—in principle—all 13 ritually related tribes), no descent group is either matrilineal or patrilineal, or axiomatically exogamous. However, exogamy and sex line descent are but some of the formal means for restricting membership in lineages. Like Polynesians, Kwakiutl had found other means to accomplish the objectives of social segregation. Empirical difficulties still remain. In fact, extant genealogies present a confusing picture of aboriginal social organization. Finally, there is the question of retaining continuity with established sociological terminologies and usages. To retain continuity I adhere mainly to Boas's terms without, however, abandoning the concept of segmentary lineage structure—which does not, after all, depend on labels.

Boas recognized only the formal existence of tribes, which he identified as villages, and tribal subdivisions, which did not resemble any formal social category he could recognize. Quite sensibly he fell back on Kwakiutl nomenclature, and called the tribal subdivisions *numayms* (from *numema*, "same kind," "fellow tribes"). In early writings (1897:328) he considered the *numayms* to be "clans"; he never thought they might be lineages. But then Boas did not recognize any Kwakiutl descent line as a lineage, even though he had before him the Gwasela tribal history which chronicled an unbroken succession of 23 generations from the founding ancestor to the present. The absence of strict exogamy and of strict unilateral descent had convinced him the Kwakiutl descent groups were special and unlike either clans or lineages.

Nevertheless, the Gwasela tradition of tribal genealogical continuity does, in fact, authenticate the presence of lineage as a central concept. The absence of exogamy or of sex line unilinearity is for Kwakiutl, as for Polynesian societies, only of secondary interest. With the Gwasela tribal history as direct evidence, and with the repeated declarations of the Hunt texts on the necessity for unbroken continuity with founding ancestors as corroboration, there is no difficulty in recognizing, even from fragmentary traditions, that lineage is the central principle. Boas did not see lineages at all, but neither did he take note of the Gwasela history. Moreover, he was captive of the sociological orthodoxy that lineages had to be exogamous and either matrilineal or patrilineal.

Ritual Congregation.　　Though Boas recognized a community of interest and of ritual association among 13 Kwakiutl tribes, he did not concern himself with its organizational structure. In this respect, also, he remained within the conventional sociological tradition, in this instance of ignoring organizations that lacked formal leadership, as well as political and economic functions generally. He listed the membership and cited Kwakwakewak as its common name, but saw no basis for regarding these tribes as a community. Actually by conventional criteria this community could be considered a tribe. Its members speak the same language, they occupy contiguous territory, they share in a common order of rank, they are closely intermarried, and, finally, they are totally involved with one another in ritual property exchanges.

Boas's unwillingness to consider this enlarged community as a "tribe" is curious because it is, in fact, so designated in the Hunt texts. Boas, however, had translated the Kwakiutl word *gwokelot,* which means "fellow inhabitants of the houses," as "tribe," even as he recognized that it really meant "village." However, it had already become customary to speak of Kwakiutl villages as "tribes," and Boas followed suit. In the Hunt texts the *gwokelot* that come together in ritual are spoken of as *lelqoala* or *lelqwalele,* terms translated by Hunt as "tribe." Hunt, it should be said, also translated *gwokelot* as "tribe" (as he did *numema,* "fellow tribes"). The texts, nevertheless, do employ a segmental terminology—*lelqoala, gwokelot,* and *numema*—that corresponds to the model of overall lineage organization that I have suggested, or more conventionally to a taxonomy such as tribe, village, lineage.

Since Boas and other scholars have already preempted "tribe" for what is a village, it would be less confusing to find another term for *lelqoala.* I suggest "Ritual Congregation" as an appropriate description of the actual character of the community of 13 tribes. Other Kwakiutl-

speaking tribes, Koskimo, Gwatsenox, and Lasqenox, also join in Kwakiutl ritual. But since they are not part of the common system of ranking, they remain outside the real ritual congregation.

The Ritual Congregation has a dual composition that is simultaneously hierarchical and oppositional. In this respect its structure conforms
to parallel ritual interests in the gradation of powers and in the antagonism of powers. All 13 are ranked in order of ritual precedences. But
the first four stand in antagonistic opposition to a group of four lower-
ranking tribes. This group of eight tribes is to be considered as an internal moiety set up for specialized ritual purposes. The two pairs are not
named, and are not, of course, exogamous groupings. The opposition
they represent is not openly cosmological, but seems to represent rather
the rivalry between older and younger brother, a rivalry the Kwakiutl
as well as Polynesians regard as natural.[1] In a broader sense fraternal
rivalries, and the antagonisms between the first four and the second
four ranking tribes suggest an opposition between higher and lower
categories in nature, and between men and spirits. In this respect the
internal moiety has a conventional cosmological basis.

Hierarchy and antagonistic opposition are complementary modes of
social unification. Each implies the ritual incompleteness of the individual tribes. Each also stands for a mode of relationship with spirits. The
ancestral spirits do not engage with one another except in a fixed order
of precedences. At the same time, the higher and lower orders must
forever act out their eternal hostility. I discuss the religious nature of
this hostility in Chapter 8.

Since the Ritual Congregation has no "political" character, it has no
chief. Nevertheless, the chief of the highest ranked tribe is a central
ritual figure, not as an organizer or director, but as a religious and
ritual focus, and as the center for ritual compliance with the obligatory
ritual cycles. The basic unity of the Ritual Congregation arises from the
original conception of a living community reconstituting on earth the
primordial spirit world. No less substantially, the Ritual Congregation
is unified through a system of generalized intermarriages which inter-
laces all the separate descent lines. Finally, through bilateral kinship
the entire Congregation becomes a grand kindred. Warfare, accordingly,
was with outside tribes (Boas 1897:424).

The constituency of the Kwakwakewak Ritual Congregation by order
of rank is:

1. Gwetela
2. Qomoyaye
3. Walas Kwakiutl
4. Qomkyutis
5. Mamaleleqala
6. Nimkish
7. Tlawitsis
8. Matilpe
9. Awaitlala
10. Qweqsotenox
11. Dzawadenox
12. Haxuamis
13. Guawenok

(Boas 1925:83–85)

In antagonistic opposition the villages were paired against each other in this manner:

1.	Gwetela	against	5.	Mamaleleqala
2.	Qomoyaye	against	10.	Qweqsotenox
4.	Qomkyutis	against	6.	Nimkish
3.	Walas Kwakiutl	against	7.	Tlauitsis

(Boas 1966:81)

The Tribe (gwokelot). In what its editor considers the "definitive account" of Kwakiutl social organization, Boas wrote:

> The tribes are groups inhabiting one winter village each and acting on many occasions, as in war or rituals, as units. They are village communities often bearing the name of the locality they inhabit. (1966:41)

From his knowledge of the Northwest Coast, Boas felt that the contemporary village communities were largely the regroupings of the *numema*, which to his mind were the original villages (see 1897:334; 1966:46). The Kwakiutl traditions state that *numema* dispersed for one reason or another to join with others in new villages. These villages would not then have a segmentary lineage organization. Only the *numema*, which Boas sometimes called clans or gentes, would have had a lineage structure. In that event the original village communities would

[33]

have been lineages. Actually, the contemporary village community is not totally different from its original form.

The family traditions support the supposition of an original segmentary organization resembling the classic form of lineage, but only partially. Around 1895, the tribes or villages had a dual structure: one group of its lineages *(numema)* represented fraternal branches and the other, one or more unrelated branches. Boas did not fail to recognize the complex structure of the tribes. In what is clearly his most authoritative analysis of Kwakiutl social organization he wrote:

> We may therefore say that in the concept of the Indians, the tribe consists of a number of divisions, each of which is derived from one ancestor, but which includes also individuals of different descent who at an early time joined the ancestor. In other cases there is no such relation, the lines representing disconnected local groups. (1920:114)

From the native point of view, the tribes were formed around a noble line that bore the name of the original ancestor. In some cases, this name was also the name of the tribe. This line, as Boas observes, represented the "real" members of the tribe. The other families became associated with him at a later time without having been descended from the same ancestor (ibid). The concept of a core of the "real" and highest-ranking descendants of the founder to which separate lower ranks and commoners affiliate is the central feature of Kwakiutl lineage structure.

The organization of the Gwetela, the first tribe of the Ritual Congregation, is illustrative of the basic concept. The founder was Matagila. His firstborn son, who inherited the name, founded its first-ranking *numema,* the Maamtagila ("the Matagilas"); the second son founded the Loyalatlawa; the third left after a quarrel to found the Maamtagila lineage of the Matilpe tribe. The Kukwakwum (the "real" Kwakiutl) and the Sentlem, the fourth and fifth lineages, "came down" separately, but nearby, and joined the others. These two were evidently not fraternal, but were linked nevertheless by a comparable bond of propinquity (see Boas 1966:39, 43; Boas 1921:949, 938–951 passim). The two lowest-ranking lineages, Laalaxsendayo and Elgunwe, were a common fraternal pair, who came as later adherents. Finally, the third-ranking Gexsem came in very late as refugees from the Walas Kwakiutl (Boas 1921:804).

The special circumstance of postcontact times, when *numema* dispersed and joined other tribes, does not obscure the original principle of a composite structure built around a core of authentic founders. The Kwakiutl may have never had in mind a "pure" lineage. The history of the Gwasela, a closely-related tribe, brings out what was probably the ancient Kwakiutl concept of lineage. That concept bears upon what Boas had observed, namely the integrity of an original descent line and its connection with other descent lines. In the examples just cited, the tribes consisted of authentics and later comers. In the Gwasela history, there is still another perspective on this type of formation. This history does not concern itself with the formation of its own subdivisions, but rather with its success in founding branches of its original line among many other tribes through successive intermarriages and subsequent transfer of a forebearer's residence to the tribe and lineage of the bride.[2] When all achieve the Gwasela aim of being represented among all the noble lines of all the tribes, all tribes are then by design conglomerates. Only the direct lines of original founders need to retain their genealogical purity.

The Lineage (numema).   "Notwithstanding the relative stability of the tribes," Boas wrote, "the tribal divisions must be considered as the fundamental units" (1920:115). The lineages are indeed fundamental in representing the genealogical constituencies of the tribe. The founding line of the tribe is represented in its top-ranking lineages. As a constituent of the Ritual Congregation the tribe is represented by its chief who is, in fact, the chief of its ranking lineage. But even though the top lineage chief stands for the whole tribe, the tribes are nevertheless the named entities, the ritual units, in all major ceremonies. The question, then, of which section of the social structure is fundamental must take account of social context. Considering the major importance of intertribal ritual, one might well claim that the tribes are the fundamental units. The issue as to which units are more fundamental is actually irrelevant since we are dealing not with separate social units but with an integral structure.

The lineages compartmentalize members of the tribe, fundamentally by rank, thus sustaining the identity of the first founder. The lineages are the separate repositories of all names and inherited valuables; they are the holders of lands and resources and are, accordingly, the compartmentalized sources of the tribe's wealth. Compartmentalization is primarily a religious concept that gives necessary recognition to the individuality of separate descent lines, each of which stands, of course, for an individual founder and his successive incarnations. When tribes face each other within the Ritual Congregation they are represented only by their leading lineage, through the office of its chief. Within the constitution of each tribe, however, all the subdivisions are revealed, prismatically, as essential components. The tribe is in its own right a smaller ritual congregation of separate lines from separate founders.

Each *numema* is further divided into distinct family lines, understandably so, since tribe and lineage are but larger and smaller versions, respectively, of the same concept of organization. As a case in point, the Gwasela family history deals with tribe, but is indistinguishable with respect to genealogical construction from a lineage history. Boas's description of *numema* composition shows that he recognized its formal resemblance to tribe:

> The house stories also suggest that other individuals, not descendants of the ancestors, are members of the numayma. It seems fair to assume that the direct descendants of the ancestors form the nobility; others accepted as members form the common people, also called the house men . . . of the chief. (1966:43–44).

A possible implication from Boas's observation that *numema* members might, therefore, be strangers to one another should be judged in the light of kinship bilaterality. Boas did not get specific information on the extensiveness of the kinship community among Kwakiutl. We know, of course, from marriage preferences that all tribes and hence all *numema* were fully interconnected as in-laws. By the rules of Hawaiian kinship (all cousins are siblings, and all uncles and aunts are fathers and mothers) the affinal kin were then recognized as consanguineal relatives. Drucker, describing a similar Nootkan social system, said that the remotest relations were considered. If a man had but one actual relative in a distant tribe he considered all members of that tribe his kinsmen (1951:274).

It is almost certain that when Kwakiutl joined themselves to other tribes as entire lineages, or to other lineages as new members, they did so as kinsmen. The distinctions among lineage members are not by kinship as such, but by genealogical relation to the original ancestors. But Boas is too schematic as he outlines the social composition of each *numema*. It is not only the direct descendants of the lineage founder who form the nobility, but newcomers as well. The direct descendants were the "real" chiefs. Only those newly arrived adherents who held no ancestral names were commoners. At the same time, insofar as there were not enough ancestral names to transmit, the surplus offspring of direct descendants were also commoners. The central feature of lineage has, nevertheless, been clearly defined: The *numema,* like the village tribe, is organized around a kinship core that represents the direct line, through the linearity of primogeniture, from the original founder.

In this structure of core and periphery, only the center would appear to stand for the lineage. The presence of adherents creates an impurity of genealogical composition. For this reason, as well as for the more fundamental consideration of the bilaterality of primogenitural transmission, there has been an understandable reluctance to regard the *numema* as a lineage at all. At issue, as I have suggested, is the perspective from which one observes the *numema.* Conceptually, the numema is a lineage that retains within its own composition the names, that is, the ancestral beings, that belong to it.[3] Sociologically—that is, from the point of view of personnel—the *numema* composition is so heterogeneous that it becomes questionable whether it is a descent group at all. If sons and daughters who separate at marriage have equal rights to inherit an ancestral name, and if, by the same token, children may inherit such names either from the father or from the mother, by what means does the *numema* sustain its continuity? Boas resolves these issues brilliantly by disclosing the structure of the *numema* from the Kwakiutl—nonsociological—perspective.

> The structure of the numayma is best understood if we disregard the living individuals and rather consider the numayma as consisting of a certain number of positions to each of which belongs a name, a 'seat,' or 'standing place,' that means rank and privileges. Their number is limited and they form a ranked nobility. . . . These names and seats are the skeleton of the numayma, and individuals, in the course of their lives, may occupy various positions and with these take the names belonging to them. This becomes particularly clear when an individual occupies positions, and, therefore, has names in different numayma. In such a case, if he should be host as member of the one numayma, he would call out the names of the second numayma, the guests, and among them his own name as member of the second numayma. (1966:50)

The *numema* is eternal. Its names are like masks whose bearers are privileged to wear them, but who are not themselves "real" persons. From this point of view, the person holding the name is only an impersonator. Sociology, nonetheless, is far from irrelevant. The bearer of the name must have proper credentials. He or she must be of noble birth, and must have a legitimate claim through kinship or direct bequest. In postcontact times, especially when there were more available names than noble claimants, assignments to *numema* were quite feasible; names were even granted to commoners. As a rule, it was members of chiefly families who collected names in numerous *numema,* no doubt in the spirit of self-aggrandizement (see Boas 1925:99–103 passim). But those who acquired names that would be otherwise vacant were keeping them alive; they were benefactors of lineages that might otherwise face extinction.

In the precontact era of relatively few available names, eligibility for inheritance was regulated by rather strict genealogical conditions. For the seat or rank of chief, which never left the lineage, only the firstborn male or female was eligible. If the firstborn was male he occupied the rank and retained a permanent residence in the lineage. If female, she held the name as though she were a man (Boas 1925:105). She could not move, as is customary, to the residence of her husband without depriving her father's lineage of the office. Residence rules are not absolute, so a woman in her masculine role as bearer of a man's name could continue to reside in her natal lineage. Her children would then be considered as belonging to her line. Her eldest son would eventually inherit her rank and name and presumably residence in her lineage (Boas 1966:52).

Boas is vague on the implications of what is an apparent conflict between preference for patrilineal descent within the lineage and the obligations of unrestricted primogeniture. Curiously, the Hunt texts also offer little on the subject. They present chiefly lines from an exclusively patrilineal point of view, as though the laws of chance that would make women chiefs half the time were not working. Hunt is explicit in his insistence that the "house name" or seat went to the firstborn male or female (Boas 1921:831), but offers few examples of female successions. Conceivably, Hunt had in mind current conditions when he spoke of primogeniture; the prevailing practices may have been, judging by the genealogies, more strictly patrilineal. For example, in the Gwasela history the narrator comments on a chief who was "unfortunate because his child was a girl" (ibid:866). When a boy was born it was he who then received the important names and privileges. The passing over of a firstborn daughter may have been more common than Hunt had imagined.[4] Informants told Boas that a younger brother had a prior right to a chiefly name over a firstborn daughter (Boas 1966:52).

Despite a preference for patrilineal succession, the concept of names as distinct from their bearers did open the gates of succession quite wide. A man could inherit the lineage chiefship from his wife's father (Boas 1921:851), and his firstborn son would accordingly find himself in the line of succession within his mother's lineage. This type of matrilineal succession was in order when it was the mother who had succeeded in primogeniture to her father's chiefship. Evidently, although the evidence on this point is not entirely clear, it was impermissible for an office to go in primogeniture from a woman to her daughter. The succession had to revert to a male as soon as possible.

A rule of unrestricted primogeniture is so fully in keeping with a concept of simple bilaterality that outsiders can be forgiven their bafflement over an equally determined Kwakiutl preference for patriliny. The strong feeling for patriliny—it is clearly not a sociological axiom—emerges in the genealogical histories, in the preference for patrilocal residence at marriage, and in the device of converting the female holder of a man's seat and name into a social and metaphysical male. Within the metaphysical sphere of ancestral spirits the son who is taking the seat of his mother is actually taking the seat of her father, and is then in the line of firstborn male descendants from the founding ancestor. Sociologically speaking, and in terms of the human personnel of lineages, the succession is, of course, matrilineal. In the Kwakiutl social order a double state of affairs is almost inevitable. The spiritual content of the *numema* remains constant; the human content is destined to experience inconstancy.

The sentiment voiced by some Kwakiutl that the ideal family should have a firstborn son and a secondborn daughter (Boas 1925:101) speaks for the common human aspiration for a simpler state of affairs. The genealogies testify to social disturbance created by the shifts of people from a father's to a mother's lineage. What the lineages feared most was loss. Intrusion was a gain. A woman as chief—even in male guise—upset traditional expectations by drawing men out of their *numema*, when in fact the aim of marriage was for men to draw women out of their place.

The evasiveness of the genealogical records on the theme of social matrilineal succession does perhaps suggest the presence of a sensitive area where two great principles inevitably clash. But this opposition of principles can reasonably be seen not as a flaw but rather as a vital characteristic of the Kwakiutl social system. Social anthropology is accustomed to studying closed systems of clans and lineages. The Kwakiutl system represents simply another variety of these systems, a variety that allows for greater personal opportunities to move into more advantageous social positions. I have introduced the rubric "status lineage" to describe such a system (Goldman 1970). By separating primogeniture from patriliny the Kwakiutl system opens outward and gains in flexibility. By eternally retaining the core names, the lineages cannot lose their essential form. This arrangement defines the dual character of lineage structure—the metaphysical center remains rigid like the trunk of a tree, the social periphery moves outward like branches touching and interlacing with those of other trees. Combining form and movement, stability and opportunity, the Kwakiutl lineage structure follows a classic natural model.

The model of lineage I have described is still incomplete. We have considered its core of firstborn descendants, those who hold the "house seat" belonging to the chiefly or senior line. Patrilineal preferences are strongest for these seats. All house seats are associated with names that may not leave the lineage (Boas 1920:360). But it had evidently become customary to assign lesser seats more freely. The firstborn claimed the house seat of the paternal lineage. Subsequent children were transferred, if there were vacancies, to seats in the maternal lineage (Hunt ms. 14:1512). Shifts of children from paternal to maternal lineages may be considered as exchanges in the form of adoptions, return gifts, in effect, from the paternal lineage, which has been the heavy recipient of treasures from the side of the wife. Boas, to be sure, also sees the other side of this exchange—which is comparable to the formal system of adoptions in Polynesia—from the point of view of the child, who will find in its mother's *numema* the status not available to it at home. The benefits, nevertheless, are mutual; transferring persons from their patrilineal center adds considerably to the maternal stock. From the point of view of personnel the free transfer of secondary positions, usually from paternal to maternal lineages, is an expression of bilaterality, in keeping with the principles of the kinship system. But since the transferred persons become the impersonators of ancestral beings who belong irrevocably to another lineage they are, to all intents and purposes, adopted persons. Adoption is a specialized mode of bilaterality.

A more conventional bilaterality, by which a truly dual connection between father's and mother's genealogies is realized, is associated with names other than the house names. These are the names, also of great value, that move among affinal relations. Insofar as all persons have ritual and social significance only as members of lineages and tribes, all names, the house names and the names given to affinals, must be considered as lineage properties. Each class of name has its distinctive structural role. The house names define and segregate the lineages since they are, in fact, the substance of the lineages. The other class, which go out of the lineages, serve to connect them all through an all-encompassing network that is ultimately a single grand genealogy for all 13 tribes. Again, we have the image of trees and interlaced branches.

All the genealogical records of early times describe a system of double naming (see, e.g., Boas 1921:845). At birth and at later stages in its life, a child received simultaneously a name from its father's side and a name from its mother's side. As a rule, a boy received male names from his father and his maternal grandfather, and a girl received female names from her father's mother and her mother's mother. The names, other than the paternal, are not the house names. They do not stand for the seats or ranks of the lineage. They are of the family genealogies. They represent the fundamental bilaterality of genealogical connections and, of course, serve to link together a person's paternal and maternal lineages. Whether these bilateral connections are of equal value is a question that can not be answered without a better knowledge than we now possess of the Kwakiutl scale of values.

Apart from the names, which stand for ancestral incarnations and are thereby valued according to a special and intangible scale of merit, there is the distinction between residence and nonresidence. Residence depends on possession of a house name, which conveys an office and ritual privileges and is the principal prerogative of paternal lineage membership,[5] and thus conveys a major value. On the other hand, names from the maternal side certify a connection that carries Winter Ceremonial privileges, another major value. From the Kwakiutl perspective, the concern may not be with equivalence but with complementary relations of great value to both sides. Ritual connections through residence are in complementary balance with ritual relations obtained from outside.

Lineage exogamy must be considered from the standpoint of complementary relations exclusively. Kinship respects would deter only marriages within the nuclear family and would certainly not bar weddings within the natal *numema*. If the classificatory terminology of the Hawaiian kinship system, which gives persons an enormous range of siblings everywhere, were to set the rules of marriage, the Kwakiutl would have had to seek mates from distant tribes.

Since terminology did not distinguish between kinsmen of maternal and paternal lineages, the source of a strong preference for exogamy must lie in other than kinship interests. I discuss these other interests in Chapter 4. In anticipation of that discussion, I observe at this point that each lineage is a permanent repository of certain valuable properties or treasures, and is involved through marriage in their interchange. Exogamy guarantees the uninterrupted flow of treasures and names among all components of the Ritual Congregation. Examples of occasional endogamy, of close marriages within the *numema,* illustrate this preoccupation even more effectively. When circumstances demand it, families arrest the outward flow of their names and treasures—a defensive strategy—by marrying within (Boas 1920:361; Boas 1921:781). In either case, marriage regulates the flow of what are, of course, life-sustaining valuables. In many instances, the Kwakiutl entered into sham marriages with a dog, with the limb of one's body, with the name of an ancestor, or even with the name of a close relative (Boas 1897:359) so as to regulate the movement of such vital forces. In normal vital circulation, one set of names and treasures moved down the generations and within the *numema,* another moved outward.

Unlike the tribe, which is essentially a ritual organization, the *numema* seems to have a double character. It is a ritual entity; it is also a socioeconomic entity. The lineage chief is a ritual leader and a director, at the same time, of hunting and food gathering. The lineage as an organization is the "owner" of all valuable resources. The fishing grounds, even the mountain trails leading to mountain goats, are owned in common. In short, the wealth of the tribe—the source of its ritual life—is held in custody by its several subdivisions.

In the etiquette of ritual relations the tribe must request its *numema* for the foods, the skins, and the cedar bark mats with which to carry out its ritual obligations. Within the total sequence of events that constitute a ritual entity, it is what we choose to call economic activity that marks the initial phases. Since distributions of skins and robes and foodstuffs are essential to all ritual celebrations, the accumulation of these products is, therefore, part of the ritual chain of events. The deep ritual meanings of properties and foods will become clearer in later chapters. At this point I call attention to the ritual aspects of accumulation of properties, and the tribe (that is, its senior or top-ranking lineage) be-*numema* are the primary producers and accumulators of necessary tribal properties, and the tribe (that is, the senior or top-ranking lineage) becomes the point of concentration, and then of distribution. The distinction between such processes involved in the circulation of goods—as accumulations, concentration, and distribution—has an important ritual significance, as I demonstrate particularly in Chapter 7. Of immediate interest in connection with social structure are the specialized roles of tribe and *numema* within this process. There are minor rituals when *numema* deal only with their fellow lineages of the tribe. But in major rituals, the center of concentration and then of distribution is the chief who stands as tribal head. In ritual it is the tribes that look outward, and the lineages, as vital dependents, that look inward. If we think for the moment of the ritual uses of property as a form of nourishment—an idea not at all alien to the Kwakiutl—then we may say that the tribes feed the Ritual Congregation, drawing upon their *numema,* and the *numema* feed the tribe.

It is as primary nourisher of the tribe, and ultimately as the source of the nourishment of all, that the *numema* has a special economic role. But this role is economic only from the standpoint of a sociological taxonomy, which readily chops up the cultural totality into decultured segments, such as economy, social structure, government, and religion. To the extent that the products of the hunt, of fishing, and of berrying feed into the ceaseless ritual cycle, the economy, so-called, becomes a phase of that cycle. It is not the products alone that enter into the ritual cycle, but the totality of "economic" activity. The manner in which the hunting of sea and land mammals, for example, is a ritual action, and not merely a ritualized economic event, is demonstrated in Chapter 9. One need only bear in mind that Kwakiutl, like all precontact American Indians, conceived of the hunt as a personal and as a spiritual encounter between animals and men. Since the two parties to the encounter occupied different cosmic realms they engaged each other in a ritualistic manner. Needless to say, animals have their special and constant role in Kwakiutl ritual. Consequently, one may regard the hunt as an initial ritual phase of all ceremonies at which property is distributed.

Only from a perspective of religious ideas can one begin to understand the extraordinary violence with which the *numema* defended its economic resources, even against friends and neighbors. Each lineage owned tracts of land, including demarcated tracts of offshore fishing grounds, the boundaries of which were considered inviolate. When encountered, trespassers, including those from neighboring lineages, were engaged in mortal combat (Boas 1966:35). So violent a defense of territory cannot be ascribed to economic territoriality, certainly not for a society so well-to-do in food resources. Extreme territoriality seems more appropriate for Northern Athabascans and Algonquians, who faced real threats of famine. The issue in defense of territory is the manner of response to trespass. The idea that trespass must lead to a death, and not merely to a quarrel, implies a mystical attitude, a view of a territory as a sacred precinct pertaining exclusively to a particular descent line. To sanctify a precinct associated with produce rather than with place of origin or first settlement is to put primary stress on its value as a site of access to the nonhuman sources of life.

I would not wish to draw too clear a demarcation between subsistence economy and ritual economy for Kwakiutl, since both came equally under the jurisdiction of supernatural powers. Myth is as concerned with supernatural assistance to overcome famine as it is with the theme of riches for feasts and distributions (e.g., Boas and Hunt 1905:7). In each case, the life of the people in what we would call the real sense and in the spiritual sense is at stake. It is the invasion of a source of life—a spiritual trespass—that provokes a proportional response. In the final analysis, the *numema* does not, in fact, possess dualities of function such as sacred-secular or ritual-economic. The duality is rather in the religious sphere; it is primary collection and primary distribution. Territoriality in its total Kwakiutl context is to be considered a defense of the religious obligations of the *numema*. More specifically, the concept of territory posits a mystical unity between a genealogical line and sources of nonhuman life, an idea that appears in a new form in the sphere of ritual distribution and exchange.

The *numema* is also the primary custodian of major properties other than land and its produce. I use the term "custodian" rather than "owner" advisedly, because these other properties, such as the ceremonial house, names, and heraldic carvings, are actually connected most directly with individuals who are the immediate "owners" of names. Properties other than land are, strictly speaking, attributes of a name and in that sense the name—an ancestral incarnation—is the true owner. The names, however, belong more broadly to the line of the founding ancestor of the *numema,* and they can not go out of the line of descent. Even though they may be bequeathed by their individual owner, the *numema* fellows' approval is customary. They must remain within the *numema* because they are the emblems of ancestors. The name, itself an ancestral emblem and source of all related emblems, which may be physical properties (boxes, dishes, carved columns, house), and nonmaterial properties (songs, dances, exclamatory sounds, and a variety of other ritual privileges), is in the custody of the lineage as a corporate body.

Only designated names are in the custody of the *numema*. Others have more complex associations. The names that are transmitted to in-laws must leave the *numema*. Such names and their associated emblems belong to persons. But in genealogical reckonings they are associated ultimately with many lineages. In short, one set of names is preserved within the *numema*, and thus preserves the coherence of a descent line. Another set goes out to interlace with other descent lines and serves to preserve the coherence of the Ritual Congregation.

The characteristic *numema* is organized around a senior core, a noble family line, and possesses therefore all the emblematic properties that give it ritual standing. But there are also commoner lineages, which seem to be incomplete structures. Lacking authentic names they have a minimal ritual role, and are as close as possible to a basal secular level. The few commoner *numema* mentioned in the Hunt texts are poorly described, perhaps for the reason of lack of ritual role (see Appendix 3). Several lineages of the Gwetela are of commoner ancestry exclusively and are known derisively as "slave numayms" (Boas 1921:1096). As "slave" lineages they would, of course, be outside the religious concerns of the congregation. Lacking rank, except for a chief, they would have a relatively amorphous internal structure. Nevertheless, they come within the Kwakiutl concept of social structure, which always postulates a sacred core and a periphery of adherents in the category of a laity. The commoner lineages are to the tribe what the commoner members are to their lineage.

III

RANK

The term for a chief's seat within the Ritual Congregation supplies an important clue to what the Kwakiutl consider rank to be. The word is *tlaqwe* (or *tlaxwe*), which also means "to stand" as well as "strong" (Boas 1921:1436). To stand is the opposite of lying down, which Kwakiutl commonly employ as a general metaphor for being subdued and inert. In some senses, it means being close to a state of death. People who are shamed take to their bed and sulk, usually as a prelude to a series of adventures which will bring them salvation through the gift of supernatural powers. Hence, rank is a socioreligious representation of the vital state of being, and in this respect alone Kwakiutl and Oceania share a common view. Rank is normally inherited. From the religious standpoint, inheritance may be described as follows. The ancestors who are the primary sources of vital powers transmit these powers to qualified recipients, who then have the privilege of representing them, or even more basically, of incarnating them in a metaphoric sense.

Kwakiutl appear to emphasize in transmission the active element of acquisition. Heirs are not passive receivers. Even though they are eligible by birth to receive the supernatural powers of the ancestors, they require preparation to be worthy of them. The point of view in transmission is shamanistic. As Boas observed, "The receipt of valuable supernatural gifts, particularly of a house, makes the recipient a chief" (1935b:54). In similar fashion, the acquisition of supernatural powers often brings with it gifts of wealth, the power to restore life, and the death bringer (ibid:175). These are all spiritual properties associated exclusively with chiefs. The house, as I explain shortly, is of special importance as the sacred container of the lineage. Myth does not depict the normal way of becoming a chief; it calls attention, however, to the fundamental principle of rank as the shamanistic acquisition and possession of supernatural powers. Chiefs are not true shamans.[1] They have the title of shaman (*paxala*) only during the winter ceremonial period. Throughout the year they are the official patrons of shamans, as though they were in charge of the shamanistic arts. While there is no identity between shaman and chief, the analogous qualities are strikingly revealed in the privilege of shamans, even if they are commoners, to distribute property, a privilege usually reserved for chiefs (see Boas 1935b:40).

The shamanic model defines the inner quality of the chief. The hierarchical order is an ancillary matter. Since there is no suggestion in the texts that the powers themselves are graded, it may be assumed that gradation is viewed by Kwakiutl as a supplementary quality. Thus while the powers themselves are simply qualitative, the person occupying a graded seat imputes to them his own degree of worth. A death bringer in the possession of the highest chief has presumably more weight than it would when held by one of lower rank. In this respect, the Kwakiutl system differs from the basic Polynesian tradition, which attributes gradation of rank to the inheritance of supernatural powers *(mana)*.

In Polynesia, the absolute association between *mana* and seniority generated a coherent order of graded rank. Among Kwakiutl, rank and powers are separate qualities that must be brought together by the proper application of rules of hereditary transmission. The Kwakiutl do not imagine the rank order to have evolved naturally. They think of it as having been established by divine fiat. According to one tradition, the Creator set up ranks at a time when the animals could still talk (Boas 1897:339); according to another, the lineages and tribes were ranked at a seal feast by a human chief (ibid:383). The two traditions are evidently supplementary, the first dealing with the initial order of all personal ranks, the second with their later and humanly devised grouping by lineage and tribe. The texts do not specify the exact relationship between the ranking of persons, which includes a total of 658 names among the entire Ritual Congregation, and the rank order of tribes and lineages. In the case of one fully described property distribution, the order is by tribe, and the blankets are in the name of the 658 rank holders (see Boas 1925:83–85). Each tribe has its own internal order of names, which may or not be the original order of the preordained ranking of names.

From a religious standpoint, the separation between commoners and chiefs is close to absolute. They occupy different realms of spiritual existence, and in this limited sense form two classes. Rank, which implies more limited distinctions of degree, applies only to the class of chiefs. Chiefly hierarchy serves to define a religious order of precedences in eating, in seating, in ritual procedure generally, and most important in the distribution of property. Violation of the order is a serious offense, as though the natural order itself had been disrupted. In fact, the natural order would seem to be the probable source of the rank order. As the Kwakiutl explain, the eagles eat first among the animals. By living within the natural order men retain their connection with the mythical state, when men were still in the form of animals.

As a counterpart of the animal world among men, the rank order would tend to be stable, although Boas and later scholars thought they saw in Kwakiutl social life a restless contention for ranks and powers. They inferred from the angry language among chiefs during certain property distributions that "potlatches" were the instruments for obtaining higher rank at the expense of less prosperous participants. Hunt, however, rejected inferences of open status rivalry and mobility of rank. In one text he says, "Now that finishes our talk about the eagles, [an order of chiefs], and the head chiefs of the numayms of the Gwetela, for they never change their order" (Boas 1921:824). An immutable rank order belongs mainly to the precontact period. After 1849, and especially because of great population decline, prospects for formal social advancement brightened for the Kwakiutl, but even then only to a limited extent.[2] As late as 1915 the rank order was still cherished as inviolable. Writing of that period, Curtis has said:

> the comparative rank is so firmly fixed that the people rarely consent to a change in the relative position of any two chiefs. In some instances a gens low in the scale has usurped the place of a higher one, but this has always resulted

[48]

in long continued strife and dispute throughout the tribe; in other words, the procedure does not meet with undivided public approval and hence is to be regarded as an exception to the rule. (1915:41).

The rank and the rank holder are consorts, so to speak, and not identities. Rank is not for Kwakiutl a sociological abstraction. It is specifically the holy order of the founding ancestors, a primary order of existence that cannot change without causing grave disruption. It is possible for incumbents who incarnate ancestors to lose honor, but the ancestral ranks continue their march down the generations unaffected. How indifferent the original rank may be to the nature of its momentary conveyor is suggested by the custom of temporarily giving an ancestral name to a dog or to one's own arm for the sake of keeping it active. Under special conditions almost any material conveyor serves for a ranked name—except a commoner. Normally, the quality of the name, the grade of the seat, matches the quality of descent.

The pattern of descent, whether by primogeniture, seniority, or sex line, has its own religious significance. The transmission of supernatural powers can hardly be regarded as a mechanical social process, since it involves so profound a ritual event as the reification of ancestors, and the consequent passing on of their vital powers. Primogeniture and seniority—the prominence of a line descended from or related to the firstborn—convey the powerful qualities of primacy. Sex line defines separate qualities of masculinity and femininity, adding the component of sexuality to the pattern.

Primacy is universally revered. The firstborn child, the first animal of the season killed, the first fruits of a crop, the first menstruation, the first inhabitants to arrive, the first ancestors—all have special merit and the powers of freshness. The first are the beginnings of a sequence, and are hence the primary sources of powers. They bear the seeds of destiny. Beginnings are recognized as entrances into new domains and so involve, commonly, rites of passage. The recognition of the firstborn as special is perhaps the single most characteristic feature of descent systems throughout the world. In its respect for the firstborn, Kwakiutl is in the traditional mold. Respect for senior lines, on the other hand, has not been carried as far among the Kwakiutl as it has been, for example, in Polynesia. There the firstborn is said to be the one who leads the way. As the leader from a prehuman into a fully human status, following parturition, he is the natural leader of his line.

Among Kwakiutl, the chief is called *gyigame*,[3] which means literally "being in front" (Boas 1947:360). *Gyiu* refers to the prow of a canoe and to the forehead. Thus the seniors are in the forefront. The imagery of chiefs as the heads, as the forward parts of the body, is repeated in the ritual distribution of parts of an animal at a feast. The front is reserved for high chiefs, the middle section for lower chiefs, and the hind quarters and tail for the common people (Boas 1921:750). The crown of the head, moreover, is the seat of the soul. In corresponding fashion, the chiefs who represent the first ancestors and have therefore dual qualities as person and as ancestral spirit are, by analogy, the souls or the vital elements of their descent groups. The match between firstborn and ancestral spirits establishes the appropriate balance between two sets of primacies and two sets of powers. When this balance has been achieved, little is lost in the process of transmission. It is presumably in the interests of achieving such a balance that Kwakiutl insist upon the firstborn as the exclusive occupant of the seat and name from his paternal lineage.

Only the first four children of a chief inherit rank. The fifth child, the traditions say, is treated like a slave or a dog (Boas 1940:361, Boas 1921:1097). The number four stands for completeness. Beyond lies the menace of excess. The hunter who is granted the magical powers to kill mountain goats must limit himself to four. At the same time, the man who can restrain the temptation to go beyond the excess number of four is believed to have great powers. Thus the first four children possess the supernatural powers, the others lack dual qualities. They are merely human, and hence are not authentic persons. The fifth child is not literally a slave, but as a nameless and unranked being is of the common people.

The role of gender in rank seems to give preeminence to the masculine side; women, when they hold the ranking seat in the lineage, do so as men (Boas 1925:105). Nevertheless, the pattern is based upon full recognition of both sexes. Through the male line men receive basic rank, and through their female line they acquire supplementary powers and ritual privileges that serve to complete the requirements of the rank. Women receive their own titles, powers, and ritual privileges that qualify them as members of the nobility. Only masculine names, however, are graded. Thus since women are, in all other respects, members of the elect, but do not hold a rank, gradation must be regarded as a specialized attribute of status. Gradation, among Kwakiutl, has indeed the most specific connection with distributions that involve relations with the animal world (see Chapters 7 and 8). For reasons I offer later, such relations are opposed to connotations of sexuality. We may say therefore that gradations of rank involve men in ritual relations that are specifically asexual.

Basic rank defines a position held in the name of a lineage, and is linked with the particular name known as the "house name." All other names held by a person convey special ritual privileges, and represent various ancestral and supernatural beings. Only the house name, which carries the special privileges of distributing property and the office of chief, reifies directly a lineage ancestor. Since all lineage ancestors were men, all ancestral house names are masculine. Thus though women inherit basic rank names through primogeniture, they act as temporary conveyors of a purely male line. This is not to say that Kwakiutl descent is simply patrilineal insofar as social status is allocated. The system of descent is dual. Basic rank through male names is but part of the cargo of supernatural treasures carried down the generations by chiefs. Another part is acquired only through marriage and is a matrilineal contribution to a man's children. Each line transmits its own type of powers, and makes its own contribution to the totality of status. One mode of transmission is asexual because it replicates masculine beings without reference to marriage. The other mode is based on marriage and is thus fully sexual.

Speaking in broader terms, one may say that social status among Kwakiutl concerns itself with the supernatural powers that conserve, vitalize, and perpetuate the life of the community. Men and women of the nobility are the conservers and transmitters of these powers. In ritual behavior each sex line depicts the two separate and interdependent sources of life, which in the most elementary terms are, of course, food and sexual reproduction. Graded rank, the province of men, the hunters, concerns itself with food primarily, as in the tradition that attributes the beginnings of the rank order to the first distribution of food among the tribes. Nongraded rank, essentially the province of women, has as its primary concern the theme of human resurrection and continuity through sexual reproduction. From this cosmological perspective, standards of social status taken from the model of European aristocracy are hardly applicable to the Kwakiutl. Nor can we say unequivocally that because men are the real chiefs and are formally ranged in hierarchical order that they hold the "superior" social position.

If the graded men have the exalted privilege of dealing in animal skins and in copper shields, the nongraded women have comparable standing as the bringers of the great Winter Ceremonial. As an order of relative strengths, rank falls naturally within the sphere of masculine aggressiveness and predatory acquisitiveness on the analogy of the eagle who eats first. By contrast, the nongraded status of noble women is associated with the concept of brides as passive. The bride is the source of great powers, but it is the groom as a member of a ranked order who demonstrates the capability of taking her. As the most highly esteemed masculine trait, aggressiveness is a most admired trait in general among Kwakiutl.

The relation of ranked noble men to nongraded noble women has a parallel in the general relationship between chiefs and the common people. The commoners are also outside the sphere of gradations. But the parallel is with respect to a single dimension of the status system, the aforementioned association between grading and aggressiveness, and nongrading and relative passivity. In principle, the commoners are ritually passive. In hunting, which has for Kwakiutl great ritual significance, the chiefs are the active killers, and the commoners are the assistants in the chase. Conceivably, at an unvoiced level of consciousness, commoner males may be equated with the feminine character and acquire thereby a special tinge of inferiority. It is an equation that sets off two classes of males, and clearly yields unmistakable connotations of superiority and inferiority. Between men and women, on the other hand, there is no common scale of evaluation. The sexes do not compete since they are on different tracks.

Graded noble men are therefore qualitatively superior to nongraded commoners. The superiority of the nobility rests, of course, upon substantial religious grounds. The chiefs are the links with the myth world, the original source of supernatural powers. They alone sustain the vital connections between the present community and its beginnings. As the incarnates of the ancestors they alone have a double existence as persons and as spirit beings. The chiefs are the "real" people (Boas 1921:357). They are real because they are complete; they combine in their person the past and the present. Most important, they are the monopolists of primary powers and thus the designated leaders and the only proper hunters of land and sea mammals.[4]

Among hunting peoples it is not unusual for the aggressive encounter with a dangerous animal to have higher prestige than the more passive trapping. This common principle of status applies to Kwakiutl, but there with a specifically religious rationale. What the Kwakiutl evidently have in mind is to establish a parity between the personal and spiritual qualities of the hunter and his prey. The beasts of the sea and of the forests occupy in the Kwakiutl imagination hidden and sacred realms. The sea is the source of life-giving wealth, and the forests and inland rivers and lakes are secret sources of other powers. The animals are their representative populations with whom a correct ritual etiquette is obligatory. The chiefs are most qualified to engage the animals on their own terms because they too are linked with the animal realms. One of the beliefs about the afterlife among Kwakiutl is that the souls of sea mammal hunters go to rest among their prey at sea, and those of forest hunters go to live among the wolves.

The encounter between the chiefly hunter and his prey seems to involve a vital interchange. The animal yields its life for the welfare of the hunter and of his community. The hunter dedicates himself in turn to the rituals of maintaining the continuity of the life cycle for all. In many instances the hunter does submit to ritual preparations for the hunt not, as it is often thought, to insure his success, but as the correct and courteous way of meeting the animal who is going to make him a gift of its life. Imputing to the animal a willingness to die shows no intent to gloss over the aggressiveness in the act of killing. The Kwakiutl chiefs epitomize the aggressive spirit.[5] They seek out the grizzly bear to acquire from him his fearlessness and his relentless anger (Boas 1930:194).

As an aspect of chiefly character, natural aggressiveness is sublimated to a ritual state. Aggression, the natural state at the point of taking an animal's life, is elevated to the broader ritual stance of opposition to the forces that threaten human lives. At this level of consciousness, the chief as fearless, feared, and awesome is again in the mold of the shaman, who is a successful healer by virtue of his militant stance of antagonism against menacing spirits. A man has become fully a chief when he is feared. The history of chief Lasotiwalas ends:

> Now [Lasotiwalas] *had the name "Chief Who Obtained Everything" after he had grown up to be a chief in every way. There is another name, "feared," for the chief who has obtained everything. Now this is the end.*

> (Boas 1925:357)

As the chiefs are double, part human and part ancestral spirit, so their chiefly qualities have dual aspects. The human side is often arrogant and assertive, angrily defensive of social superiority. The spirit part is in parallel, but at a higher level. There is a social and political reality to the prideful status of the Kwakiutl chief. This humanly real side is rather modestly displayed, however, compared with the metaphoric extravagance required by the religious portrayal. Chiefs who overstepped the political limits by a display of avariciousness were liable to violent removal. But in the ritual setting, the chief who inspired fear was said to be admired.

Boas was silent on this subject but Codere (1957) insisted that Kwakiutl society was graded by rank rather than by class, and that differences in status shaded off imperceptibly from top to bottom. This surely was not, as I have shown, the Kwakiutl view of their community. The chiefs are the real people, the commoners are the tail end of the kinship line, and the fifth born, the superfluous for whom there were no more names left to transmit. Commoners are related to chiefs by kinship, but not in the religious qualities of greatest interest. Commoners are called *bek* or *begwanem*, "people." Nevertheless, they share in the common amenities of eating and housing. The striking Polynesian separations based on the sanctity of the body and the possessions of chiefs are missing on the Northwest Coast. Still, chief and commoner are separate castes in some respects. Normally they do not intermarry, and they are apart in all major religious rites. Some ambiguity as to the status of commoners exists, however. As intrinsically human, they are in essence the common substance of all life, including the ancestors.[6] At the same time, they are totally of the earth, which is after all the realm of choice for all ancestors, most animals, and many supernatural beings.

Slaves (*qak*) were a full-fledged caste. Captive aliens, they had no kinship connections with their new homes, and no genuine ties any longer with their original tribes and villages. As persons violently torn loose from their roots, slaves existed in a state equivalent to being dead. Being on the margins of death they were by Kwakiutl standards the proper sacrificial victims for cannibalistic feasts. The ultimate destiny of persons who were otherwise employed in menial tasks was thus to serve as food, and slaves were, in effect, reduced to the lowest level of generality. Commoners were at least accorded the honorable differentiations of kinship and lineage, and held a circumscribed but definite place in ritual distributions. Slaves were totally undifferentiated except by gender. The slave had become a fully generalized symbol of human life comparable to the animal. If the slave had been reduced to being the counterpart of, say, the seal he had the higher ritual value as being human.

In summary, the main categories of the social community are counterparts of spiritual realms, each distinct and closed to the others, connected only by ritual relations that serve to sustain their separation. The order of chiefs is a closed system that can never be enlarged beyond the fixed number of names. The order of commoners is open-ended and subject, at least hypothetically, to unlimited demographic expansion. The order of slaves, finally, is limited by cultural restraints on excessive violence and ultimately by the natural balance of forces. In the original scheme, the nobility were limited to some 10 percent of the population or less. Only in postcontact times, when in some locations there was a surplus of names were the barriers between chief and commoner breached. Even then, the high ranks were relatively immune to status rivalry.

Rivalry inheres in every system of human inequality, including that of the Kwakiutl. However, their reputation for intense social invidiousness is not altogether ill-founded. A common refrain in family traditions is contempt for those who claim equal or superior rank. The Gwasela narrator sings:

> *Therefore I feel like laughing at what the lower chiefs say when they try to claim higher rank than what I have—I, who had in the beginning an ancestor who was a chief who gave away property at a feast.*

(Boas 1921:841)

This refrain is mild by comparison with others in the songs of ancestral impersonation. The problem has been in locating the contexts in which such sentiments are lodged. I deal with this subject in Chapter 8. For the moment it is sufficient to say that a ritual rhetoric of invidiousness is not to be confused with a status rivalry that promotes social mobility. But if class and basic rank were originally beyond competition, the status system as a whole was not entirely closed to movement. In the acquisition of supplementary names, which are distinct from the closed list of 658 basic ranks, there was ample room for maneuver. Marriage offered the widest opportunities; it brought in new names from the side of the bride's family, and gave access by way of adoption to basic ranks in her lineage. Polygyny, allowing up to four wives, multiplied acquisitions of names and privileges, and thus added to personal prestige and to spiritual completeness. Bilaterality, the range of which expanded through marriages, made it possible to pick up a spare name, or a higher rank among relatives who were childless or had fewer than four children. A less conventional but still proper means for acquiring names and supernatural powers outside the normal course of inheritance

was through war and personal murder. In Kwakiutl doctrine, the killer—
but only of the proper class—has the right to usurp the names and
privileges of his victims.

The Name (tleq). The name is the essential ingredient of religious
worth. The basic social division is between those who possess real names
from a power-granting donor, and those whose names are, as Hunt
remarks derisively, "made up." To lack a real name is equivalent to
being without a full complement of soul, for the name is one form
of soul.[7] As such it has existence on its own, although it needs a material bearer to be complete. In the primitive world, names are commonly
considered to be spiritual attributes, and are often held in secret for
fear of loss or injury at hostile hands. The loss or weakening of a name
is equivalent to soul loss and equally feared. The Kwakiutl doctrine of
names has evolved as a special version of the widespread tradition. In
the setting of aristocracy where the name is held by persons of notable
powers there is no need to hide it fearfully. In any case, it has its own
powers and its own existence as the spiritual essence of ancestors.

Postcontact conditions demonstrate the relative autonomy of the name
with startling clarity. Because of a surplus of names, men began to hold
basic rank in several lineages where they had acquired additional names.
The new owner held title, but the names, by lineage law, retained their
separate residences. A box, equivalent to a house, was set for each basic
rank name, and when property was distributed it went to the name,
entering its box. When the owner gave blankets to all the lineages he
included his new names among the recipients. Literally, he was not giving to himself, he was giving to the names. Conversely, when he was
a recipient he would receive from the box bearing his names (see Boas
1925:89, 103). An even more striking demonstration of the autonomy
of the name is in the right of a man to "marry" a name owned by
his mother as a means of receiving the powers and privileges that pertain
to that particular name, and can be transferred only through marriage.
This type of marriage as well as those with a dog or an arm seem reasonable if the name is considered a corporate entity whose own rights are
inviolate. These examples are, of course, anomalous because they do
not stand for the traditional requirements of matching of name and
recipient either through lineage descent or by marriage. Nonetheless,
they are convincing demonstrations of the nature of the name. The

relations between persons and names are fully reciprocal. The name cannot fulfill its power-laden destiny without a carrier, the person without the name is incomplete. From this point of view alone, the analogy between body and soul can hardly be ignored.[8]

If names, as it is said, existed in the prehuman myth realm, their initial existence was as pure nonmaterial being. Kwakiutl speculation on this question stops short of elaborating the nature of pure spiritual existence. The concept of preexistence is little more than an intimation. Myth and family traditions always link names, persons, and powers. Thus the name has concrete associations. Each has a history. The names that confer basic rank are part of the history of the founding of the lineage. Secondary names are included in later histories that narrate how the early ancestors met supernatural beings and were given their names and powers. Those names pertaining to the Winter Ceremonial were always received later. Along with the very important feast names, without which a person is as dead, they are gifts of the father-in-law that were originally acquired from supernatural beings.

In view of the special attention the traditions give to the details of the encounter at which the name was acquired it would be reasonable to assume that a name by itself is not a sufficient possession. The content of the name is revealed by the ritual setting in which it is displayed. The ritual setting invokes the tradition of acquisition, which is part of the traditional heritage of the lineage. It recalls the supernatural being who was the original donor, and it displays symbolically the powers that came with it. The name itself is part of a four-element packet of powers, and it would be contrary, I believe, to the Kwakiutl conception to attach importance to the name alone. The name bearer must be identified with the primary event as an incarnate of the founding ancestor or of a later ancestor who had entered the secret realms of the supernatural beings to get their names and powers. In the display of the name, the original event mentioned in song and dance is reified. The shamanic power quest of the original is repeated in each succeeding bearer of the name. It is probably fair to conclude from the ritual patterns that in subsequent transmissions of the name the donor has become metaphorically equivalent to the original supernatural being. This relationship would account for the characteristic gift pattern enunciated by Mauss (1954) of the superiority of the giver over the receiver. In the magisterial role of benefactor there is an intimation of divinity.

Acquiring many names is a spiritual obligation. Kwakiutl did not collect names as though they were honorary degrees. By reifying the name the bearer was giving the ancestor and the supernatural being life among men. In return he insured his own life and indirectly that of his lineage fellow. The sociological formulation that would say that with each new status a Kwakiutl chief assumes a name appropriate to his new position needs to be modified to acknowledge his becoming identified with new spirit beings. He does not collect new names, he lives through them and has different capacities through each.

Hunt describes the names of the head chief of the leading lineage of the Gwetela in the following manner. The head chief is Maxuyalidze. With this ancestral name he is head chief and he invites the tribes. He has a "man's name," Place of Obtaining Property, which represented him before he became head chief, when he had only the privilege of giving property to his own tribe. He has a young man's name, White Goose, and a child's name, Found by Good Luck. He has a birth name and two Winter Ceremonial names, one as a Seal, another as a Sparrow (Boas 1921:825–826). Other chiefs have, in addition, feast names and warrior names, the latter acquired after the killing of an enemy.

Although in the legendary period names were acquired through random encounters with spirit beings, in contemporary times the principal names are acquired routinely in the course of personal maturation. Again the spirits and the person are matched. In the absence of any indication in the texts that there are special spirit beings who are appropriate for the very young, for youths, and for mature men, it might seem that it is human history that grades the spirits. There are no specific references to a likely possibility that once a grading has been established it continues down the generations. Only a logical deduction about the system implies that when chiefs divest themselves, as they must, of their names, they start by giving away their own child name, for example, to a child or grandchild. There is no doubt, of course, that the head chief name goes only to the next head chief.

The seven principal names of the Gwetela chief also represent seven ritual stages in his successive movement toward the pinnacle of his due rank. It is perfectly legitimate to describe this aspect of the rank order as a system of age grading. At birth, the infant receives a name that is but the name of his place of birth. All children born at Fort Rupert are first named Tsaqis (Fort Rupert). In contrast to a spirit name that has associated powers, a place name is relatively inconsequential, but not without symbolic significance. The place name memorializes the spot where the ancestor first settled on this earth. Implied in this naming is an equation between the ancestor's becoming human at this locality—in a sense, born—and, of course, the birth of the child. The significance of this name arises thus from its recapitulating the historic first appearance of the ancestor. The second name, and often the third as well, came as a pair, one from the paternal and one from the maternal grandparents, in recognition of their joint possession of the grandchild. In Kwakiutl belief, the grandchild is the promise of the line's continuity (Boas 1930:181).

The second name comes after 10 moons, a period recognized by the Kwakiutl as the normal gestation period, and marks ritually the new birth of the child in direct association with spirit beings. At this time the child is painted with red ochre, the common symbol of aliveness, and is decorated with arm and leg bands that link it to the Thunderbird (see Boas 1932a:201) and thus to the Sky World and to the Winter Ceremonial. Four days later the leg and arm bands are removed and the child receives its fourth age grade name. After each of these namings small local distributions of property are made in the name of the infant. After four years the child distributes red ochre among the young of his village and receives his "paint name." He has advanced to being a donor of low-grade power. Years later as a youth he "spreads out" by receiving a name that permits him to distribute property, that is, animal skins, within the lineage. Four years later he receives his first Winter Ceremonial name, and is linked thereby with a new set of supernatural powers, the gift of his maternal grandfather. Finally, if he is to be a high chief, he assumes his father's basic rank and is then qualified to distribute property to all the tribes. For a detailed account by Hunt of the rituals of accession to basic rank, see *Contributions to the Ethnology of the Kwakiutl* (Boas 1925:113ff).

Since one person at a time bears a particular name, acquisitions by the children involve self-divestment on the part of parents and grandparents. At some point, a parent will have stripped himself or herself (girls receiving names from mothers and grandmothers). When the chief has yielded his basic rank, at the mature age of 35, he has closed out the period of his own spiritual rank. He has become a reduced human being, akin to but not actually a commoner, for the history of his names clings to him. In the natural course of events, the chief will have divested himself of all names, by the time his firstborn has reached maturity. When he has become "the old man of the house" (Boas 1925:229) his house is dismantled, and his heir builds a new one to prepare for his impending marriage and the start of a new cycle.

What has seemed to many to be an unseemly appetite for personal fame and the acquisition of honorific names is rather a solemn concern with the social responsibilities of carrying forward at the propitious moment the legacy of powers—nothing less, in fact, than the life of the lineage and tribe.

The propitious moment, in the religious sense, is when donor and receiver are at their high point in religious powers, before the donor has begun to decline and after the receiver has been prepared. It is undesirable for a name to be transferred after death, although Hunt reports such a case. The unattached name is in danger of dying out (see Boas 1897:359; 1925:101). Chiefs on their deathbed quickly summon an heir to pass on the names before it is too late. We know of one exceptional case where names that had been held by dead relatives were revived. The recipients were not of high rank. They were the two children of a woman who had herself inherited her father's seat after he had died and so left her husband's lineage with her children to return and occupy her father's place. Having no other names to give her children she resurrected, as Hunt remarks pointedly, "the seats of those who were dead" (Boas 1921:967).

We have been considering the name as alive and as a supernatural power. It is also visualized as having weight and mass. Thus at the rites of transfer of a copper from one tribe to another, a chief who is offering blankets for the copper says:

Now you have seen my name. This is my name; this is the weight of my name. This mountain of blankets rises through our heaven. My name is the name of the Kwakiutl. . . .

(Boas 1897:349)

The name is set forth in proportion with blankets, which towering like a mountain are a link with the sky. The mountains are one of the traditional access routes to the heavens. The equation of a name with blankets, which in the early days were animal skins, implies a three-sided relationship that includes the personal bearer of the name, the supernatural donor at one side, and the high pile of animal skins at the other. The bearer is thus an intermediary between the ancestor, who had been in animal form, and the skins, which are the forms of the animals. It is with respect to this relationship, one may argue, that the assumption of a name demands the immediate distribution of animal skins. Indeed the Kwakiutl say that the distribution "fastens on the name" (Boas 1925:111). This expression seems to mean that the distribution completes the relationship between the name bearer and his ancestor. In short, the ancestor does not simply transmit a name to a descendant without involving the animal world. This transaction expresses the Kwakiutl conviction as to the indissoluble connection between men and the animal world, a connection that may have its source in the bond between the hunter and his obliging game. Since the pact of a mystical reciprocity is between hunter and animal, it is understandable why women are not distributors of property, and why women as females do not carry the ancestral seat name. The image of blankets (animal skins) reaching to the sky carries forward the basic theme of a cycle in which the ancestor, returning his own animal form to the sky acts to initiate, through a human descendant, the reaching up of earth-based animal forms to the same place.

Finally, the name serves to define the qualities of the supernatural donor himself. Most names are epithetic and characterize the original bearer as strong, as predatory, as masterful, and as menacing. The entire roster of chiefly names merits close study as a guide to Kwakiutl thinking about the nature of chiefship. The following sampling of names from one tribe, the Mamaleleqala, is illustrative: Creating Trouble All Around, The Great One Always Alone in the World, Four Fathom Face, Making Potlatch Dances All the Time, Copper, From Whom Property Comes, Giving Wealth, Giving Food, Giving Potlatch Everywhere, To Whom People Paddle, Whose Body Is All Wealth, From Whom Presents Are Expected, Great Mountain, About Whose Property People Talk (Boas 1897:339–340). I have, however, bypassed this particular line of investigation.

The epithets of all 658 names, representing original ancestors and their seats, would seem to sum up Kwakiutl character. In Kwakiutl belief this character is seen to have been preordained, not evolved in the course of what might appear to the alien outsider to be a history of stormy status rivalry. The ancestor says:

These will come to be the names when I come to take my place in this world, when I come being a man in this world coming down here.

(Boas 1935b:66)

What the Kwakiutl chiefs carry with them is not their own character but that of their founders. The name is not a guide to personal character, but to the collective representation of the tribe or lineage. Accordingly, the concept of name as a soul is not to be taken in the personal sense. The personal soul is distinct. The name stands rather for the collective immortality or continuity of the descent line. The personal soul departs at death to join with owls or other animals. The name soul remains forever among men. It animates the lineage and, if basic, may not leave it. As in a marriage, the name and the person consort for the purpose of perpetuating the spiritual side of the lineage. If it is a marriage, it is a nonsexual union. This type of union is to be visualized, I believe, within a more comprehensive pattern that includes actual marriage. Within this pattern each element has a complementary role in carrying forward the ancestors and their descendants.

Nothing in the Kwakiutl texts, I must remind the reader, specifically denotes the name as a soul. The concept of name soul is an implication from the texts, which unquestionably attribute spiritual qualities to the name. I have taken the term itself from Eskimo, whose attributions to the name are similar to those of the Kwakiutl. There are good historical reasons for assuming a common religious substratum to Eskimo and much of Northwest Coast culture, so that Eskimo usage can illuminate Kwakiutl. The Eskimo view of the name as one of several souls that belong to a person is so widespread in the arctic, ranging from western Alaska to eastern Canada, that it may be one of the very early Eskimo-Indian religious traits. Among Eskimo, names are the spirit representatives of the ancestors, and live again in each new generation of bearers. The name adds powers that give strength and help avert illness. Powers are cumulative; in addition to the name acquired at birth, men and women try to obtain as many names as possible (see Rassmussen 1931:214–220 passim). The principal difference between Eskimo and Kwakiutl concepts is with respect to access and transmission. The Eskimo concept is more or less egalitarian, the Kwakiutl spiritually aristocratic.

Crests.   The family tradition usually begins with an ancestor coming down to earth, taking off his animal mask, and becoming human. The mask then becomes the emblem or crest *(keso)* of the lineage he has founded (Boas 1897:554).[9] The crest takes the form of a mask, some other wood carving, or a painting depicting the ancestor in his animal form, the original of which has returned to the place of origin (Boas 1935b:78). Therefore, the crest corresponds to the name as one of the two noncorporeal attributes of the ancestor. It accompanies the name in hereditary transmission and yields another type of power. For example, the lineage that has a particular animal for a crest will obtain that animal easily (Boas 1932a:233). However, this aspect of the crest seems less important than its emblematic value to the Kwakiutl, who possess other means for getting animals. As an emblem the crest completes the reification of the ancestor. The name represents him as a human being, the crest stands for his original animal (or other nonhuman) connection. Together, mask and name accurately define ancestors and their noble descendants as double. If the name is to carry powers it cannot do so without the presence of the crest.

In the light of mythological references, it is the mask that is the quintessential form of the crest. For Kwakiutl a mask is a disguise only in the ultimate metaphysical sense of being an appearance behind which is a deeper reality. The mask, which may cover the forehead, the entire face, or the entire body, is imagined as the visible outer form of all life. In myth the animals that deal with persons wear their forms as full body masks or coverings when they are behaving as animals, and remove them when diving for power or dancing in the Winter Ceremonial. They then appear in a human inner form. Basically, the masks stand for natural diversity, the inner form for consubstantial unity. As naturalists the Kwakiutl are far from disparaging natural diversity, and the mask for them is no mere outer trapping. Outer is as essential as inner. The sky itself is thought of as a man's mask looking down upon the earth. As the counterpart of the name soul the mask would be the form soul of beings. Vocabulary directly supports the attribution of soul to mask. Thus one of the terms for soul in Kwakiutl is *begwanemgemtl*, which means literally "person mask" (Boas 1927:390). In summary, then, persons noble possess three kinds of soul: a personal soul, a name soul, and a form soul. Commoners have only a personal soul.

Name and mask are collective spiritual qualities temporarily lodged in a person. Other forms of crests, such as carved house posts, heraldic columns erected outside, and wall paintings, are less directly personal. They are more closely associated with the house than with its residents. The house, while belonging to a chief, has a separate existence and its own emblems. Its separateness derives from its special function as a residence of the lineage. It is both a lineage house and a ceremonial structure that contains the lineage members and their guests in ordinary residence, and as spirit beings. Family traditions often describe the house as one of the supernatural treasures that came down from the sky,[10] or rose up out of the sea. It is a traditional gift (in myth) from the father-in-law (see Boas and Hunt 1905:184–185) following the marriage of his daughter.

Among supernatural treasures, the house comes within the special category of containers that includes canoes, boxes, dishes, and animal skins. The idea that all forms of life and forms of vital force occupy a house or some container is widespread in North and South America, and is probably related to observations about wombs, nests, eggs, pupae, and animal shelters of all sorts. The Kwakiutl speak of the body as the "house of the soul" (Boas 1921:724). By analogy, the house is the body or container of its own content of living force, namely the spirit incarnate of the lineage ancestors. When a parent dies, they say "the house is dead or broken" (Boas 1888:210). This analogy arises naturally from Kwakiutl imagery in myth, which presents a picture of the house as alive, able to swallow people, and holding the tribes in its hands (Boas 1921:1279). The front walls and the doorway of actual houses are usually painted in the form of a great devouring mouth that swallows the guests (Curtis 1915:8).

Traditional houses were built of red cedar planks and logs. Wood is the natural building material on the Northwest Coast, but for Kwakiutl trees are living beings; like animals, they make a gift of their bark and planks to men. The red cedar in its obvious associations with blood is a sacred tree. Its bark is a major source of supernatural power for shamans and in the Winter Ceremonial. By implication, the house is a potent container. Early houses on the Northwest Coast, including Vancouver Island, were raised some 30 feet above the ground on a cradle of timbers. The house had to be entered by ascent along a notched pole. Its floor, accordingly, was a deep pit, surrounded by a raised platform upon which the separate sleeping quarters and secret ceremonial chambers were built (see Niblack 1890:305). Similar houses are described in the family traditions of the Kwakiutl. The construction of the house seems to be in accord with mythological themes. The requirements of ascent and descent suggest movements from the middle level of earth, up to the sky, and down into the underworld of ghosts. There are, in fact, ritual occasions when the roof of the house is specifically identified with the heavens. For example, the great transverse roof beam, to which warriors tether themselves during the Winter Ceremonial, is said to be the Milky Way. The so-called Cannibal Pole, the great symbol of death and resurrection, is set in the house to project through the roof as a link to the sky. The association of the house floor with the underworld of ghosts is more uncertain. It is suggested by Puebloan structures of *kiva* and *sipapu* that connect with the underworld, and by Kwakiutl associations between ghosts and the fires that are set upon the sunken floor.

More certain is the connotation of the house as a spirit associate of the lineage chief. Houses are named, which suggests they are form souls of the lineage. The life span of the house is that of the chief during his official tenure, that is, as long as he continues to incarnate his ancestor. When the heir takes the name, the old house is torn down plank by plank and given away, and a new house is built. The new house is built in stages over a period of four years that correspond by analogy with the rites of elevation of the heir.

IV

MARRIAGE

"Marriage among the Kwakiutl," Boas wrote, "must be considered a purchase, which is conducted on the same principles as the purchase of a copper" (1897:357). The idea of "purchase" can not be accepted as a serious explanation for what is really a complex series of ritual exchanges between the parties of the groom and the parties of the bride. But, to use somewhat different language, comparing the acquisition of a bride to the acquisition of a copper shield, an object of high value, does open promising channels for analysis. Boas, however, seems to have had in mind the self-evident connection between the two "purchases" and social prestige. Coppers and brides added enormously to the reputation of the person and his lineage. Their acquisition, therefore, assumed great urgency and was the occasion for ritual demonstrations of the family honor. Copper shield and bride were valued less for intrinsic than for their symbolic values.

Although Boas astutely perceived a common principle in acquisition of copper and bride, he characteristically did not pursue its implications. To do so he would have had to seek a deeper understanding of the meaning of the coppers and ultimately the meaning of property in general for the Kwakiutl, and for these tasks Boas was less well equipped, as his statements on the nature of the "potlatch" so painfully reveal. Generalizing from a very special transaction when the recipient of a loan pledged himself to return it plus double the amount, Boas defined the "potlatch" as "the interest-bearing investment of property" (1897:341). This statement, albeit both naive and factually incorrect, is, of course, understandable as an early appraisal of a custom well out of range of positivist Western thought. Unfortunately Boas never corrected his initial impression even though his own voluminous field data on the subject flatly contradict him, and this unfortunate statement remained in his notes for his definitive ethnography, which was to represent his last thoughts on Kwakiutl.

As Boas plainly saw, the nature of ritual exchange is central to marriage. If exchange is but a commercial transaction enveloped in the ritual trappings of a primitive society, and the purchase of a copper is but one of the grandiose forms of exchange, then marriage would also be commercial. Most writers have acknowledged, however, that Kwakiutl commerce was in the interest of social prestige. Thus, in calling attention to common principles of purchase of coppers and brides Boas had nothing more in mind than the commerce of prestige.

Coppers and brides are indeed related acquisitions, and both are involved in rank. But since rank is for Kwakiutl an organization of religious qualities, coppers and brides must also be recognized as acquisitions in the religious sense. To arrive at Kwakiutl meanings we must turn away from the a priori opinions of Boas and later writers and go directly to the genealogical records, the "family histories" as Boas calls them. There are 20 or more family histories, all collected in text and carefully translated by George Hunt. The 23-generation history of a Gwasela family is the most comprehensive; some histories are comparatively fragmentary. But since each history is the authentic record of family honor, special attention is paid to marriages. The Gwasela history is of unusual interest because it portrays what seems to have been a changing pattern of marriage ritual, a ritual that includes, of course, the transmission of treasures and associated property. The narrator, a Gwasela woman, seems concerned that the listener understand the period during which events occurred. When exchanges come to be in woolen store-bought blankets rather than traditional animal skins, she explains the change by reminding her auditor that at that time the

Hudson's Bay Company had opened its post at Fort Rupert. Of course, there is no way to evaluate the historical accuracy of her narrative. Let us say, however, that this family history, and the others with which it agrees on main ideas, represents an authentic Kwakiutl viewpoint on the basic forms of marriage and the course of their development. Since to attempt a summary of the histories as they deal with marriages would be cumbersome, I have drawn upon them for what seem to be basic principles in marriage. Interested readers have access to the texts for forming their independent judgments.

The Gwasela history begins by identifying the ancestor as a whale traveling about in a canoe, which is his whale body. When he steps out of his canoe he has taken off his whale form and has become human. He builds houses at two different beaches and assumes a new name, Stranded Whale. Having established his fully human personality, he settles down. He is assisted at once by Sintlae, the ancestor of the Sintlae lineage, who has descended from the sky with his wife and daughter. They introduce themselves, and then Stranded Whale asks for the girl, saying: "I wish to marry your princess O brother so that our names may be really together" (Boas 1921:837). The girl then sits beside Stranded Whale and they are married. The father-in-law transmits two names to his son-in-law as a marriage gift. When a son is born the father-in-law gives him a name; his own father gives his son his own original name together with a house. Stranded Whale then gives his father-in-law his whale form as food and receives in return a canoe (which is not given the connotation of a whale). As a result of this simple exchange, Sintlae and his daughter receive new names.

This account of a first marriage is interesting in several respects. The bride and her father come to the house of the groom, an unusual procedure. In all subsequent Gwasela marriages the groom voyages by sea to acquire and bring back a wife. There is no connotation of bride price and there are no property exchanges, other than the reasonable quid pro quo of a whale canoe as food for a canoe as means of conveyance. The real issue in this first marriage is the first acquisition of names from outside. Subsequent Gwasela marriages involve more complex exchanges and a greater variety of acquisitions. If we choose to consider the first marriage as prototypical, we may conclude that the acquisition of names—of name souls—is at its core. Subsequent marriages add new names and other treasures in a progressive expansion and fleshing out of the supernatural properties of the chiefly line. All acquisitions other than the first names are acquired by a masculine journey outward to bring back the bride.

The second marriage in this genealogy is to a wife from a distant tribe. On a trip of exploration Stranded Whale again meets a chief and the chief's wife and daughter. Stranded Whale accepts the daughter as his bride, and gives up to his second father-in-law the traveling canoe he had received from his first father-in-law. He receives as his wedding gift a house, the speaking posts of the house, the name of the house, a personal name, four house dishes, two slaves, and 55 animal skins as "the blankets of [the] wife" (ibid:840). Later, the father-in-law provides 50 seals for a feast to still another tribe at which the "blankets of the wife" are given away in the "first potlatch" of the Gwasela. When a child is born the father-in-law brings more animal skins, this time to be given away to guests when the names of the child are announced.

Acquisitions through marriage eventually include coppers and Winter Ceremonial dances, but not, as a rule, family crests. Boas, however, offers a family history of the Qomoyaye in which a crest is transmitted by marriage (1897:336–337). This crest, it should be noted, was not a primary but a secondary acquisition by the ancestor after he had been established on earth. The ancestor had met the dangerous giant crane, Hoxhoq, and made it his lineage carving. A Qweqsotenox chief was able to acquire the carved *Hoxhoq* by marrying the owner's daughter. Later, a Gwetela chief obtained the same crest from the Qweqsotenox by marriage. It would seem, therefore, that a crest that is not an original property of the founder may enter the cycle of transmissions through marriage.

The ritual aim of marriage for the groom's side is always twofold:to add weight to a rank by acquiring new names and wealth, and to complete the assembly of supernatural gifts and powers of the lineage by adding essential ritual complements. According to myth, which usually states the key principles of ritual, marriage is the principal source of supernatural acquisitions (see Boas 1935b:93). The most vital such gift the bride brings to her husband is the privilege of the Winter Ceremonial, about which I need say only this for the moment: It conveys a group of powers quite distinct from those transmitted from within the lineage. The paternal lineage conveys ancestral powers, marriage brings in additional powers associated with specifically nonhuman supernatural beings.

The ancestral powers, to anticipate a fuller discussion of the subject later, are essentially parochial; they guarantee the perpetuity in full vigor of the lineage. The powers of the Winter Ceremonial are socialized; on the small tribal scale, they are universalized. They represent the chiefs as shamans, the guardians of the full Ritual Congregation against death. Death is visualized by Kwakiutl as Man Eater or another destructive spirit. As the conveyor to her husband of the shamanic powers of the Winter Ceremonial, the wife draws him out of the narrow and restricted confines of his descent line and provides him with the more worldly forum of the shaman. Herself an outsider, portrayed as an acquisition from across the sea, she endows her husband with an external spiritual dimension. The idea of an external spiritual dimension is taken directly from Kwakiutl imagery. In the many ceremonial songs about chiefs' capabilities the constant themes are those of moving about the world (see Boas 1925:187), of seizing the crests of all the tribes, of moving from one's own sphere outward into others.

Thus to the themes of accretion and completion Kwakiutl marriages add the dominant chord of exogamy, which sounds the universal obligation to move out of parochial confines. Kwakiutl see the exogamic obligation as a spiritual matter foremost and as practical sociology—forming alliances with other families—only secondarily. In all the many records of marriages the talk is of spiritual acquisitions. The father-in-law appears as the guardian of great treasures. He is the human counterpart of the supernatural beings who are compelled by legendary heroes to yield up their powers. In the legendary incident, as in marriage, an alliance is formed, a basic alliance of donor and receiver, an alliance where the donor is equivalent to a supernatural being, and the recipient replays the part of the mythical hero.[1]

Each family history gives an account of dual acquisitions, first of the family crest and then of treasures from marriage. The first acquisition results from the asexual metamorphosis of the founder from animal person to true person, and the second from marriage. Marriage takes place after the metamorphosis. In almost all instances, the initial as well as subsequent marriages are masculine acquisitions. Kwakiutl sometimes regard marriage as a military adventure, speaking of "making war against all the princesses of all the chiefs" (Boas 1897:359), leaving no doubt whatsoever of its masculine emphasis. The military imagery is not a reflection of "bride by capture," but is rather a restatement of a mythical exploit and the capture of powers. The bride and all that comes with her are *tlogwe*, including the children (Boas 1927:391). It is in this context that we finally understand the literal meaning of *tlogwe* as "coming down to the beach" (Boas 1935b:99).

[70   ]

The warlike imagery in marriage is to be understood in religious terms. As religious concepts, warfare and marriage share the common metaphor of quest for supernatural treasures. By killing an enemy within his own cultural tradition the Kwakiutl acquired his name and powers. They took what belonged to a distant and alien lineage and entered it into their own. As in marriage a principal objective of war was the acquisition of Winter Ceremonial dances and powers (see Boas 1905:240). Warfare and marriage meet only on the issue of acquisitions. Beyond that they part company. Warfare actually broke connections. The names taken in war were torn forcibly from their own genealogical chain. Marriage, on the other hand, interlaced the two lines.

Thus warfare and marriage are equivalent in terms of concepts of acquisition and subsequent transmission of powers, but divergent and perhaps complementary with respect to concepts of linkage. Marriage and warfare are analogs of the spirit quest with respect to the elementary pattern expressed by going out into alien and dangerous territory, encountering a source of supernatural powers, obtaining them from him or her, and bringing them back for the benefit of the community. We may then consider power quest, warfare, and marriage as three integrally related modes of transferring supernatural powers from their primary sources into the lineages of activist males. The three modes of transfer establish interlineage links (marriage) and new links between men and supernatural beings (power quest), and transmit the links between men and supernatural beings from one community to another (warfare). In marriage, finally, the father-in-law, the great magisterial donor of treasures, is analogous to the supernatural donor.

On the strength of such analogy we may go a step further and suggest that just as the gain for the father-in-law in marriage is the privilege of entering into the domain of the acquisitor son-in-law, so the gain for the magisterial supernatural beings is also in entering the domain of the acquisitor human. In several legendary instances, primary supernatural powers are gained directly by marriage with supernatural beings (Boas 1935b:93). The power quest and marriage have a dual character in that both donor and receiver acquire comparable benefits. The donor is magisterial as benefactor. At the same time, he allies himself to and becomes the equivalent of his recipient, who now bears his name. The recipient for his part shifts at once from petitioner to the magisterial position of at least partial identification with his donor.

Boas suggested a second duality in acquisitions. The animal persona, the internal source of the crest, yields its powers once and for all. But the supernatural beings whose treasures move only through marriage are recurrent figures; connections with them must be repeatedly sought after and renewed. In other words, the theory of magical acquisitions matches the realities of transmission—the patrilineal line is the constant, and the female side the endlessly renewable.

This view of the female side is in harmony with the sociology of marriage. Brides live as a rule with their husbands' lineage, and the aim of one lineage is to marry into all others. All the family histories illustrate precisely the same pattern of spreading the marriage net widely to encompass the outside world. The Gwasela genealogy shows that after 23 generations this tribe had married into almost every other tribe. The Kwakiutl pattern of nonrepetitive marriages is distinct from the type Lévi-Strauss (1969) describes as "restricted." In such types, rather common in the primitive world, clans, lineages, and other kin groups bind themselves to a series of restricted exchanges, sometimes going so far as always to choose a spouse from the same group (ibid).

Restricted marriage exchanges seem to pursue an idea of an exact matching of qualities in marriage, not qualities of person, but of origins. Kwakiutl marriages, which are generalized rather than restricted exchanges, have broader and more ambitious aims. One aim is indeed to match groups' qualities, and that is accomplished by equating the rank of groom and bride. The other is to accumulate diverse qualities of the high grade until all that are available have been garnered. Other systems of aristocracy, such as those in Polynesia, pursue a policy of concentration of the highest degree of quality to the point of brother-sister marriages, as in the Hawaiian Islands. There, the incestuous marriage fused two highest lines to a point of spiritual incandescence. For the Kwakiutl the ultimate aim in marriage is reached when one lineage can show that over the course of generations it has brought to itself all the powers and treasures the myth world has to offer.

Lévi-Strauss visualizes both marriage forms, the elementary and the generalized, as operating through cycles of reciprocity. The former follows a cycle of simple reciprocity where A gives a wife to B and then B returns a wife to A (or in some instances A is the constant wife-giver and B the constant groom-giver). The latter works through a more complex cycle of exchanges in which A gives a wife to B and B gives a wife to C and then C (or D or E) returns a wife to A. This concept of marriage cycles is predicated upon a rationalist view of the sociology of marriage which says that since marriages are a means of social bonding, each link must have equal opportunity. The concept of marriage cycle is not necessarily that of the native, but is a sociological deduction about the logic of closed systems of exchange. The viewpoint of Kwakiutl is not cyclical; it is monopolistic. As the narrator of a family history says: "Therefore I am full of names and of privileges. And therefore I have many chiefs as ancestors all over the world" (Boas 1921:844). In another text: "I am [L] who marries all around the world" (ibid:847).

The monopolistic aim connotes an aggressive attitude toward acquisition, an attitude that might account for ritual displays of antagonism between the parties of bride and of groom. Acquisitive aggression is also countered defensively by endogamy, since families marry within to safeguard their precious treasures against what they conceive to be a predatory attack on their vital substance. Kwakiutl lineage endogamy is not a "rule" of marriage; it is manifestly a defensive strategy, basically an ignoble, though allowable, mode of self-preservation. Endogamy was rare; who would boast of it? The strong lineages were, in the image of the eagle, predatory in acquisition. None could refuse them a bride. They were also polygynously free to take up to four brides, thus quadrupling their external acquisitions.

Those who were in the position of givers of brides were not correspondingly weak. Kwakiutl promote marriage exchanges through a balancing of powers. The strength of the acquisitor who has the power to extract what he wants is more or less matched by the giver, who has both the abundance of powers to give and the opportunity to penetrate another lineage. The donor of the bride is undoubtedly, as Mauss (1954) justly observed, the *magister*. But the second proposition of the equation does not follow in marriage, because the receiver is in no sense the lesser, or *minister*. In marriage, each side fulfills its necessary role, the male line to appropriate new spiritual powers and treasures so as to complete itself, the female line to give up, and by giving acquire a foothold in another lineage and eventually in all.

Ultimately, giver and receiver meet on the same ground, the ground on which all original spirit qualities that had first existed are recombined in the genealogies of the important lineages. The social bonds are forged through the completion of dissimilar but complementary aims. In Kwakiutl eyes the natural order is fulfilled when the natural dualism of uniqueness and of commonality is carefully preserved. That is, marriage merges certain properties held by a male line and by a female line, but at no point in the merger is the uniqueness of the masculine core of the lineage compromised.

When Boas described marriage as "purchase" he misrepresented its

Kwakiutl significance totally. Marriage inevitably follows the example of biology as a mode of sexual reproduction and transmission. Culture modifies the purely biological example by equating the lineage with the male sex, and so instituting lineage exogamy as metaphor for bisexuality. At the same time, the transmission of names and powers is set forth as the cultural parallel to the biological transmission of physical features. Or, we might say of Kwakiutl, they count upon nature to transmit the physical qualities through biological reproduction. The task of transmitting spiritual qualities they, as spiritual descendants, take upon themselves.

It is necessary, of course, to identify central interests of a culture if only to discover the common ground that the central interests of all cultures occupy. The entire configuration of thought and action within which central interests are embedded is, nevertheless, our own central concern—it is the totality that represents the cultural reality. If transmission to the next generation is focal, the complex of ritual and social activities that initiates marriages and that sustains the continued relations between the side of the groom and the side of the bride enables us to understand exactly what it is that is being transmitted. The significance of a name, for example, as of any other cultural artifact, derives from its context. I turn now from the general orientations of marriage to its ritual context.

The rituals of marriage concern only the chiefs, for they alone have anything of value to transmit. Saying that all others simply "stick together like dogs," Kwakiutl deny marriage to commoners, thus clearly defining marriage as a peculiarly spiritual relationship irrelevant for those who lack full spiritual qualities.

Marriage is also a stage in the elevation of the heir, coming after he has received his seat in the lineage. It will establish him, as it once did the founding ancestor, as the initiator of a line. Unmarried, he remains but a parental product, and the product of his lineage and tribe. They are all the makers of his road and hence the managers of his marriage. From a sociological position, we recognize the vested interest of family, lineage, and tribe in the gains to honor from a good marriage. From a religious point of view, one sees these interests in a different light. The groom, still an incomplete being, cannot be the central figure in the marital acquisition. In his first marriage, his father and the related chiefs act for him. He himself lies on his back in the house of the bride as an inert figure, not speaking, not moving. The bride is correspondingly an inert mass, sitting heavily within her house (Boas 1897:360). The groom's marriage will bring him closer to completion. And for this new stage in his elevation his fellow tribesmen and his father-in-law, who heads the opposite side of tribesmen, join forces. His side has already done for him all it could do. They now call upon the father-in-law: "You who hold the world, we have come to get some treasures from you" (Curtis 1915:122).

The treasures that are demanded from the father-in-law are of two kinds. One set is similar in kind to those already possessed by the lineage of the groom, the other set is new. The former include animal skins, canoes, copper shields, and slaves, the latter include names (especially feast names), houses, house posts, crests, feast dishes, abalone shell ornaments, and Winter Ceremonial privileges.[2] The duplicate treasures have no special connotation as belonging to a male or female line. They enter into general circulation. As soon as they are received by the groom's side, together with the new and supplementary treasures, they are immediately set into general circulation among the tribesmen of the groom. The supplementary treasures are held until they are given up again at another marriage.

Feast names (see Boas 1921:786), and Winter Ceremonial names that may be rendered as the supernatural statuses of feeding the tribes and of endowing them periodically with supernatural power are special marriage treasures. Other names also move via marriage as the female contribution to obligatory bilaterality of name souls. In all early genealogies, a name given by the father to his child is matched by the name given to it by its maternal grandfather.

House dishes usually come in sets of four, each dish carved in the image of a creature of great power. In their totality they represent the great animals of sky, sea, and earth, and certain supernatural beings (ibid:1047). One lineage, for example, possessed two eagles, one grizzly bear, and one wolf dish; another had sea otter, killer whale, beaver, and whale; a third had Thunderbird, Qolos (the mythological younger brother of Thunderbird), a whale and a beaver; a fourth had two double-headed serpents—the awesome Sisiutl; a fifth, the cannibal ogre, Dzonoqwa, along with a grizzly bear, a whale, and a killer whale; and a sixth, to complete a mere sampling, had a whale, a killer whale, a sea lion, and a seal. Curiously, few traditions deal with the origin of the feast dishes. The killer whale, a popular dish form, is explained in one lineage narrative as a commemoration for the owner who as a sea mammal hunter expected to have his soul join the killer whales after his death (Boas 1921:715). But a seal dish held in another lineage supposedly memorialized nothing more than the killing of a seal.

These were not ordinary utensils, but part of the treasure trove of a chief, who announced from whom he had received them in marriage as he set them before his guests. Feast dishes are known by several terms. The most general is *hamaatse,* meaning a receptacle for food. They are also known as *tlogwelitl,* apparently from *tlogwe* (treasure). Some were as large as seagoing canoes, carved like a canoe from a cedar log or made like a box of kerfed boards (Hawthorn 1967:215–216). One double-headed serpent dish measured 20 feet by 3 feet. Others were no longer than 2 feet. Each dish served six guests (Boas 1925:57).

We may approach the interpretation of the symbolic meaning of dishes from several angles. The first clue is from language. As *tlogwelitl* they are identified immediately as supernatural treasures; indeed, in myth these animal and spirit dishes are present in the houses of ancestors and of supernatural beings (Boas 1935b:51). The dish as receptacle suggests an analogy with all other receptacles such as houses, boxes, and canoes. Thus we may regard dishes as form souls for food, which, at least during ceremonial feasts, have the vitality of the animal who had proffered it. The form souls are analogous to crests in that the animals they stand for are generally the great custodians of provender from the realms of sea, land, and sky. But to think of the dishes given in marriage only as associated with food is to miss the true dimensions of Kwakiutl imagery, which characteristically reaches into ultimate issues of life and death. Thus Dzonoqwa (Wild Woman) is a man-eater, most often depicted as a female with enormous breasts and a cultivated hunger for children—a common Kwakiutl image of the double nature of powers. The double-headed serpent, the dreaded Sisiutl, is a war image, an armor for its possessor and at the same time a terrifying weapon that turns those who look upon it to stone. Thunderbird and his brother Qolos are the rulers of the birds of the sky (as distinct from the birds of the earth) and are the enemies of the double-headed serpent. For Thunderbird the Sisiutl is a salmon—that is, from the supreme perspective of heaven the formidable Sisiutl is himself nothing but food.

Perhaps, most revelatory of deeper religious meanings associated with feast dishes is the figure of the Wolf. The Wolf, indeed a chief of the inland forest, is also the most formidable figure in the category of animal spirits. He is a conqueror of Thunderbird, a restorer of life, a major tutelary spirit of shamans, and a founder of the Winter Ceremonial. In one myth he is said to be the chief of the myth people (Boas 1935b:154). I have brought out enough to suggest that the feasting dishes transferred to the groom by his father-in-law are treasures symbolizing a range of life-conserving powers, from the elementary act of eating to the metaphysical issues of death and resurrection. I have already said something about the religious meanings of the house, the copper shields, and the Winter Ceremonial as marriage gifts, and shall say more about these treasures later. The feast dishes alone reveal the extraordinary value the Kwakiutl attach to what they receive with a bride.

In visualizing marriage as a purchase, Boas evidently had in mind contemporary postcontact customs when store-bought wool blankets had indeed become ritual currency. In modern marriages the groom could give blankets and receive, together with other gifts, a return gift of blankets. Boas thought the marriage exchange could be expressed simply in terms of blankets, and even more precisely by way of a quantitative ratio. Without offering a survey of examples, he said the father of the bride returns three times the price paid by the groom (1897:359). The genealogical traditions dealing with precontact marriage do not verify a fixed ratio of exchange. Many accounts of property exchanges ignore bride price altogether, but detail scrupulously everything received from the father-in-law. Such an omission from family histories told from the masculine side implies the relative unimportance of bride price in marriage. In any case, taking account only of material property, no ratio can be established because most of the goods given by each side are of different kinds. The groom's side gives animal skins almost exclusively; the bride's side gives animal skins, canoes, slaves, coppers, abalone, food, fish oil, feasting dishes, speaking posts of houses, crests, names, and the songs, dances, names, and powers of the Winter Ceremonial. Considering only animal skins, which might represent equivalents in exchange, there is still the difference in kind, and no denominational system. Sea mammal skins, especially otter, are most valued, but there is no fixed rate of exchange between sea otter and deer skins. Each side gave what it had and was not obliged to match. The canoe appears as a commodity in marriage exchanges, a commodity of great value, but there is only one example of its being given by the groom's side, and that was early in Kwakiutl history. The records of marriage exchanges reveal most forcefully a preponderance of giving by the father-in-law. This giving is so one-sided that by comparison bride price can only be thought of as a solicitary opening of negotiations (see Appendix 4).

Preponderance of giving by the maternal side is in proportion to ritual obligations of transmission of emblematic properties, all of which move one-sidedly to the son-in-law. The bride price *(qadzedleme)* (Hunt ms. 14:2249) is offered only once, while the return payments may be made as often as six times, once as an immediate return, once when the Winter Ceremonial season is to open, and thereafter at the birth of each of the first four children. The first return marriage payment *(wawatlkale)* may match, as Boas observed, the bride price payment (1966:54). As the bride price complements the emblems of the groom, the immediate return payment complements those of the bride. The payments in her behalf represent the mat she sits on, her carrying straps, her mantle, and other emblems of her worthiness. A very heavy payment of complementary properties *(qotexa)* accompanies the transmission to the son-in-law of a copper and of Winter Ceremonial privileges, that is, rights to impersonate one of the Winter Ceremonial spirits.[3] The copper, when converted after a "sale" into animal skin blankets, helps defray the heavy "costs" of feasts and property distributions that accompany the exercise of Winter Ceremonial privileges. Finally, substantial payments of complementary properties accompany the bestowal of maternal names on successive children.

The material property given as *qotexa* is referred to in the texts as *yäklelwas,* a term translated by Hunt as "bad things" (Hunt ms. 14:1634).[4] The term has not been explicated, and Boas did not speculate as to the sense in which these valuables are to be considered as "bad." Important clues come from the meanings of the stem *yak* and from the ritual setting for the *qotexa.* I discuss the meanings of *yak* in Chapter 7 and refer now only to two basic meanings—"property" and that which is killed. Within the context of the Winter Ceremonial the latter aspect carries a connotation of antagonistic ecstasy. The cognate expression is probably *yakalitl,* which means "to get excited" (see Boas 1921:1393, vocabulary lists).

In speaking of marriage exchanges I follow routine sociology. Still to be discovered are the religious meanings behind the property exchanges. For that purpose I turn again to the family histories.

In a very early Gwasela marriage already referred to, the groom gave one canoe and received at once a set of speaking posts for his house, a "potlatch"-inviting name, a feast name, four feasting dishes, two slaves to take care of the dishes, 50 seals for a wedding feast, and as the "blankets of the wife," 10 sea otter, 25 marten, and 20 black bear skins. After the birth of a daughter, the mother-in-law gave one of her names to the child along with 10 sea otter, 30 marten, and 10 black bearskins. After the birth of a second child, a boy, the father-in-law gave a name to his son-in-law and a name to the child together with 4 sea otter, 10 marten, 7 black bear, 35 mink, and 50 deerskins. In this early marriage no Winter Ceremonial dances are mentioned, an important hint that the Winter Ceremonial had perhaps not yet arrived among the Kwakiutl. But the records are emphatic on the considerable disproportion between a "bride price" of one canoe and a return of 221 assorted animal skins (ibid:840ff), not counting other forms of material and non-material property.

More characteristic of a later but still precontact period marriage is the following example of exchanges. The groom's side gave 10 black bear, 4 marten, 25 elk, 4 lynx, and 11 marmot skins. The father-in-law gave a name, a copper, a male and a female slave, a "Cannibal" and a Grizzly Bear dance, the dance names, and a "cannibal" pole. Later, at a Winter Ceremonial, the father-in-law arrived bearing new gifts—100 dressed skin blankets, 4 slaves, 4 large canoes, a copper, a "Cannibal" dance, a Rich Woman dance, a Frog War dance, and all the dancers' names. After the birth of a son the father-in-law brought a name along with 40 mountain goat blankets, 25 mink, 30 marmot, 4 grizzly bear, 4 marten, and 100 deerskins (see Appendix 4).

We return now to the question asked earlier: Do the Kwakiutl distributions constitute a system of property exchanges that accompany a marriage? The disproportion between so-called bride price and dowry is not of crucial importance. Exchanges need not be symmetrical. All depends on our interpretation of the totality of the ritual events in marriage, among which the property distributions are but one set.

Marriage ritual concerns itself basically with the transmission of supernatural treasures, a transaction involving both sides in different ways. The side of the groom initiates and completes the transaction, intiating by going out and requesting or compelling the father-in-law to yield his daughter and her associated powers by a display of their own powers and treasures (see Boas 1925:237ff); then completing by returning home and displaying what had been secured. The bride's side is concerned with the heart of the matter, with direct transmission of many and varied powers each of which must be given due notice. The property distributions accompany each ritual display of treasure, not as a "validation" but as an inextricable aspect of the display, in the way in which the thunderclap accompanies the lightning bolt.

What places the emphasis on the exchange of goods between a buyer and a seller is our own merchantile mentality. For traditional Kwakiutl Indians still in possession of their own religion, and still free from the white man's commerce, marriage was a religious event. The animal skins that changed hands were not property as the Hudson's Bay Company store understood the term. They were objects of unusual symbolic value, and integral to the religious meanings of the marriage. The meaning of property in Kwakiutl culture is the subject of a later chapter. Here it is necessary to say only that the animal skins are distributed by groom and bride sides not in direct exchange, but in respect to the rituals of transmission. Exchange has the specific meaning of something given in return for something else. In marriage there is exchange, not of property, but of rights—of religious rights, to be exact. By yielding certain of his treasures a man acquires rights to establish a joint descent line. Marriage exchange is the acknowledgement of bilaterality, as is well known. In exchange both sides demonstrate worthiness to share joint supernatural powers.

In these demonstrations, the groom's side has only to identify itself as lineage and tribe and the groom as person, an event that calls for a comparatively small distribution of animal skins. The bride's side has to exhibit and to transmit a great deal of religious treasure and is therefore obliged to distribute a great deal of complementary property. In those marriages where no mention is made of distribution by a groom's side, I assume that identification has been a minor matter. In the Gwasela family history, the first marriage of the ancestor himself illustrates the point. He gives the canoe which is actually his form soul (identification), a gift of fundamental significance. Gifts to the father-in-law of animal skins in later generations demonstrate the worthiness of the groom's name and of the names and powers of his sponsors. This demonstration seems to be solely for the benefit of the father-in-law, judging by the fact that he does not distribute the gift to his own lineage or tribe. In one instance he returns intact what he has received from the groom (Boas 1921:845). On the other hand, all the animal skins, and coppers that are converted to animal skins, given by the father-in-law are for distribution by the son-in-law to his own lineage and tribal mates, by way of displaying the treasures received in marriage. Displays associated with many treasures and encompassing many tribes are costly.

The display of marriage treasures creates a new connection between a man and his son-in-law that is in some respects filial. The filial connection at the spiritual level is expressed in the strong patrilineal focus of the marriage gifts. To be sure, the bride is the carrier of the treasures; it may be said that through his mother a man receives another set of names and other privileges. Nevertheless, as the family histories tell it, the man receives from his father-in-law for himself and for his sons. Daughters receive from their maternal grandmother. While marriage is undeniably bilateral, it sustains bilaterality by forming still another male line, creating a connection that parallels the filial. The new connection is symbolized by the father-in-law when he gives the property that is distributed by his son-in-law in honor of the treasures received. To mark the difference it is the groom, now in a more mature phase, who distributes the property given by his father-in-law. Even though he is giving away what was given him, his position as a new, active center of distribution elevates him substantially, but not all the way.

The final steps in elevation come when he distributes on his own and in honor of his true patrilineal names and powers. In accordance with Kwakiutl rules of symmetry of status, the young woman arrives at a corresponding level through rituals of first menstruation. To honor her emergence as a potential procreatrix she wears an abalone blanket and hat and holds a copper to her side (ibid:701). On marrying a chief she is titled *modzitl*. Marriage is a stage in her elevation as well and comes immediately after completion of her puberty ritual (ibid).

The transmission of treasures and of animal skins is, as I have said, the most important ritual transaction in marriage. In some examples no other ritual events are mentioned—whether because the informant thought other events were inconsequential or because no other events occurred, we are not sure. We do know that many marriages involved ritual dances at the house of the bride, and that the dramatic enactments were themselves owned as valuable mythological treasures. This aspect of the marriage ritual was therefore not standardized. Each lineage followed its own forms and respected the forms of all others.

Nevertheless, the forms described by Boas and in the Kwakiutl texts do convey one constant theme—namely, antagonism. As indicated earlier, the marriage acquisition is analogous to the acquisition of powers from mythological beings. Just as the pattern of encounters with these beings is itself varied—some very friendly or casual and others violently and dangerously antagonistic—so with marriage rituals.

The situation then is that certain tribes enact with each other the roles of antagonist. Since for Kwakiutl, antagonism expresses supernatural powers at the highest level, the tribes engaging in it are not enemies but friends. They have no quarrel with each other. Rather they have joined forces to portray dramatically the idea that some of the treasures received in marriage must sometimes be won by force. Realists to the core, and close observers of the true natural order, the Kwakiutl do not conclude romantically that *all* treasures must be fought for, that all encounters with supernatural spirits are dangerous, that all brides must be overcome by supernatural forces. The conclusion is that contest as a part of the natural order must be given ritual recognition.

Contest is a test of the powers of the side of the groom against those belonging to the bride, her household, and her tribesmen. Referring to marriage parties the texts imply two equations, one a matching of tribes and the other a matching of the great powers of the suitors against the weight or heaviness of the bride. The first equation matches the number of tribal chiefs of the suitors with those of the bridal party; the second matches the aggregate of their hereditary supernatural powers. Of one party of suitors it was said, "They are so great, that they obtain what they want, on account of their greatness" (Boas 1921:1053).

The dramatized ritual contests follow mythological texts. Sham battles with stones depict the war theme. Climbing an incline to reach the bride who is on the roof of her father's house sets forth the idea of a bride reaching to the sky atop a mountain. Or the bride may be behind a wall of fire, or in a house with a snapping jaw such as is inhabited by many supernatural beings. A more consistent theme of contest is that of overcoming the heaviness of a bride who has been rooted immovably to the floor. A display of the combined supernatural treasures owned by the chiefs acting for the groom is finally able to shake her loose. In a marriage between Mamaleleqala and Gwetela (an antagonistic relationship), the suitors show such supernatural treasures as a magical hunting bow, a magic sea mammal harpoon, a shamanistic quartz crystal, and various family crests (see Boas 1897:360; Boas 1921:1022ff, 1054–1057).

An equation is implied between the weight of the immobilized bride and the formidable powers that overcome it. In general, Kwakiutl equate the powers of rank with heaviness. The man elevating his son makes his son heavy. The bride for whom marriage to a chief completes her own elevation to the noble rank is perhaps heavy in like manner. In the case of the bride, however, the imagery of weightiness is refracted in several directions. Her immobility evokes the image of the woman rooted to the center of the earth in the house of Man Eater. In myth she helps seekers of supernatural power to overcome Man Eater. In her heaviness the bride is seated on a mat, her "marriage mat," a euphemism for a quantity of property. Her blanket and her carrying straps are also euphemisms for the portion of property she brings to her husband. Mat, blanket, and carrying strap are associated with weight, supporting weight, enveloping it (perhaps as skins envelope the animal), and transporting it. These items have high value. In one marriage the mat was said to be worth six slaves (Boas 1921:1040). In another, the carrying strap had the value of an expensive copper and 300 blankets. Her blanket may be covered with precious white abalone shells. This valuable blanket is said to be her "heaviness." Transferring it to the groom gives him all that her heaviness implies. Chiefs are made great through their marriages, the Kwakiutl say. The marriage ritual specifies how this is done.

Of the treasures and goods transferred to the husband in marriage, part is reckoned as the marriage gift of the father-in-law and part as pertaining directly to the bride, as aspects of her person. Among these, the abalone shells and the coppers have a special symbolic significance. Copper is a form of wealth used by men, but brought to them by women. Copper is an energetic commodity, kept in motion, moving in marriage and between tribes and endlessly converting its value into animal skins. Abalone is a more stable form of wealth transferred only in marriage. The red copper and the pearly white abalone are linked symbolically as female insignia. During her pubescent isolation a princess wears an abalone blanket and hat, as she later docs at her wedding. She has a copper at her side so that she "may easily get coppers to carry on her back to her future husband" (ibid:701).

A Dzawadenox myth sheds some light on the meaning of abalone. The daughters of a chief go up to the sky where the eldest marries the son of Abalone of the World, receiving as a wedding gift four baskets that perpetually refill, one with dressed skins, one with woolen blankets, one with coppers, one with food (ibid:60ff). The house paintings of Abalone of the World suggest with whom he is associated. They are Sun, Moon, and Thunderbird, the heavenly trinity. In this tale, abalone is a treasure source from the sky, or upper world. In other myth contexts, abalone is associated with the Salmon, who is also known, among his many other properties, as an abalone maker (ibid:676). These are not contradictory ideas. They reveal rather a concept of unity between sky and sea. The same idea applies to copper. Although copper has its basic source in the sea, it is also a product of the sky.[5] A tale from the same tribe speaks of the origins of copper. A Dzawadenox ancestor married Copper-Making Woman, the daughter of Copper-Maker (Qomogwa), the underwater god of the sea (see copper in Analytical Index).

Unlike the abalone shell with its fixed locus in the sky, copper is a mobile and generative symbol, reaching out like the chiefs themselves to encompass multiassociative meanings. The word for copper is *tlaq*, which means "red," not an innocuous term for tribal societies that have worshiped red ochre as the blood of the earth from the beginnings of history. By direct association, copper is salmon, the recurrent life-sustaining food of the sea. It is the reflection of the setting sun on the sea and thus a bridge or a ladder that spirits climb to reach the sky or descend to reach the earth. Like the sea itself copper is healing; it is a life-bringer and a death-dealer. It can fan the flames of a fire, and it can quench a fire. The copper is like a person. It has a human torso shape. Its upper section is considered the head and face, the longer lower section the body. Women carry it on the back like an infant (ibid:1025); men hold it in their arms, as they would a child. Alive, as a spirit being, the copper has a name like that of a chief.

Coppers are broken, that is "killed," and they are later pieced together, restored to life in a miracle of resurrection. The living status of the copper is actually undefined. If the copper is a life form, it is a general form that includes the salmon and the human being. When a copper is "killed," it is struck with a wedge like a sacrificial slave. Thus, it is like a chief and also like a slave. In one context the copper is the blanket of an infant, to keep it warm in its cradle. In another context it is harpooned like a whale.

In Western eyes the protean dimensions of copper have been reduced to one term, wealth. If we are to retain this term for traditional Kwakiutl, we must ignore all gross national product connotations and recognize it only for its vitalistic and animistic meanings.

What the bride brings to her husband, to his lineage, and to his male line, is an incomparable treasure, a boundless wealth. A man says to his son-in-law, "Now listen to the supernatural power of your wife" (ibid:1005). At bottom, at the most rudimentary level of imagery, marriage is the miracle of sexual reproduction elevated by the Indians to a principle, which is abstract and metaphysical even though it is called to mind by concrete images.

Marriage is one set of events in the ongoing stream of the life of the tribes. It arises as an ongoing phase in the elevation of persons—in itself a metaphysical process—and provokes in turn new developments and new movements in several realms of existence. In Kwakiutl religious thought, all vital actions reverberate in all associated realms. What has happened in the myth world must find a sympathetic resonance on earth. The realms of sky, earth, sea, and underworld must be made to respond to one another either by parallel or by antagonistic actions. The bride bringing with her, or causing to be brought with her, the great treasures of the myth world and of all the cosmic dimensions provokes a vast and corresponding response in all the associated realms. Whatever is brought is set in motion, is put into a circulation that, like the bloodstream, brings warmth, life, and vitality to all quarters. The copper, itself a vital force, moves at once from the groom among the tribes, provoking everywhere enormous responses. The bride brings the Winter Ceremonial and thus provokes a literal revolution in the life of the community. When the winter whistles are sounded, the community is transferred from a secular existence and is propelled into an ultimate intercourse with a world of spirits. The women dancers, it is said, are "the mothers of my tribe. They carry all the winter dances" (Boas 1966:208).

V

WINTER
CEREMONIAL:
I

The principal sources of information on the Winter Ceremonial are the family histories, Boas's, volume on religious life (1930), and, of course, Boas's great work, *The Social Organization and Secret Societies of the Kwakiutl.* The family histories, all of which were collected by George Hunt in the Kwakiutl language and translated by him with utter literalness, and then edited for greater intelligibility by Boas, are the authentic sources of the Kwakiutl viewpoint. They describe the ceremonies in their official context, which serves to authenticate the social standing and the supernatural treasures and powers of each family. The narratives are for Kwakiutl ears. They assume Kwakiutl understanding, although in some instances Hunt, aware of his anthropological obligations, elicits explanatory comment.

I have used the original, unpublished Hunt manuscripts as well as Boas's edited and published version. The two sources are not all that different. In many places, however, the Hunt manuscript is more precise in rendering Kwakiutl meanings. For example, Boas characteristically converts Hunt's "secret" to "sacred." "Man eater" is converted to "cannibal," even when the man-eater is not a human being. Boas prefers general anthropological terms to Hunt's elementary but more descriptive English. Boas speaks, for example, of "initiates" and "half-initiates." Hunt, more specific, speaks of "go through the rules" and "not go through the rules." Boas, inexplicably, does not in many instances publish Hunt's translations of native terms or names of persons. For example, Boas speaks of certain dancers as *Kwexilak*, when Hunt has already meaningfully translated the word as "board fast beating," an important idea since fast and slowdance tempos have ritual significance.

Apart from their descriptive content the family histories are important because they reveal the Kwakiutl idea of necessary sequence of events, of the line of development from myth time to the present, from the "true" events that had transpired at the Beginnings to their simulated presentation in present-day ritual. Kwakiutl insist on distinctions between the present and the mythical past, and between the reality of ritual and its mythical reality.

Boas's writing on the Winter Ceremonial may not be noteworthy for clarity of exposition, but it is masterfully detailed and therefore faithful to Kwakiutl thought. His 1897 work has two sections; a general and explanatory treatise is followed by notes on his firsthand observations of a Winter Ceremonial held at Fort Rupert in the winter of 1895–96. In the first section he attempts to synthesize all he has learned about the Ceremonial from informants, from myth narratives, and from family histories. Thus he fuses, and to some extent confuses, historical periods, the earlier precontact conditions and the newer situation of trade goods, trading language, and the consolidation of the tribes at Fort Rupert. Boas wrote this section before he had collected the bulk of his materials on the subject. The eyewitness account, on the other hand, is of one piece; though postcontact it is a rich expression of Kwakiutl culture. It is, as Codere remarked, the work of a brilliant and dedicated observer.

For background on the analytic essay that follows I have drawn only upon native narratives. No summary can possibly improve on Boas's description of the actual performances, which is readily accessible in the new edition edited by Codere (1966).

The basic idea of the Winter Ceremonial is to display inherited supernatural powers as a demonstration of the prowess of a line, and as a

means of promoting the collective welfare by bringing supernatural powers into the community. The ritual structure arises from the individual
but orchestrated enactments of myths of original acquisition of the
supernatural powers. All traditions differ as to the nature of the original
powers and as to the nature of the original encounter. Hence all rituals
also differ, but only in details. Their common ritual theme is the introduction (initiation) of a young novice to the supernatural donor, which
removes him from the human realm, and his subsequent recapture by
his co-religionists. The ceremonial involves the entire community, some
as spectators, the rest as actors. In 1865, 400 of 1000 at Fort Rupert
were spectators only (Curtis 1915:155). All acting roles are finely differentiated, almost in the manner of rank gradations.

The actors form two grand divisions, Sparrows and Seals, each differentiated by grade or rank within itself. Sparrows (*quequtsa*), broadly
speaking, are the officiating officers of the entire Ceremonial. Their
chief, who may indeed be a common man, heads the Ceremonial, not
merely in an administrative capacity but as a chief shaman who "has
no fear" of any supernatural events that occur. Seals (*meemqat*) are in
the front line as direct contacts with the spirit donors of the supernatural
powers. Except for their chief, Sparrows are all former Seals. They have
gone through the course of initiation and impersonation, and now as
restored human beings are equipped like curing shamans to guide no-
vices through their spiritual ordeal.

In keeping with their human standing Sparrows are organized by age
grades as follows:

Boys	Nuisances
Youths	Killer Whales
Young Men	Rock Cod
Older Men	Sea Lions
Chiefs	Whales
Old Men	Koskimo (a foreign tribe)
Head chiefs	Eaters

(Boas 1966:175)

Seals represent the supernatural spirits, which numbered 53 in Boas's
list and 63 in that of Curtis, recorded some 25 years later. Curtis
confirms Boas on a rank order of spirits, but a generation later the

ranks are only approximately the same. Both lists agree in giving highest rank to the class of man-eating spirits and their human dance impersonators (Curtis 1915:156–158; Boas 1897:498–499). A general characterization of spirits impersonated by dancers should suffice. The top-ranking group includes (following Boas's list) the war spirit and a variety of man-eating spirits and their animal and humanoid helpers. A middle group includes fool dancers (warrior figures), Wolves, Thunderbirds, Whales, Killer Whales, Otters, Dogs, Ravens, Sea Monsters, Mink, Sunrise, and Salmon. The low group includes Eagle, Shaman, Ghost, Wasp, Salmon, Property Distribution, and at the bottom, Eagle Down.

No list or rank order can be final, since new dances are constantly being incorporated into the Ceremonial from marriages, and may replace older ones in importance. Thus the *hamatsa* dance representing the Man Eater at the Mouth of the River became the major ritual of the Winter Ceremonial among the Kwakiutl in relatively recent times, supplanting the earlier *hamshamtses* (Man Eater of the Woods), which then became mainly a woman's dance. The *hamatsa* is always male. Curtis's list gives the sex of each dance impersonation. By his list, men generally impersonate the violent land mammals, ferocity in war, the powerful birds of heaven, Thunderbird, Monster Crane, Raven. Women impersonate sorcery, military invulnerability, and some of the great mammals of the sea, the deadly Killer Whale and whales, as well as the Salmon and Rich Woman (Qominoqa). The latter two are the great symbols of wealth. Several dances are by either sex; most are male.

All the spirit-impersonators fall into two hierarchical divisions. The highest are *laxsa* ("gone into the house") and include all dancers who come under the influence of Man Eater at the Mouth of the River (Baxbakualanuxsiwae), namely, *hamatsa, hamshamtses,* Grizzly Bear of the Man Eater, Kinqalatlala, the female attendant and flesh procuress of the Man Eater, and Qominoqa. *Laxsa* refers to having gone into the house of the Man Eater to receive from him powers and dance instructions.[1] In ritual, these dancers actually "disappear" into the woods and need to be "captured." All other dancers are *wixsa.* They have not gone into the house, they have "only leaned against the walls" (Boas 1932a:212). They need not leave the ceremonial house at all.

The *laxsa* having "disappeared," and representing also the most powerful and dangerous forces, become the focus of ritual attention. They must be "recaptured" and "tamed" by strenuous efforts.[2] Among the *wixsa,* some are also subdued, mainly by song, but others simply exhibit their dance and songs. In all Kwakiutl Winter Ceremonials the Man Eater, either *hamatsa* or *hamshamtses,* is central. The ritual unity that finally emerges from disparate and individually owned dances is achieved through the symbolism of his figure.

The Sparrows are a society of shamans, the Seals are their clients. As a permanent, expansive, and corporate society the Sparrows are grouped by age, representative of the individual growth cycle, primarily a sign of their position on the human side. As a transient but stable grouping of individual spirits the Seals represent a generational cycle; membership moves from man to son-in-law to grandchild. Sparrows are directors of action, managing the invitations, the seating, the order of dances, guiding the "taming" of the spirit-possessed, instructing in songs, and so on. Seals are passive (though energetic in action) replicas of their spirit tutelaries.

The hereditary managerial posts in the Sparrows are all masculine and transmitted by male primogeniture. The privilege of dancing a spirit impersonation, however, comes mainly from the female line, that is, from the wife's or mother's father. These formal oppositions are then expressed in the ritual antagonisms of biting, teasing, scratching. Sparrows resist the efforts of *laxsa* Seals to give up their arduous calling. They punish ritual error, a missed dance step, a false word in a song, improperly using a summer name, and the like. Ritual error is a powerful concern because Kwakiutl understand the Winter Ceremonial, as a whole as a series of contests between persons and spirits, and as supernatural power contests between rival tribes. The presence of power can be demonstrated, of course, by accomplishment, but also by ability to overcome. Whoever commits an error is said to be overcome. If the error is serious the victim is as dead. At very least he must begin all over.

With this skeletal structure of the Winter Ceremonial dances in mind, we may pick up the essential inner details from the texts. Hunt recorded part of a family history of the Qomkyutis tribe of the Fort Rupert Kwakiutl. This important text deals with an ancestral chief, Waxapalaso, and the acquisition of *hamshamtses* and hence an early pre-*hamatsa* tradition (see Boas 1921:1121–1179, also Hunt ms. vol. 5 same pagination).

Waxapalaso lies on his back in his house thinking what to do when he recalls a remark of a Qweqsotenox, "Look out for the one of our tribesmen who has a great treasure!—I mean Head Winter Dancer—for he will go around our world to play with the people of supernatural power, all around the world." In the morning he scolds his still sleeping son saying: "Don't you think of Head-Winter-Dancer, the great shaman, the great war-dancer, who is famous all over the world, and who is looking for a great shaman to play with? I mean you ought to rise and wash yourself in this good river [Tselgwad]." He then strikes the youth with his fire tongs.

The son, Xaxosenaso, leaves the house intending to kill himself. At the cascade of the river he comes upon a rock with two holes, and recognizes them as the eyes of Dzonoqwa, the Wild Woman of the Woods. A voice urges him to enter the eyes, saying, "Then nothing will be too difficult for you." Xaxosenaso scrubs his body vigorously with hemlock branches while sitting first in the right eye and then in the left eye. After he has washed both sides of his body, the voice commands him to dive four times, staying under water a long time: "then you will obtain what makes you strong, so that nothing will be too difficult for you." He dives deep, and stays under for a long time. When he comes to the surface he has fainted. The text explains, "for he had been dead, and came back to his senses" (ibid:1125).

Entering the forest he tests his newly won strength by twisting a spruce tree with his hands. Suddenly, a strange man appears before him and counsels him: "and you shall always purify yourself in the morning and in the evening so that no harm may befall you." Xaxosenaso just stands there, in the words of the text, "as though he were out of his mind" (ibid).

He continues his sacred journey, walking up toward the headwaters of a river. Nearing the source, he comes upon the prize treasure. He sees a large, angry-looking human head, and knows that he has found Head Without Body. The head tries to frighten him with changing expressions. Finally, it opens its mouth to show the head of a man within. Its mouth remains open, and it utters the great cry of the *hamshamtses* dancer. At this the man within the mouth jumps out as a *hamshamtses* dancer. He squats in the traditional dance posture, his outspread arms trembling. Then he rushes upon Xaxosenaso to take a bite out of his arm, and jumps back into the mouth of Head Without Body, who immediately disappears.

A disembodied voice tells Xaxosenaso that he has just obtained the *hamshamtses* dance as his treasure, the Head Without Body as a crest, and the name, Nanogwis, One Man Eater. The voice directs him to show his treasures, that is, to give a winter dance, and to do what the *hamshamtses* dancer had done to him. He starts down the river, pausing along the way to purify himself. He scrubs his body with hemlock branches and dives into the river four times. Whereupon another voice directs him to still another treasure. A Thunderbird is revealed to him sitting on a rock. He says to it, "I came to obtain you, Great Supernatural One, as a treasure." Thunderbird takes him under his wing and flies with him around the world. Bringing him back to the same place he assures Xaxosenaso that with his help he would match the powers of his rival among the Qweqsotenox, Head Winter Dancer. "And if he discovers that you are not an ordinary man," Thunderbird tells him, "he will come at once to make war upon you; and as soon as you want me to help you, sing my sacred song:"

> *Burn them, burn them, burn them you who burn the world! Hail, hail, hail, hail, hailstorm is brought by you!*

(ibid:1130)

When Xaxosenaso approaches his village, he does not know that he has been away four years. He hears someone singing near the river. Going toward the voice, he comes upon a small man who escorts him to a large winter dance house. He sees within it all that had happened to him in his meeting with Head Without Body, but this time in the format of a dance performance. Head Without Body is represented by a secret room painted with a head design. The *hamshamtses* dancer comes out from the doorway wearing a revolving head mask. The speaker of the house tells Xaxosenaso that all he has seen within is his new treasure. He is shown other treasures. A woman dancer, Wilenkagilis, dressed only in hemlock branches, and known as Great War Dancer, acts out the disemberment of her own body. She urges a reluctant Xaxosenaso to dismember her. Her body recaptures its head and limbs and she is whole again. Her next trick is to throw her supernatural power on the dance floor. It brings a flood that puts out the fire. At that moment, the house and all within disappear, and Xaxosenaso is left alone. He sings her song:

> *I was taken to the other side of the world, I was taken to the other side of the world, by the great*

supernatural power. I was taken to the other side of
the world by the great supernatural power.
I received everything, I received everything, from
the great supernatural power. I received everything
from the great supernatural power. We, we!
I have everything, I have everything, belonging to
his supernatural power. I have everything, I have
everything belonging to his supernatural power. We, we!

(ibid:1136)

Finally back home, Xaxosenaso says nothing of the great supernatural treasures he has brought back. But the people are alarmed to learn that Head Winter Dancer of the Qweqsotenox is coming to them. Their shaman tells them, however, that Xaxosenaso has the name of Wilenkagilis, the War Dancer, as well as great supernatural powers; they are reassured and happy. The Qweqsotenox arrive with their champion, Head Winter Dancer. They come wearing cedar bark neck and head rings. They are feasted, and the contest of powers begins. Dancing naked to fast time, Head Winter Dancer throws his supernatural power on the floor. It brings a flood and puts out the fire. The hosts are unmoved, and the flood recedes and the fire is relighted. Head Winter Dancer allows his head to be cut off, and it is restored. But Xaxosenaso shows his superior powers, and the Qweqsotenox and their champion are forced to leave in shame. But they have not escaped, for they are subsequently killed by the Thunderbird song their conqueror sings against them. Now called Wilenkagilis, Xaxosenaso is feared by his people because of his great supernatural powers. The people, as the text says, desire to be his slaves. They work for him and bring him everything he wants, food, water, firewood, and canoes (ibid:1147).

For a final display of his supernatural treasures, the new Wilenkagilis request his father to sponsor a Winter Ceremonial. In preparation, he returns to the place where he had first met Head Without Body. Living alone in the woods, he scrubs his body with hemlock boughs, and dives into the river mornings and evenings. After four months of ritual isolation he has a dream, in which all that had happened during the first meeting is repeated. Now he returns to show his treasures at an actual winter dance.

Sponsorship is called "begging for one's life" (ibid:1153). The Sparrow chief lays his red cedar bark ring on the dance floor and says to the congregation:

Go on and consider whether you wish to remain alive. Then you will take up this red cedar bark and give a winter dance next year. If you do not take it up, you will die where we are sitting here.

(ibid)

Whereas the Sparrows are all retired Seals, their chief has never been initiated as a Seal. He is usually the son of the preceding chief. To retain the connection with the Seals, however, his initiation is announced, and is about to take place when he is suddenly snatched back. The supernatural power is said to be frightened away, and it is possible to induct him instead as a Sparrow. He receives a cane, red cedar bark neck rings, and a Sparrow name.

Winter dance performances reenact the encounters with the supernatural donors of the powers. The dancer is then an embodiment of the donor, and the congregation is in the position of the novice at the time of the encounter. Xaxosenaso dances as the *hamshamtses* he had seen; and as he had been bitten, he now bites the flesh of assembled Sparrows and Seals. he also displays the acquired treasures in simulated form. The Kwakiutl have often taken great pains with ingenious mechanical contrivances to make the display as realistic as possible. The Sparrows as the shamans must restore the dancer to his normal human state. The condition of possession is considered a form of madness, of being bereft of the senses, of being wild and uncontrollable like a released force or passion. As the song for Xaxosenaso, now Nanogwis, One Man Eater, says, to cure a holy madness is to tame:

We will try to restore to his senses [Nanogwis], *shamans*
We will tame [Nanogwis], *shamans*
We will quiet [Nanogwis], *shamans*
We will heal [Nanogwis], *shamans.*

(ibid:1170)

The *hamatsa* dance which replaced the *hamshamtses*, among the Kwakiutl, is in the same man-eating tradition, but more violent, and consequently, more highly valued. The *hamshamtses* was then relegated to the women, as more in keeping with its relative tranquility. The great spirit Face Without Body is a passive being, literally immobilized, and his *hamshamtses* is no more than an arm biter. The patron of the *hamatsa* is the most formidable and frightening of supernatural beings, Baxbakualanuxsiwae, Man Eater at the Mouth of the River. His dancer, the *hamatsa* is ravenous, an eater of whole, freshly killed bodies, of decayed corpses of relatives, and a biter of arms as well. *Hamshamtses* is a solitary dancer, but *hamatsa* is part of an ensemble that represents the great Man Eater and his retinue of spirits.

The ritual design remains constant whether the dancer is *hamshamtses* or *hamatsa*. I cited the Xaxosenaso narrative because it seems the fullest, and illustrates most completely the stages of ritual development, beginning with the primary encounter and the display of supernatural powers as actual, to the dream encounter and the simulated display of powers in pure ritual form. A Hunt Text from the Awikenox (Wikeno), a northern Kwakiutl tribe, demonstrates the basic similarity of the pattern in the case of *hamatsa* (see Boas 1921:1222–1248). Among southern Kwakiutl, the tradition is basically the same. The following narrative is from Nakwaxdax, but involves an Awikenox chief (see Boas 1897:396–400).

Nakwaxdax tribesmen are disappearing mysteriously. And when the four sons of chief Nanwaqawe leave to hunt mountain goat he warns them to avoid the houses of the grizzly bear and of the Man Eater. The youths, of course, ignore the warnings. They come upon the grizzly bear, engage him in combat, and kill him. They continue on their way and come to a house from which red smoke issues, the mark of Man Eater. They go in and find a woman seated on the floor. She says to them, "I am rooted to the floor. I will help you." She tells them they are in the house of Man Eater, and how to kill him. They are to dig a fire pit, fill it with hot coals, and cover it with boards as a trap. Man Eater arrives crying *hap!* (eating) in a state of excitement. His body is covered with mouths. He lies down, and jumps up again in a newly excited state, calling out *hap! hap!*, and then retires into his secret room. His attendants come out and dance. They are Great Raven and Giant Crane. When they finish, Man Eater comes out with his female attendants, several Kinqalatlalas and the Qominoqas. When the dancing Man Eater steps on the fire trap, one of the youths pulls aside the boards. Man Eater falls in and is burned. At his "death" the women also die, but the Crane and Raven only faint. The youths seize the ritual ornaments and paraphernalia, the masks, the whistles, and the cannibal pole. The rooted woman instructs them in their uses, and teaches them the songs of Man Eater.

They return home with their new possessions, and fetch Nanwaqawe their father. The rooted woman instructs him in the Man Eater ritual. She teaches him the names and songs of Man Eater and of his associates, and finally reveals herself to be Nanwaqawe's daughter. Nanwaqawe would free her, but dares not cut her deep-set root for fear of killing her. She advises him to return home and present the *hamatsa* dance.

Two new elements enter the Winter Ceremonial by way of the *hamatsa* legend; one is the killing of the tutelary, Man Eater, the other is the mediation of a woman in the process of transfer of powers. The act of killing transposes the winter ritual on to a new level: from mere biting to devouring; from being, in effect, born from the tutelary from whose body the dancer emerges, to becoming his conqueror; from being but a one-man-eater (Nanogwis) to being an insatiable devourer. The presence of the *hamatsa* elevates traditional ritual antagonism to higher levels. The presence of the rooted woman, the human daughter rooted within the house of the devourer of men, as an internal opponent is, of course, the mythological setting to marriage, still another phase in the cycle of transference of powers.

The *hamatsa* dance does not enact the killing of Man Eater. It presents him rather as resurrected, and in his voracious aspect. Since the *hamatsa* is a human being, he is literally a cannibal. His state of being is, nevertheless, ambiguous. He is human, but he is also mad, and possessed by the Man Eater spirit; and it is the spirit that is the devourer of men. To sustain this conception of *hamatsa* dancer as a spirit being, he is made to vomit every trace of the human flesh he has swallowed. In one sense the vomiting signifies, ritually, the miracle of resurrection. At the same time, the human being must be free of the taint of cannibalism. Even his excrement is closely studied for traces of human flesh. The *hamatsa* does not return to the normal human condition for a full year, among some Kwakiutl tribes for as long as four years. During this period he does no work; he may not gamble, nor engage in sexual intercourse. Boas made the interesting observation that the restrictions upon the *hamatsa* are like those imposed on young women who are menstruating for the first time (1897:538). The *hamatsa* and the menstruant are both separated from the domain of men, perhaps for similar reasons, each as a representative of the powers of death. The dancer symbolizes death the devourer, the menstruant is the symbol of the wounded being who could bleed to death, but will, in fact, recover and become a life giver.

As the highest stage of shamanistic achievement, the *hamatsa* initiation can only be approached gradually. As in other North American Indian shamanistic initiations, the *hamatsa* has advanced through the world of spirits, impersonating others for six years before he is ready to meet the Man Eater. Only the *hamatsa* disappears for the full four months duration of the Winter Ceremonial. Thus the season opens with his disappearance and closes after he has been brought back and temporarily subdued. He is but one of some 50 spirit incarnates. But his role is ritually and thematically central. As he is for the moment the Man Eater spirit, the congregation must be ritually clean to capture him. There is a special affinity between him and the ghost dancers; but anyone in the house may unexpectedly hold the power to capture him.

The *hamatsa* is accompanied by the retinue representing the spirits dwelling with Man Eater. While all form a single thematic ensemble, the male dancer is always paired directly with Kinqalatlala, a slave of Man Eater, and his procuress of bodies. Her dance signifies that she is both his feeder and his tamer. She carries a mummified human corpse to a drum inside the house, and from there feeds its flesh to the dancer and to all former *hamatsas*. In another dance she moves before him, facing him and drawing him into the house, gesturing with outstretched arms, palms up. She sings:

I am the real tamer of [Baxbakualanuxsiwae]
I pull the red cedar bark from [Baxbakualanuxsiwae's] *back.*
It is my power to pacify you when you are in a state of ecstasy.

(Boas 1897:527).

The dancing of the procuress is slow and restrained, that of the *hamatsa* alternates between the excitement of rapid tempo and the subsidence of the slow drum beat. He is excited when he is naked and crouching low. His outstretched arms tremble and he is poised to attack the congregation. When standing, and fully dressed, he is in the human state, and is then quiet.

[97]

VI

WINTER
CEREMONIAL:
II

Human beings have always seen the darkening of the days as the
frightening drift into death, and have fought against the dying of the
light as for their life. The energy of ritual fills the void of the night,
as though dusk to dawn were the true arena where the struggle for
life must be fought. Daylight can take care of itself; the darkness must
be subdued and tamed and made to turn back by the powers that human
beings have won for themselves. For northern tribes, winter is the long
night, the descent into darkness and death. For the tribes of the Northwest Coast, winter is the sacred season when all other work is put aside
to fight the night, the darkness of death which can be made to yield,
but will never let go on its own.

The Kwakiutl Winter Ceremonial is a kind of shamanistic festival,
a dazzling display of powers, a pitting of human powers against the

powers of alien supernatural beings, or, as the people often say, a time to see what the supernatural powers will do. On the human side there are two principal groups of protagonists: the chiefs, who for the occasion are called the "shamans," and their children, boys and girls who are sent out to meet the supernaturals face to face. In diversity of incident and symbolic representation the Winter Ceremonial is bewilderingly complex. At some point or other, all supernatural powers the people possess and all their supernatural donors are brought out for display in song and in masked dances. In the course of the sacred winter season almost the entire content of myth on the acquisition of powers is dramatized in a kaleidoscope of image and sound, apparently uncoordinated in detail, as each set of dancers carried out its own portrayal on its own ground within the great dance house. Everything that goes on, however, carries out one elementary ritual theme: The young are allowed to be seized by supernatural antagonists and the "shamans" try to bring them back. When the young return afflicted with holy madness, the shamans cure them, restoring them to their ordinary state.

Curing shaman and Ceremonial shaman are identified in the same title, *paxala*.[1] The Ceremonial shaman is the curing shaman translated to the more general and hence higher level of ritual performance. The bringing down of *nawalak* so that the community may be assured of life for another year is basically the curing ritual socialized. Only in the most general sense, of course, is the Winter Ceremonial the magnified and socialized version of the curing ceremony. The elementary shaman is at the bottom of it, but the very magnitude of the Winter Ceremonial is itself a new phenomenon. The Winter Ceremonial is shamanistic, but in a guise where the central concepts of shamanism are asked to deal with all the major concerns of Kwakiutl culture—with lineage, with rank, with marriage, with distribution and exchange, as well as with all relations between men and spirits and between men and animals. The Winter Ceremonial has, of course, the central shamanistic theme of overcoming death. At the same time, it has a broad cultural compass, befitting the grandeur of the theme. It stands for that side of the culture that faces the coming of the night.

The shamanic model for the Winter Ceremonial is readily discovered in the surrounding area, among northeastern Siberians, Eskimo, Athabascan, and Algonquian, and Salishan peoples (see Eliade 1964). In essence the shaman is a special person who has been able to recover from a mysterious affliction that has brought him close to death. Fellow shamans aid his recovery and prepare him professionally to become a healer and to command other powers. This rather mundane experience, in itself common enough, is transformed into a more profound religious event. Illness and recovery are metamorphosed into a concept of a dangerous journey from the human world of the living to the spiritual world of the dead, and—most important—to return home. To cross what should be an absolute divide and return safely is an exceptional feat confined to the exceptional person who has been chosen or accepted by the spirits. The shamans are the human emissaries who are to set up the means of continuous intercourse with the world of the spirits.

Shaman and spirits form a bond of interdependence. Each at some point possesses the other, the shaman acting as agent of his spirits, the spirits as agents of the shaman. Each in a sense sacrifices some part of its original identity for the sake of the new and mutually advantageous relationship. The spirits consort with human beings and respond to their commands. The shaman becomes established as a marginal person who straddles the boundaries between his own kind and the universe of spirits. The nature of his original disorder marked by trance, vision, faintness, epileptoid seizure, wasting illness, the common signs of impending death, define his marginal state. The marginal state is volatile and ambiguous and, therefore, very dangerous. The shaman is compelled to battle. He must prove himself or define himself by demonstrating his powers, demonstrating to all as well as to himself that his spiritual connections are still reliable. He is at the border between his kind and the spirit world as a defender of the human community, an aggressive assignment.

There may be a parallel between the pattern of relations between shamans and spirits, and between hunters and animals in northern North America. Each pairing involves a system of intercourse between two realms, originally joined in the primal myth era and now separate and hostile, but obliged to intersect and to collaborate. Animals offer their lives, their flesh to human beings in return for respect and human collaboration in preservation of their species. Human beings, too, give up their flesh when they enter the spirit world, often at the hands of spirits who are hunters of lives. The shaman secures the safety of the souls, a link in preservation of the species. Eliade offers the important observation that the shamanic aspirant gives animal spirits his own flesh to eat (1964:108), implying thereby a parallel with hunting. The parallel is perhaps rather self-evident, since the spirits with whom the shaman consorts, with whom he establishes a common identity, are the animals of the original mythic state (ibid:93). Ultimately the two patterns of relationship are not parallel, but intersecting. The shaman mediates both.

The shaman of the Winter Ceremonial is a transformed version of the primordial shaman described by Eliade, and equally a transformation of his curing counterpart among Kwakiutl. The transformation deals with the issue of directness of the shamanic experience. In primary curing, shamanism is an experience personal and mystical, that is, immediate and spontaneous encounter with spirits. The shamans of the Winter Ceremonial, however, have themselves had no direct or immediate encounters with spirits; they inherit the primary experiences of their antecedents.

Boas wrote of the transformation of the traditional North American vision quest from an individual experience to an accomodation to hereditary rank (see 1897:336). This may be taken to mean the power of the social system to transform the religion. For the Kwakiutl, however, transmission by marriage and by descent along the lines of aristocracy adheres to religious principles. It is not sufficient to say that shamanism comes under the influence of the social system, rather, elementary shamanism has become evidenced by association with those other sources of supernatural powers that belong to chiefs. Hereditary shamanism is not unusual in this region, in any case, so that Kwakiutl only formalizes an acknowledged practice. The decisive innovation is insistence that marriage symbolize the bridging of the divide between the home world and the alien realm, and that the father-in-law as donor stand as an equivalent to the supernatural spirits. It is in this sense, of course, that the father-in-law is the great magister.

In the Winter Ceremonial the process of initiating the acquisition of generalized shamanistic powers starts at marriage, at a point when the groom is nearing the peak of his powers, and is simultaneously on the verge of becoming a full-fledged chief. His course is precisely opposite to that of the curing shaman, who must first descend to illness and to the crisis of death. This inversion defines precisely the distinction Kwakiutl imply between commoner and noble shamans. Nobility transcends common suffering. As Kwakiutl often say, it is the "little ones" who must struggle. The curing shaman is one of the "little ones" and it is he who submits to suffering and to self-divestment. The noble faces the spirits from a posture of strength. His rank has already advanced him to a plane of equivalence with the supernatural being.

The Kwakiutl call the Winter Ceremonial *tsetseqa,* a word Boas initially translated, too crudely, as "fraudulent, pretended, to cheat" (1966:172), saying that: "Even in the most serious presentations of the ceremonial it is clearly and definitely stated that it is planned as a fraud" (ibid). Boas is left with this wry thought: "The peculiar attitude of the Indians towards the whole ceremonial makes it difficult to understand its fundamental meaning" (ibid). The crudity is in the choice of such words as "fraud" and "cheat" for rites of such extraordinary religious importance as the Winter Ceremonial. The proper translation of *tsetseqa* finally appears in his posthumous grammar (1947) where *tsekweda*, based on the same stem, is given as "imitated." Thus the label defines the ceremonial aptly as a simulated event. One should not conclude hastily that a simulated or theatrical performance is not thereby religious.

The concept of *tseka* (the stem) has distinctive native overtones of meaning. Thus in an earlier stab at translation Boas suggested "secrets" (1897:418). Among the neighboring Heiltsuq (Bella Bella), whose dialect is only slightly different, *tseqa* refers to shamans and to the Winter Ceremonial. From Heiltsuq usage Boas derived still another meaning, "exalted" or "unusual." Taking all these suggested meanings into account, one arrives at an idea of hidden things, in the sense that the ceremonies deal with secret matters that are always hidden and can be experienced, therefore, only in a simulated form. The masks, the whistles, the ornaments, the dramatizations of mythical events simulate a hidden reality, a reality that does not literally exist on this side of the cosmos, belonging only, as the Kwakiutl always say, "on the other side." The idea of simulating hidden things is one of profound religious sophistication, a recognition of the ineffable.

In contrasting the Winter Ceremonial with "true shamanism" I had in mind general patterns of arctic shamanism, the historical model for the Kwakiutl. Unlike his more mystical and more spiritual counterparts, the Kwakiutl shaman relies heavily on elaborate tricks in his public demonstrations. He devises hidden trapdoors and partitions, and uses strings cleverly to manipulate artificial figures. He is in appearance the modern magician, and when his tricks through clumsiness are exposed he is humiliated. Hence, the curing shaman is an avowed simulator too. Is he a fraud? The possibility of fraud cannot be dismissed. Yet all shamanism relies on some tricks, on extraction of foreign crystals or worms from the body of the patient, on ventriloquism that suggests the presence of spirits in the vicinity, on sleight of hand and hypnotic suggestion. In some respect all shamanism is a simulated theater of spiritual mythology. Siberian tribes perhaps voice the feelings of many shamanistic congregations when they speak of contemporary practices as decadent. The original ancestors, they say, had real experiences with the spirit world. They actually did all the things shamans now pretend to do (see Eliade 1964:68).

The concept of decadence, which is clearly pertinent to a consideration of Kwakiutl shamanism and the Winter Ceremonial, probably states historically the more fundamental idea of an increasing separation between an original mythical state of being and a contemporary reality. All mythical states of first origins are by the nature of religious thought set in a pristine world no longer directly accessible. Founding ancestors remain connected with their descendants, but across a decided barrier, a barrier growing increasingly impenetrable. What is referred to as shamanistic decadence is but an acknowledgment of distance as a function of aging. In their views of shamanism and of the Winter Ceremonial the Kwakiutl acknowledge the gaps between the true spirit world at the time when men were still in animal form, or had just emerged, and the present. What was real then is simulated now.

In using terms such as "simulated" or "theatrical" we run the risk of seriously misrepresenting the Kwakiutl idea by secularizing what they specifically identify as the opposite of the secular. The summer season is known as *baxus*, translated by Boas as "secular" (1897:418), and is said to be the opposite of the *tsetseqa*. In the summer, the Indians say, the *baxus* is on top and the *tsetseqa* is on the bottom (ibid). In the winter the positions are reversed. The winter ceremonial season begins as a rule in our November and ends after January. It is a bracketed solstice observance, but not, strictly speaking, sidereal, for the season is launched not on a fixed day but always by the social event of transmitting winter dance privileges. These are, of course, handed over in the winter. The point is nevertheless made, and emphatically: The act of transmission initiates the Winter Ceremonial period even before the season has actually started. The distinction is important because it verifies the shamanistic analogy of having a mystical experience triggered by an extraordinary event; and it separates Kwakiutl ritual timing from the astronomical traditions of Plains and Pueblo Indians.

The appearance of the Winter Ceremonial season totally reverses the order of human existence. People then represent another form of being. They abandon their summer names and their lineage affiliations as though they had returned to an existence prior to the appearance of human beings. In the winter they are organized in animal societies, and, of course, as varieties of supernatural beings. No one then is, strictly speaking, a human being, and no one accordingly belongs to a lineage, for the Kwakiutl the quintessential organization of human beings. They live under a new spiritual jurisdiction, under dangerous spirits who punish remorselessly any lapse of ritual decorum. The winter condition does not actually duplicate the prehuman condition because it is unrelated, by design, to the lineage origins. What it seems to duplicate is a general state of being when human beings reestablish close contact with a spiritual existence by an act of identification. The house becomes a spirit residence, the people become simulated spirits, and the great supernatural spirits come to live among them as among their own kind.

I believe we can satisfactorily distinguish between so-called genuine and simulated participants and events. The impersonations are artifice, but the power brought by the spirits is genuine. The power of the Winter Ceremonial is *nawalak,* the most positively identified concept of supernatural power that the Kwakiutl voice. Boas compares *nawalak* with "holy" and with the Algonquian concept of *manitou* (1927). It seems to be, judging from contexts, the power associated with the unusual forms of life. Thus simulated actions, by establishing identity with the sources of power, acquire the powers.

The semantic problem of contrasting simulated actions and genuine powers is self-evident. Implied is a religiously impossible equation between spurious recipients and genuine donors. Kwakiutl have no sense of charity; for them, a genuine donor can give only to a genuine recipient. Religious logic compels the conclusion that in the context of the Winter Ceremonial the simulated is not the profane. In no sense is it the antithesis of the holy. To receive *nawalak* from the supernatural, petitioners must be on the proper plane. While they are not, and cannot be, fully equal to the supernaturals they impersonate, they have raised themselves to a level of sanctity or, better still, of ritual purity at which they can receive powers. Actually, Kwakiutl follow a common ritual procedure in all transmissions: The recipient prepares himself by seeking identity with the donor. The viewpoint of *tsetseqa,* of simulation, seems to be that a true identity is not, and indeed cannot be attained with the supernatural beings. They remain distinct from human beings just as the ancestral founders, the animal-masked humans, are now eternally distinct from their human descendants. The Kwakiutl who told Boas the Winter Ceremonial was presented as simulation were surely not denigrating a ritual of great importance. They were stating, I would imagine, a position of true religious humility: Men can imitate the gods, they cannot be the gods. Imitation, even in tribal societies, is flattery. Among Kwakiutl, as in all animist religions, the gods are seen as attracted to their own kind.

If the impersonators are not genuine spirits but genuine impersonators of spirits, what about the *nawalak* that is received? The Kwakiutl view is that a well-conducted ritual brings the actual supernatural beings down into the house (Boas 1930:69), which then becomes the abode of Healing Woman (ibid:121). They bring with them the *nawalak*, but not, of course, in the same form as in myth. In myth, the *nawalak* powers are both extraordinary and specific, restoring the dead to life, killing enemies effortlessly, accomplishing miracles in hunting, acquiring wealth, curing, and so on. On earth the miracles of myth are not altogether discounted, yet deferring to reality the congregation expects only general benefits. They speak of the period as "making the heart good" *(aikegela)*, as wiping the slate clean of the ailments, the troubles, and the rancors of the secular time, and as "bringing down from above" (Boas 1897:418), a conjunction of ideas about general benefits brought down from the sky world. A more specific benefit is the shamanistic preservation of life. Thus at the end of the season someone must at once promise the festivities for next year or else "we will die" (Boas 1921:1153).

Reality compels a compromise with the extravagant promises of myth, but not at the sacrifice of the fundamental premises of religious logic. The generalizing and softening of specific and extraordinary powers does not, we assume, violate the authenticity of a primeval condition; its reality cannot extend to contemporary conditions. The man can never again be the child, the tree can never again be the seed. Time is an authentic condition. The aim of myth is not to overcome time by fusing in superficial fashion present and primeval. On the contrary, myth insists on the implacable and irreversible separation between that which started a cycle and that which continues the cycle.

The viewpoint of myth, as deeply rooted in the human consciousness as is the incest taboo, is that history must move forward from its origins. The connection with beginnings is not to be broken. Even more imperative is the distinction between present and beginnings. The incest taboo remains a powerful psychic compulsion for similar reasons. Deepest incest revulsion among human beings is for the mother and son connection, which implies a return to the source of origin. Common to origin myths and to the incest taboo is the Orphic idea that life in its growth moves out and away from its primal sources. Return is fraught with the danger of rejecting life. Those who violate the incest taboo are dead, metaphorically. Since they are already "dead," it is reasonable for religious societies to treat them as such—expelling them or killing them.

The inescapable counterpart of the incest taboo is the sacred obligation to retain connections by endowing them with deep significance. The Garden of Eden is never again to be reentered, and never to be forgotten. And the Kwakiutl idea of simulation is unusual only in its remarkable explicitness. Like the biology of growth and development, gradations are recognized between (1) the supernaturals themselves, (2) the ancestral beings who acquired powers from them, and (3) the contemporary people who now simulate the earlier pristine conditions. Simulation, however, is no casual matter. It seeks identity, even through danger, but dares not make identity absolute. The initiate enters the realm of the supernaturals, but as a differentiated human being who is firmly tied to others on the human side who will pull him to safety.

Simulation of powers and of beings is the familiar sacred-profane distinction. Kwakiutl semantic sophistication enables us to understand a more subtle distinction, in which sacred-profane represents a gradation through which the sacred reaches toward but need not encompass the truly divine. By recapitulating the myth Kwakiutl gain a substantial benefit. But they are not mystics; and they do not delude themselves with the belief that what had been at the Beginning can ever be regained. They simulate the mystic doctrine through metaphysical enactment of the return to first and enduring principles. Apart from the simple positive good of the ritual series, the enactments have perhaps the more constructive benefit of setting forth the cultural metaphysics, using the language of visual symbols and the irresistible power of mimesis to impress upon all the meaning of Being. For the student of Kwakiutl thought, the Winter Ceremonial is the gateway to hidden meanings, its symbolic structure the Rosetta stone to an undeciphered code.

As Lévi-Strauss has so cogently reasoned, all myth versions are authentic. Each tells a part of the whole story. According to several traditions, the Winter Ceremonial first came down from the sky. The Dzawadenox tale cited in Chapter 4 about the marriage of a chief's daughter with the son of Abalone of the World attributes the origin of the rites to the celestial trinity of Sun, Moon, and Thunderbird (Boas and Hunt 1905:58). A Qweqsotenox tradition is more specific and attributes origins to Thunderbird, who is called Head Winter Dancer. The attribution of origins to the Thunderbird, who in myth represents the birds of the Sky World in their ever-losing combats with the birds and beasts of earth, is in keeping with major religious themes. In the former version the rites are brought to earth in marriage, thus authenticating the act of transmission. In the latter version, Thunderbird and his wife come to earth bringing with them the winter dances. In another version it is the Wolves who bring down the first rites (Boas 1930:62ff).[2] The original source is generally in the sky, and the secondary sources are on earth where the powers had been deposited. Yet finally, there is the tradition that the Winter Ceremonial, and privileges of giving coppers all over the world, come from Qomogwa, god of the sea (Boas and Hunt 1905:85).

Stories of the first origins are, however, general, dealing only with the broad framework of the rites and not with the supernatural beings who are impersonated. In the marriage story of the Dzawadenox chief's daughter a connection is established between the winter dances and incidents of having one's brains eaten by Brain-Eating Woman and being restored to life after she vomits them out and they are sprinkled with the water of life. This brief incident contains the main idea of the rites. In stories of Thunderbird, who is also Head Winter Dancer, another connection is established. Head Winter Dancer (Tsaqame) becomes a great shaman and demonstrates that his powers are at least equal to those of Qanekelak, one of the great Kwakiutl deities, a creator and a transformer. In the presence of Head Winter Dancer and in the presence of the Winter Ceremonial itself, when it is in progress, the god Qanekelak is diffident. He recognizes an inherent antagonism of powers and acknowledges his inability to conquer. Thus the Thunderbird, qua Head Winter Dancer, demonstrates that the powers of the winter dance, powers in the province of human beings, are on a par with those of the god who created many important features of earth.

We cannot be sure to what extent Kwakiutl myth is conceptually unified. Are all qualities of Thunderbird, for example, pertinent to his role as Head Winter Dancer even when not in that specific context? Yet it is hard to escape the impression that the contexts of Thunderbird combats are related. If he is a contestant with Qanekelak in his guise as Head Winter Dancer, his heroic combats with the birds and beasts of earth, when he goes by the name of Thunderbird, may be part of a common theme. With Qanekelak he is equal, and they fight to a draw. Against the birds of earth, headed by Woodpecker, he is defeated and thereafter the thunder, a threat to life, is heard only in the proper season. The meaning of these narratives is not, I should think, that the birds, who represent the earth division, are stronger than Qanekelak and Head Winter Dancer, but rather that Thunderbird, as such, is for the moment subordinate. He is invincible, however, when he is both the great shaman and the Head Winter Dancer. The entire mythological tradition must demonstrate to the Kwakiutl how awesome and unconquerable are the powers of the Winter Ceremonial. (See Chapter 7 for Qanekelak and Head Winter Dancer as paradigms for ritual antagonism.)

Even in the course of a single season at one village the ritual series represents a great variety of supernatural beings and their powers. Not all the supernaturals, each of whom is portrayed by a masked dance and song, are presented at any one time. Boas had grouped them into four great supernatural jurisdictions: the war spirit, Winalagilis, Making War All Over the Earth; the Man Eater spirit, Baxbakualanuxsiwae; *matem*, the birds that give the power of flight; and Ghosts, who have the power of bringing back to life a person who has been killed. His classification does not incorporate all dances—for the ceremony is in fact a rapidly evolving system—rather the main religious themes they represent.

The quadripartite grouping divides thematically into pairs of dualities: War and Man Eater as death and consummation; Birds and Ghosts as flight and resurrection. In myth, Man Eater and War Spirit are older and younger brother respectively. Man Eater is the chief and his younger brother "makes war around the world" to fetch corpses for him to feed upon. They form a natural pair (see Boas and Hunt 1905:204ff). Birds and Ghosts form a different kind of pair. Birds are souls who ascend to the sky, the original source of *nawalak;* Ghosts live underground and in resurrection ascend to earth. Each pairing complements the other; all-devouring death is matched by means of overcoming it. Thus the main themes are set forth in a fairly obvious manner and repeat themselves. One of the songs representing the Man Eater states the point clearly:

[Baxbakualanuxsiwae] *made me a winter dancer*
[Baxbakualanuxsiwae] *made me pure*
I do not destroy life. I am the life maker.

(Boas 1897:508)

The major themes of devouring death and resurgent life resonate throughout the Winter Ceremonial and throughout all other rituals. In the Winter Ceremonial the theme is picked up at once in the statement of powers given as gifts by the supernaturals. These, too, come often as a set of four. They are: (1) the magic harpoon for gaining wealth, (2) the burning fire that destroys wealth, (3) the water of life that revives the dead, and (4) the death bringer usually a pointing stick (see Boas 1897:415). Again the four form two pairs: magic harpoon/burning fire and water of life/death bringer, and magic harpoon/water of life and burning fire/death bringer. The first pairing relates property to people, a theme picked up later in man-eater songs. The second pairing contrasts life enhancing and life destructive forces.

The organization of supernatural powers and the gifts they bestow are in harmony. The harmonic relation, however, is satisfyingly complex since each gift is not merely a special province of a single donor. All supernatural beings can give one or several, and often all. The statement in myth that the four gifts are usually a single treasure *(tlogwe)* helps convey the religious message of the unity of opposites, a fundamental Kwakiutl dogma. I might as well establish this point at once. For Kwakiutl, all metaphysical issues of antagonism are resolved simply and neatly by the Hegelian trick of transformation into opposites: death turns to life, life to death. As the *hamatsa* dancer sings: "I do not destroy life. I am the life maker. Perhaps the most ancient shamans, whose business it was to reverse the direction of the course from death to life, first discovered this fundamental biological and spiritual principle.

The transmission of the four gifts was a historical event. It occurred, as a rule, during a shadowy historical period verging into the decadent present, after the ancestors had assumed their human form, but at a time when their exploits were still legendary. This earlier period accounts for origins of the Winter Ceremonial and is, in this most important respect, distinct from the present era when the legendary events are merely enacted. The original recipient had met the supernatural directly and in receiving his treasures had himself become *nawalak* and possessor of the qualities of his supernatural donor. In the present era transmission is indirect, from the father-in-law who had himself received the powers in marriage, or from killing in the course of war,[3] or from killing an initiate encountered in ritual isolation in the woods. These experiences are secondary, and hence attenuated. Even the ritual enactment by the initiate of being "seized" by the supernatural spirit is a secondary and fabricated event. In other words, the legendary events are the genuine experiences, and their ownership authenticates the ritual enactment.

The dominant figure is Man Eater; his role is the exclusive prerogative of highest-ranking chiefs (see Boas 1897:411; Boas 1921:1176). Though the four categories of supernatural beings form a conceptual ensemble, all are subordinated to the central figure of Man Eater, who in his own being incorporates the necessary duality of devouring lives and of giving life. Further, he is devourer of property and sources of wealth and so binds together the ideas of life and wealth as two aspects of the same vital reality.

Myth describes Man Eater as occupying, with wife and children, a house in the woods. Dwelling in mountainous forests, a spirit region in opposition to that of sea and sky, he has his closest associations with forest beasts and flesh-eating birds. The exact details of habitat and associations vary from tribe to tribe, but the symbolic pattern remains constant. The mountainous forest is a special domain of spirits; it is not a human habitat. When the myth people were still in animal form, according to a Mamaleleqala tradition, they lived as people now do, on the beach. The interior was a dangerous zone, which people entered to seek for *nawalak*. The forest was also the ancient cemetery, where the dead were draped in trees. So the forest is the appropriate habitat for the entire Winter Ceremonial, and especially for Man Eater. The mountains, moreover, are considered to give access to the sky; arising directly from the sea, as they do in many places, they appear to the Kwakiutl to connect that realm with the sky as well.

In the Gwasela family histories a cannibal pole, Man Eater's own tree that connects him with the sky, has carved representations of the entire set of animal associations of Man Eater. The cannibal pole is also associated with the Milky Way (Boas 1897:446). It is surmounted by Eagle, the lookout who discovers human flesh. Eagle stands on the head of Man Eater, who is perched above Raven at the North End of the World, who in turn rests on Grizzly Bear, the guardian of the doorway. At the bottom is Wolf, the "scent taker" of Man Eater (Boas 1921:856).

The figures of Eagle and Wolf at the top and bottom of this "totem pole" are especially interesting for two reasons. Both are shamanistic figures, and Eagle is the figure of the highest-ranking chiefs as well; neither is considered to be in the same class as Raven or Grizzly Bear, who like Man Eater are devourers of men. The eagle is a special shamanic tutelary among Eskimos and among Siberian tribes. The wolf, however, belongs particularly to the Kwakiutl brand of shamanism. Woodman the Wolf was a high chief among the myth people living at Crooked Beach, and Eagle was a chief of the birds. Wolves are described in myth as the first great shamans and as the first to have the Winter Ceremonial. As shaman figures, Eagle and Wolf are links to Man Eater but are, strictly speaking, not of him, as indeed they could not in all logic be.

Man Eater is even more specifically located; he is at the headwaters of the rivers at the North End of the World. The north is for Kwakiutl the source of darkness, of disease, and of violent death. The rivers hold at their place of beginnings a major source of *nawalak*—seekers of *nawalak* commonly proceed upstream (see Boas and Hunt 1905:150). Man Eater moves restlessly about the earth driven by his insatiable appetite for human flesh. An entourage that includes three categories of women assists him. Qominoqa is usually his wife. Kinqalatlala is a slave. A woman who is actually human is deeply rooted in the floor of his house. The women are his provisioners, bringing him victims and corpses. Others in his entourage are Grizzly Bear, a vicious and fearless killer of men; Raven, who feasts on men's eyes; Hoxhoq the Great Crane, who devours men's brains; and a humanoid male called Haialikilatl (Benefactor), all but the last in the general category of devourers. The chief devourer is Baxbakualanuxsiwae, whose insatiable appetite is depicted by the image of mouths all over his body (Boas 1897:395).

In a fairly transparent biological metaphor, the females are the suppliers of bodies, the great provisioners. Qominoqa, Rich Woman, defines what wealth means for Kwakiutl: not objects such as trinkets, coppers, or woolen, store-bought blankets, but lives. Wealth is life. Man Eater sings: "I am swallowing food alive; I eat living men. I swallow wealth. I swallow the wealth that my father is giving away" (Boas 1897:459). I return later to this very important idea. The slave women are auxiliary provisioners. As for the rooted woman, her role as provisioner is only incidental to her human destiny as the persistent enemy within Man Eater's house. She teaches men how to overcome devouring death.

Death is tamed. Women have an important but not exclusive role in taming Man Eater. Those who feed him property also tame him by quenching his voraciousness. The brothers who seek him out and take his powers and "kill" him also tame him. If Man Eater can die and return to life, death, it must be assumed, cannot be final. Ultimately, Man Eater is tamed because that is his destiny. One of his many names is Wishing To Be Tamed (Boas 1897:398). Frightening as he is said to be, he is easily overcome by simple guile, or else he yields readily. In one story, he welcomes the hero, saying: "My dear, do not be afraid. I want to give you magical power. This is my house. I am [Baxbakualan-uxsiwae]. You shall see everything in my house" (ibid:404). All accounts, and each tribe has its own, bring out his dual qualities—his terrifying side, and the softer side, that can be made to yield to simple perseverance. Almost all Kwakiutl supernatural beings submit to the persistent suitor. The man who meets Death-Dealing Woman in a stream embraces her, and copulates with her until she promises him the usual four treasures.[4]

The encounter with Man Eater and his company is stripped of total terror from the outset, since they are all seen in the ritual aspect of dancing and singing, rather than as raw forces. Ritual is by function the reshaper, the subduer, and the tamer of all raw states. Hence the gap between the human dancers and Man Eater and his entourage is reduced from the start. The mythical encounter serves to project not a raw image of devouring spirits, but a ritual format. In the human setting, the ritual containment of ultimate raw menace is completed. Since the impersonator of Man Eater is a high chief, or the son of a high chief, qualified by birth and marriage to bring Man Eater into the human community, he is also qualified in his role of shaman and noble to be his supreme antagonist.

The power of Man Eater and of the entire Winter Ceremonial, for that matter, is concentrated in rings of red cedar bark. Worn on the head, around the neck, at the wrists and ankles, the cedar bark rings are by form alone—the magic circle—the containers of power. The circle may stand among Kwakiutl as it does among Eskimo and other North American tribes for the cosmos (or sun or moon), the ultimate container of powers. In myth the ring is represented as a container of souls and spirits, like a primordial covering. Red cedar bark is a parallel source of power by virtue of substance. It stands for the blood of the sacred tree, the tree that, like the "cosmic tree" in Siberian shamanism, ascends to the sky. The rings hold the greatest concentration of powers, but not all powers. The remainder of the *nawalak* powers are in whistles and in face and forehead masks. The masks seem to represent the form soul of Man Eater or other supernatural beings. The red cedar bark rings introduce an idea of generalized form soul, pertaining to abstract powers, perhaps to a religious idea as general as that of the Siouan *wakan* or the Algonquian *manitou*, which are essentially cosmic powers. The depicted spirit beings are presumably not the ultimate powers; like people, they are themselves recipients, but from an unidentified donor.

If an idea of a universal spirit, of a primal source of life and of its powers, does exist for Kwakiutl, it does so only as an implied possibility, not as a ritual reality. Ritual deals with the self-evident reality of universal distributions of power, but in graded degree. Thus Man Eater cannot contain within his person alone all the relevant powers, even though his symbolic character and his dual nature are complete within his figure. The complexity of the Man Eater rites alone—part of the more comprehensive plan of the Winter Ceremonial as a whole—is in accord with the doctrine of the essential incompleteness of any part of the whole. We may see in Man Eater the central metaphor for the Winter Ceremonial, but Kwakiutl are less reductive. For them, as pure imagery, the part may stand for the whole. In ritual practice the aim is to represent the totality of parts, as a mosaic. One is reminded of the Navajo dry paintings which painstakingly bring the supernatural power into being by the patient assembly of grains of sand, pollen, and other bits and pieces whose coloring and texture create symbolic designs, and finally a portion of myth to which song, dance, the sound of rattles, the beat of drum, the narrative of myth add the rest. If a portion is omitted the entire assembly, like a faulty chemical experiment, fails.

The spirit of war, visualized as Winalagilis, Making War All Over the Earth, is a younger partner of Baxbakualanuxsiwae. Equivalent as life takers, they are, nevertheless ranked in order of their powers. Man Eater is potentially an ultimate devourer. Unless he can be tamed he consumes all. His is the natural image of death leading to final decay and dissolution. He devours flesh, but also skulls, the cases of the life spirit, the hardest bone, the body's sole hope for material immortality. Dread of Man Eater may not be of mere death, but of the degradation of reduction to the end product of digestion—excrement. By contrast, the spirit of war is only a killer. He begins the task; Man Eater, who can feed on corpses, completes it. In this respect the war spirit is indeed a younger brother, the equivalent of an attendant. Man Eater's women gather corpses, the masculine war spirit is an active killer. Among the Kwakiutl of Fort Rupert the war spirit has no mask or carving (Boas 1897:394). He is a canoe figure which Kwakiutl think of as a receptacle (although the Trobriand Islanders' idea of the canoe as a swift masculine projectile-phallus may also be present), as well as a conveyance. He also comes from the north and travels about the earth never leaving his canoe. He grants the dual powers of killing and of invulnerability in combat. Toxwid, usually a woman, represents military invincibility; Hawinalatl (War Dancer) represents insensibility to pain, and impregnability; Mamaqa represents the powers of sorcery.

War powers are, to be sure, pertinent to the active Kwakiutl interest in military success. The concept of Winalagilis as a war spirit reaches, nevertheless, well beyond ordinary expediency. The spirit of war also has shamanistic associations. He is a stealer of souls (Curtis 1915:79), and is the supernatural patron who grants them their curing powers. Once again, we find the common principle: The source of the remedy is in the affliction. The death dealer is the healer. That a woman should play a key role in the war spirit configuration is in keeping with the thoroughgoing Kwakiutl dualism that controls the entire Winter Ceremonial. Even as she is the companion and aide of death-dealing spirits, she is, at least by implication, a life-giving figure as well. Her association with Winalagilis projects the war theme onto a broader cosmic scale. The female Toxwid has her powers from the double-headed serpent, Sisiutl, a double supernatural being who kills and also preserves. Merely the sight of Sisiutl contorts and kills. Those who have his powers wear him as a belt that provides invulnerability (see Boas 1897:487). The blood of the double-headed serpent applied to the skin gives it the impregnability of stone. At the same time, the serpent is seen as the salmon of the Thunderbird—not as an ordinary salmon, but rather as an incandescent version, seen by people as a blaze of light. This blaze of light is presumably the lightning flash that strikes the water, the forerunner of Thunderbird's clap of thunder. In this set of symbolic associations, Sisiutl joins Man Eater as one of the key figures in the Winter Ceremonial.

G. W. Locher has seen in the double-headed serpent the grand integrative image of Kwakiutl religion (1932). One need not go so far in reductivism to recognize how deeply the serpent, even though a comparatively minor figure in the entire Winter Ceremonial, does succeed in portraying the main themes. Sisiutl, as Locher has painstakingly shown, has wide-ranging associative connections with almost the entire spectrum of Kwakiutl religious beliefs. Through it, we see as from another vantage point the panorama of forces and spirits that occupy the great lineage houses during the winter season. As the food of Thunderbird, a primary patron of the Winter Ceremonial, Sisiutl is a counterpart of Salmon. Salmon, the food of men, is also visualized as light in its associations with copper. Copper as Salmon and as light represents the wealth of the sea and the treasures of the sky. Broadly speaking, the double-headed serpent theme is conceptually akin to the man-eater theme, in that both supernaturals control life-taking and life-granting powers. Each, nevertheless, has its own place within the total mosaic. Man Eater is the avowed and explicit devourer; the serpent, with his two mouths and his natural character of one who swallows creatures whole, is a devourer by implication only. As actually portrayed, Sisiutl is essentially the lightning bolt, the traditional war symbol. Still, the imagery of devouring is so powerfully lodged in the Kwakiutl religious imagination that the double-headed serpent cannot escape it. Sisiutl is inevitably fused or else paired with Man Eater in myth as well as in ritual organization.

In a Qweqsotenox tale, Head Winter Dancer (Thunderbird) kills a sisiutl that has been caught in his salmon trap in the form of a blazing salmon. He coats his son's body with its blood, thereby turning him into a Dzonoqwa, whom he names Food Giver Stone Body. The traditions more commonly depict Dzonoqwas as female devourers of human children. The masculine type of Dzonoqwa is a warrior who enslaves chiefs and robs them of their crests (souls). It is evidently the male Dzonoqwa who is fused with Sisiutl. Food Giver Stone Body then becomes paired with Man Eater as his warrior. He speaks to Man Eater: "I will go and make war to satiate you" (Boas and Hunt 1905:206). His war cry of *ho!* is like the thunderclap that dazes or kills all within its range. Chiefs who own the right to his war cry use it when they are "selling" a copper. In that ritual context the menacing cry of the warrior marks the transmission of a copper across a tribal boundary as an act of antagonism. Man Eater, who devours all, including coppers, remains the central figure in ritual and the eminence behind all property transactions.

Since all the great themes of the Winter Ceremonial are presented in song and dance, we must assume a special significance to these expressive forms. The dance presents the spirit characters in their characteristic motor forms, supplementing the masks which portray physical form. The songs reveal the essential nature of the beings, and the names establish their genre. In addition there are ornaments and instruments, cedar bark neck rings, eagle down, whistles, staffs, and the like. Each item is a vital (perhaps a soul) component of the being who is represented. The mission of the human community seems to be to assemble all separate components and thus to create, or rather to reconstitute among themselves, the spirit beings who would otherwise lack a human connection. Impersonation is therefore an act of creation. The human form, as in the transmission of names down the generations, is the carrier of spirit beings. In the spirit of mutuality of interchange, the human community grants life to the spirit beings who in turn are to grant life-preserving powers to them. In this respect, the Winter Ceremonial must be seen as more than a general enactment of life renewal themes. It has the more immediate purpose of doing for the nonhuman spirits of the Kwakiutl cosmos what lineage and rank do, as a matter of course, for the human ancestors.

The assembly of spiritual components to create or reconstitute a spirit being of the Winter Ceremonial provokes what the Kwakiutl call an "excitement." The excitement informs the congregation that the spirit has entered the dancer and possesses him. When the first winter spirit has arrived in this manner, the Ceremonial season has begun. The state of possession of but one man suffices to convert the entire community into an assembly of spirit beings. In due course, others will be seized by the excitement and will join in the dances. The ritual community, often intertribal, forms itself then into Sparrows, Seals, and commoner observers.

Sparrows and Seals divide the ritual congregation into opposing and antagonistic spiritual divisions. The Sparrows are the earthbound division, and having inherited office from their fathers are linked to the paternal lineages. Seals, the actual impersonators of the spirits, are the representatives of the other side, that is, of the spirit world. Having acquired these privileges from the wife's or mother's side, they are linked to maternal lineages. Only through the ritual connection can one recognize what is for Kwakiutl the religious significance of marriage. Sparrows are the officials and managers of the ritual, the Seals are their ecstatic clients. The Sparrows hold the role of shamans—the spirit controllers. Consequently, their chief is Head Shaman. Ritual antagonism between these two divisions acts to sustain the linkage and separation between what is set forth as two realms of existence. The Sparrows, as former Seals, must resist the premature efforts of those still in the spirit realm to leave it. From the texts it is not directly evident what significance the sparrow as a bird has for Kwakiutl. Presumably, sparrows represent the birds of earth, who, together with land mammals, once fought against Thunderbird and the birds of the sky and by their victory achieved the regulation of thundering. Since ritual contest is perceived as shamanistic, the Sparrows would appear as shamans against Head Winter Dancer (Thunderbird), himself a great shaman from the sky.

In the Winter Ceremonial the Sparrow-Seal antagonisms are rather complex. In the broadest sense, the Sparrow shamans are in contest against the general powers of the spirit world, of which Head Winter Dancer is representative. In this contest they are allied with Seals to see what they both can do against the great powers. In the face of such major antagonism, the oppositions between Sparrows and Seals are relatively minor. The Seals are, after all, the clients of the Sparrows, who are charged with bringing them back to secular safety.

The ritual concept of Seal illustrates a Kwakiutl penchant for fusing opposing images or opposing forces. Seal is the generic category for the 50 or more spirits of the Ceremonial who represent in their number the cosmic realms of earth, sky, sea, and the underworld of ghosts. Their designation as seals suggests at least a common denominator of identity that transcends otherwise extraordinary differences among all the spirits. That they are sea mammals who move easily between two major realms is one bridging factor. Basically, they are of the sea, thus associates of Qomogwa, and they inhabit a world that is opposite in time orientation from that of human beings. Their summer is the earth winter, so that they are always in their winter dances (see Boas 1935b:164), when they apppear among human beings. The sea, which is the source of salmon and copper, is even more generally considered to be the element that finally cures the *hamatsa* dancer and releases him from his state of possession. As the great source of wealth, the sea is the tamer of the Man Eater and of all associated spirits. Thus, once again, the principle of fusion of opposing elements is drawn upon as a mystical mechanism for counteracting dangerous forces. Kwakiutl seem to give themselves all possible advantages in their cosmic contests. The novice who goes out to meet Man Eater is paired with shaman Sparrows who are to guide him back. At the same time, he is fused with Seal, the opponent of Man Eater from within. And, of course, the frightening spirits are

[117   ]

themselves controlled and counteracted from within their own realm, and from within their own nature.

Another division within the company of Seals distinguishes between those who "go through to the other side" *(laxsa)* and those who remain within the human realm or, as the Kwakiutl say, only lean against the wall *(wixsa)*. Since dying is also spoken of as *laxsa,* they are the company of those who enter the realm of the spirits, on the analogy of the dead leaving their human habitat. In the course of ritual procedure the *laxsa* leave the house to disappear in the woods for a lengthy sojourn, returning as possessed by spirits. The *wixsa* need not leave the house at all; they retire briefly into a bedroom. Understandably, the *laxsa* are associated with the major spirits, and the *wixsa* with the minor. An unexplained reference to *laxsa* as "cedar bark boxes" suggests, simply by analogy with Kwakiutl concepts of containers, that the *laxsa* are actual possessors of great powers that need to be contained. Basically, *laxsa* comprise the joint complement of Man Eater and war spirits, the exponents of the major ritual themes; the *wixsa* are, perhaps, ancillary, but they complete the required mosaic.

Viewed in the perspective of overall structure, the grand divisions of Sparrow and Seal, and *laxsa* and *wixsa* manifest a principle of gradation, not identical with the gradations of rank, but perhaps akin to it. Social rank among Kwakiutl is, after all, a religious configuration, as a gradation of the original ancestors by criteria of power. Gradation of winter spirits is entirely comparable to the gradation of ancestral spirits. Gradation does not divide a community. On the contrary, it establishes an unbroken chain, a connection implying diminution going back to the original sources. Implied in gradation is a metaphysical mechanics that "safely" links together the most powerful and the weak. The weak are, accordingly, spared the dangers of direct association with great powers. From this point of view, the structure of the Winter Ceremonial provides an unbroken lifeline from the *hamatsa* dancer who is most exposed, to the Sparrows. The *wixsa* are an intermediary group, a bridge between the two.

The minor spirits of the *wixsa* are not necessarily innocuous; and they are thematically joined with those of the *laxsa*. The most important of the minor spirits are the fool dancers *(nutlmatl)* who are, in fact, lesser forms of war dancers. The *nutlmatl* represent the madness, the wildness, and the obscene side of war and destruction. Like similar cults among Plains Indian warriors, they are "contrary ones" doing things backward,

in opposition to conventional norms. They are figures of filth and ob-
scenity, their long noses dripping snot. They urinate and defecate in
the house and pretend to commit suicide. They are destructive madmen
who rage through the congregation, knocking people over, destroying
property, and, finally, in some instances, dismantling the entire house
(see Boas 1897:468ff). For their destructiveness, they pay with property.
An indemnity, or a pacification of the spirits of madness? In thematic
consistency, the "payment" would have a significance parallel to the feeding of Man Eater. The fool dancers as destructive forces should, by
the same principle of consistency, contain within themselves a countering
and thus a restraining force. Property-giving is an example of a counter-
force. Perhaps, the contrary behavior should be considered as another.
Thematically, contrariness expresses reversal. Rage and madness, the
fury of excess, are reversals of the common order. But if the reversal
theme is conceived of as general it can imply a movement back in either
direction. In this sense, the contrary behavior of the *nutlmatl* conveys
the counterpart theme, namely that every course of action can be reversed.

The dances and spirit impersonations portray the religious essence
of the Winter Ceremonial. It is also a period of feasts, "potlatches,"
"sales" of coppers, and returns by fathers-in-law of "marriage payments."
Are these separate or coordinated events? Boas thought the dances were
the real religious content of the Winter Ceremonial season, and the
feasts and property distributions but unrelated secular events, conven-
iently placed at a time when people were at leisure and already assembled.[5] Had Boas recognized the religious import of oil feasts and of
property exchanges, he might have come to a different conclusion about
the total religious content of the Winter Ceremonial. The Winter Ceremonial is a complex ritual organization within which the shamanistic
contests with spirits are carried out by a totality of means. I reserve
a full scale discussion of the ritual totality for later chapters. But I cannot
close this chapter on the Winter Ceremonial without at least outlining
its full dimensions.

It must be understood that the scope of a strange ritual is not obvious.
Some events are so clearly cognate that their unity is recognized at once.
Ordinarily, the conditions of space and time furnish sufficient clues as
to what are the unities. But since ritual is only akin to, but is not theater,
where the stage separates what is presented from what merely occurs,
the fact of events occurring within the same space (the village) and at

the same time (the winter season) does not in itself establish a conceptual unity. In a situation as complex as that of the Kwakiutl Winter Ceremonial, understanding of conceptual unity is ultimately to be reached through understanding of the whole nature of the religious concepts.

A most important clue to the ritual design comes from our understanding of Kwakiutl marriage. As Boas saw so clearly, the Winter Ceremonial is a response to the acquisition of rights in marriage and is indeed the occasion for what he called the return of the marriage payment. Having gone this far, Boas simply dropped the matter, failing to recognize the religious nature of marriage and of exchange. As we have seen, marriage is a climactic event that bridges the gap between two realms on what we would call the social level. In Kwakiutl marriage the closing of the gap, symbolized by the transport of a bride from across the sea, is analogous to the bridging of the gap between men and spirits. The bridging of a gap must provoke a chain of events. Since Kwakiutl symbolic imagery is biological, the chain is both developmental and circulatory. By bridging one gap, marriage leads to a new step by which the human-spirit separation is then temporarily overcome—a new and perhaps higher development, as though the ability to unify one type of realm provides the means to unify another. One developmental move demands another, and each calls forth a circulatory movement of property—coppers, animal skins (form souls), and oil. What Boas spoke of as the "sale" of a copper may be visualized "biologically" as part of the circulation engendered by marriage. The "sale" of a copper is associated with the Winter Ceremonial because it and the winter dances are both related properties that are transmitted through marriage. The dances are exhibited and the coppers are set into circulation. Oil feasts are also part of the same transaction. Fish oil, the Kwakiutl say, is given in the name of the bride. Distributions of animal skins are mandatory for all demonstrations of acquired powers. The Winter Ceremonial is also the occasion for antagonistic displays between tribes; and as I show more fully in a subsequent chapter, social antagonism is essentially a ritual counterpart of the necessary antagonism between men and the dangerous spirits.

I discuss Kwakiutl property concepts in the next chapter. These concepts, however, become clear only in the context of the Winter Ceremonial and are, therefore, most appropriately introduced at this point. The essential clue to the nature of property comes in the *hamatsa* songs. These are some examples:

I hold down your great furor,
>*great* [hamatsa] *I hold down your whistles,*
>*great* [hamatsa]

I appease your voracity,
>*great* [hamatsa]

You are looking for food all the time
>*great* [hamatsa]

You are looking for heads all the time
>*great* [hamatsa]

You devour wealth, great [hamatsa]

(Boas 1897:460)

He wants to eat with both hands, the great [hamatsa] *at the house of the one who is trying to eat all himself all over the world; but he did not reach the coppers that he was going to obtain at the edge of the world.*

(ibid)

Wealth, which stands for the vitality of the people, is indeed an integral component of the festival. Wealth satiates the voracity of Man Eater, and is quite understandably a major ceremonial theme. The festival is inaugurated by a simple ceremony of the "winter dance pole," a heavy staff some six to eight feet long. The pole represents, as Boas reports, the amount of property that will be spent by a man in behalf of his son-in-law, property such as copper bracelets, blankets, food, and grease (ibid:502). A chief dancing with the pole in behalf of the young man demonstrates that it is too heavy for him to carry. Then he sings:

The spirit of the Winter Dance came down
The spirit of the Winter Dance came down and
>*stays here with me.*

(ibid)

Thus is opened the Winter Ceremonial. When the people enter the dance house, they pass through a doorway surrounded by a ring of hemlock branches covered with eagle down. Hemlock, a cleansing agent, removes the human smell; eagle down is a symbol of wealth.

VII

RITUAL
DISTRIBUTION
AND EXCHANGE

The Kwakiutl conception of ritual distribution and exchange bears little resemblance to what has been portrayed under the heading of The Potlatch. While Boas's inappropriate view of the "potlatch" as an "interest-bearing investment of property" was never taken too seriously, his equally erroneous impression that "potlatch" gifts were usually returned with interest as high as 100 percent has been widely accepted as an ethnographic fact. With slightly more justification, scholars have concurred in Boas's representation of the "potlatch" as the means for acquiring rank.

Property distribution is indeed associated with rank, but not as Boas saw it. The misunderstanding of Kwakiutl ideas about matters we label as "exchange," "property," "wealth," and "rank" arises from the uncritical application of a European model of status relations to a totally different system of meaning. Thus the Kwakiutl expression "fighting with property," struck Boas and later scholars as a native version of conspicuous display in the game of status rivalry. Since their "potlatches" were imagined as extraordinarily extravagant, the Kwakiutl came to be a prime example of mankind's unfortunate obsession with materialistic values.

From the great store of ethnographic information so painstakingly and meticulously gathered by Boas and Hunt, an entirely different picture of what is more appropriately designated as ritual distribution and exchange emerges. I have already indicated in another context that Kwakiutl property was originally a representation of lives and not dead currency, and that value was not in mere quantity but in quality. Quantity is a value, a measure of supernatural powers and of personal force. But it is not, as has been assumed, comparable to a commercial value. Correspondingly, distribution and exchange of such properties reflect a cosmological conception of circulation, a conception that is outside the scope of sociological theory which reduces a complex concept to mechanical motions of mechanical objects.

Marcel Mauss, the master of general theory of exchange, came closer to the true Kwakiutl conception when he explained that the obligation to return a gift was inherent in the quality of the property. The gift object, he observed, held a power within itself, a power that was part of the donor's being. Whoever received a gift then possessed a valuable that was also dangerous, because alien, and dared not hold it permanently (1954:9, 10, 41). Mauss saw very clearly the magical or mystical properties of Kwakiutl gifts. He called attention to the *mana* inherent in spoons, dishes, and coppers (ibid:113) and to the mystical "cult of blankets, mats and hide coverings" (ibid:112). The power in the things exchanged, he reasoned, "forces them to circulate, to be given away and repaid" (ibid:41).

We see in the data an even more fundamental explanation for the circulation of properties. Mauss began his inquiry into the gift by asking two sequential questions: "What is the principle whereby the gift received has to be repaid? What force is there in the thing being given which compels the recipient to make a return?" (ibid:1). In this phrasing the second question appears as an answer to the first and predisposes the inquiry toward an investigation of the objects, whereas the more fundamental investigation would seek to explain principles of circulation. The power in the object is surely germane to its role in exchange, but one must ask, does it compel the circulation? If we take note of the total character of the properties to include all they represent for Kwakiutl we come to a broader conception of exchange and circulation. The objects have not only power, they have meanings by which they represent all spheres of life.

From this more comprehensive point of view the obligation to reciprocate in exchange is not in response to the specific powers in the objects but to a cosmological conception that postulates an eternal circulation of forms of being. The obligations to give and the obligations to repay are obligations to participate in this vital circulation. In the main it is an obligation of chiefs. The very same obligations of chiefs sustain the great *kula* exchanges among Trobriand Islanders and their neighbors. Kwakiutl chiefs, however, participate in exchanges as incarnates of ancestral and supernatural beings. For them, therefore, the total system of circulation encompassed a universe of men, of ancestral spirits, of supernatural beings, and through the properties that circulated, of animal and vegetable forms of life. The primary property in traditional exchanges was animal skins.

In traditional Kwakiutl belief the animal skin memorialized a creature that had allowed itself to be killed in fulfillment of a compact (see Boas 1930:193), as among Eskimo, for reciprocal benefits, which would sustain the permanent circulation of life: The animals sustained mankind; mankind would sustain them. From this point of view, which is not merely that of the Kwakiutl, but of most American Indians, the animal pelt could be no mere trophy of a killed beast, and its circulation could not serve the narrow interests of men alone. The logic of a doctrine of reciprocal relations, not to mention of primordial identities between men and animals, dictates the assumption that the animal skins and other valuables are also represented as forces in the system of circulation. Exchange involves not men alone, but also the beings represented by the so-called "currency" of exchange.

I suggested earlier that animal skins should be considered in their associations with the first ancestors as original outer forms or "form souls," which as masks and as crests were perpetuated genealogically and so have the attributes of immortality proper to a soul.[1] The Kwakiutl do not actually describe the skins given in ritual distribution as having these same mythological properties. One can claim only that in the context of myth, and in the total context of their beliefs, the skins of ordinary animals are analogous to the form souls of animals depicted in myth.

[124   ]

The animal form of the ancestor was recreated as a mask—the ancestral crest. In ritual the mask stands for the essential form of the being who is depicted or incarnated. Kwakiutl recognize a hidden reality behind the mask, but also insist that the mask may be the only reality ordinarily exposed to mankind. Thus the sky is visualized, as are all the heavenly bodies, as the "great face of a man's mask" and not as the face—whatever that would be—itself.

The animal skin is also a form, a garment that originally converts a human inner substance into animal form. In myth, animals easily slip in and out of their skins to become momentarily nonanimal (see Boas 1935b:133). From the mythical perspective, the skin is the animal's essential attribute from which, however, it is separable, in the way in which soul separates from body. When in myth, animals give their skins to humans they offer with them their characteristic animal qualities (Boas 1930:194). In one myth, the hunter who has obtained the white mountain goat skin has the power to catch other mountain goats. Thus the animal skin, *naenxwa,* which Hunt translates as "animal skin covering," and Boas renders more blandly as "blanket," is like a mask.[2] But it is, of course, not a crest. Crests are individual, and have epithetic names; animal skins are generalized, and are namelessly generic. Crests move down precise channels of patrilineal and matrilineal kinship, animal skins circulate ceaselessly among the tribes. The crest is the form soul of an ancestor who was dual (animal, or other, and human). But the skins of hunted animals are those of ordinary and unitary beasts, and therefore, in still another category of attributes, belong exclusively to the animal world. As exclusively animal, they circulate in a broader sphere.

Properties do not circulate at random intervals. They follow the life cycles of persons and the cycle of the seasons. They are interlocked with birth, with the stages of maturation, with adolescence, with accession to rank, with marriage, with succession to chiefship, and with death. When the sidereal cycle moves to winter, the circulation of properties quickens and enters an antagonistic phase. Kwakiutl visualize the cycles of growth and the cycle of the seasons as sequences of transformation of states of being, as changes in identity. At each stage in the life cycle, persons assume a new name. During the winter season all names and identities are changed (Boas 1925:111). The circulation of properties responds to and is integral with all vital transformations that are accompanied by a change of name. From a sociological view—a distortion of Kwakiutl reality—property is distributed to "validate" rank. In the total perspective, we see properties rather as one expression of vital force moving in concert with names, crests, and powers, which represent still another set of vital forces.[3]

The source of circulation is not the social order as such. The starting point is the natural order, the growth of persons, their aging, their maturation, their death, their sexual reproduction, their rearing of children, their incremental accumulation of powers, in a sense their self-multiplication, since identities (names) are both successive and cumulative. The turning of the earth, the seasonal migrations of salmon, the changes in the weather and in the length of the day are the other and related aspects of the natural order to which the circulation of properties respond. Among Kwakiutl, as among all peoples whose cultural continuity has permitted a coherent cosmological elaboration, all cycles mesh like gears, all motions respond to each other. Men complete the connections of their social order in harmony with the motions they recognize in the natural sphere. This they must do, since they recognize the social order as an integral aspect of a broader cosmic order, with which it must therefore synchronize.

The individual life cycle, plus the seasons, engenders the primary circulation of emblematic properties—that is, of a succession of beings. In the anthropological literature, what I call emblematic properties are described as nonmaterial property. But since material masks and nonmaterial songs, for example, are equally emblems of an incarnation, the designation "emblematic properties" is the more logically apt. Emblematic properties are received at each stage of the life cycle, and other properties are at that time distributed. These properties are thematically related to the emblems, and are, accordingly, complementary. Emblems of original ancestors and of supernatural beings become the property of a noble, and immediately provoke an outward circulation of animal skins, along with bark blankets, slaves, canoes, foods, and coppers. What then is the religious meaning of this fact that one form of property arrives, and another leaves?

We may start with the nature of emblems and their complements. The emblems represent an order of ancestral and mythological beings who achieve an incarnation within contemporary persons. Through human beings, these beings are themselves transformed, as they in turn transform their hosts. The complements represent still other orders of life: The order of animal life depicted directly in the form of skins

[126   ]

(coverings) and food; the order of human life reduced to the animal level, depicted directly as slaves. Canoes, dishes, and boxes are a third and living world of conveyor-containers drawn from the world of arboreal life. Coppers are from a fourth world that incorporates the three cosmic realms of earth, sky, and sea (but not the underworld).

Within the total and ongoing sequences of vital exchanges, the first or primary transaction brings the mythic world of first ancestors and of supernatural beings into connection with the contemporary natural world. Emblematic properties (mythical) are associated with complementary properties (contemporary). In this primary transaction the human being as noble (shaman) is the mediating power, the bridge, the vital connection between myth time and the present. A religious sociology of exchange ensues through the introduction of human concerns. The noble mediator is not an empty drum upon which cosmic forces beat their independent rhythms. He is himself a drum beater, a master of rhythms. He sounds his own vital interests and seeks to turn the dialectic of interchange between the mythic world and the present to his own advantage. He compels the cosmic circulation of emblematic and complementary properties to yield him long life and strength.

All Kwakiutl exchange may be seen as a quadrilateral relationship by which the myth world faces the present world in an opposition of original donors and present recipients of powers. Simultaneously, human beings face each other in parallel fashion as donors and receivers. Neither pair is independent of the other, since the ancestral and supernatural beings live in men, and men face each other in the guise of ancestors and of supernatural beings. Moreover, the primary relationship between the first beginnings (mythical) and the present, through which the endless continuity of existence is assured, is through men and their personal interests.

But the personal interests of men, specifically the chiefs, are also within the larger order. For as the Kwakiutl define rank and pride of rank, ambition and the zealous protection of inherited privilege, the status rivalries of chiefs carry forward the original plan. Nevertheless, in human agency the plan allows, as does nature, for the play of contingency.

From still another side, the complementary properties, the totally nonhuman side, face human beings and their spiritual incarnates in their movements from one person, represented by a name, to others represented by other names. As they vacate the storage box that is representative of one name they fill the storage box of another.[4] Since these properties, whether the skins or coppers, are representatives of beings their motions are equivalent—though expressive of still another relationship—to the transactions between donor and receiver. As I explain more fully shortly, donor and receiver are each in the condition of dual forces. The donor is simultaneously benefactor and destroyer, and the receivers are reciprocally the benefited and the destroyed, presumably on the model of the hunter and his animal game. Between the complementary properties and the named beings, the relationship is simply one of reciprocal completion: When these properties leave they "fasten on a name," when they arrive they fill a vacancy, almost like a marriage, if the storage box is considered an analogy of a house. In the Winter Ceremonial these same properties enter into still another relationship—with the supernatural beings.

So that we need not think of Kwakiutl life only as a bloodless abstraction, lived as religious psychodrama, we take keen note of all the evidence, even from the old days, of real human beings, beneath the masks of their incarnations, who are subjectively sensitive to honor and insult, to benefice and menace, and to obligations of social reciprocity. The persistence of the "potlatch" and of "potlatch" rivalries within a Christianized and somewhat commercialized social milieu tells us that much of the old system can be laicized and carried out on the strength of basic human motives, by pride in power, invidiousness, shame, and sensitivity to refinements of status. Within the traditional order the human psyche was embedded in a total religious matrix. The lust for power and mastery, as we would speak of it moralistically, was for Kwakiutl as real and necessary as the savagery of the grizzly bear. The contemporary Kwakiutl psyche is, perhaps, now disembedded. But who can say how much of the older religious and naturalistic ideas remain?

A general conception of the "potlatch" as a religious phenomenon was put forth by Lenoir as early as 1924, and a year later by Mauss. Lenoir's essay, which has been largely ignored, is particularly penetrating on the magical and religious nature of the "potlatch." Lenoir saw, for example, the religious connections between "potlatch," warfare, and the mystical combats of the Winter Ceremonial. Mauss arrived at similar conclusions, but from a more general perspective. Mauss saw the necessity for placing Northwest Coast exchanges in a new perspective that would go beyond the legalist conceptions of contract emphasized in the writings of Davy (1922) and Adam (1922). In reply to these he wrote:

For the potlatch is more than a legal phenomenon; it is one of those phenomena we propose to call "total." It is religious, mythological and shamanistic because the chiefs taking part are all incarnations of gods and ancestors, whose names they bear, whose dances they dance, and whose spirits possess them. (1954:36)

He added, however, that the "potlatch" was also economic, and a "phenomenon of social morphology," and a form of legal contract (ibid). Nevertheless, he considered the obligation to take part in gift exchange as religious: "In the things exchanged at a potlatch there is a certain power which forces them to circulate, to be given away and repaid" (ibid:41). Lenoir had come earlier to a similar conclusion in describing the Indian exchanges as the distribution of "social mana" (1924:240).

Mauss's discussion of exchange on the Northwest Coast, though brief and general, is incisive and sweeping. He did not confuse the Indian with the modern bourgeois, and he did not mistake Indian property for currency. In giving and in exchanging goods the Indian, as he recognized, was consorting with spirits, using a medium that was itself alive with spiritual power. Mauss sought only to uncover the essential principles of exchange, pointing others toward the further and deeper explorations of their reaches and meanings. One need not accept all of his judgments to acknowledge that to look further one gratefully stands on his shoulders.

Yet Mauss's influence on students of the "potlatch" has been curiously incomplete, considering the justly deserved renown of his *Essai sur le don* (1925). Boas evidently had no formal occasion to consider Mauss's views on the "potlatch," since his last explicative article on Kwakiutl was published as early as 1924. Thereafter Boas dedicated himself to publishing a series of unevaluated Kwakiutl texts. Had he been deeply impressed by Mauss, however, he might have referred to him in the Kwakiutl manuscript on which he continued to work. Nor is there reference to Mauss in Ruth Benedict's widely known essay on the Kwakiutl (1934). Barnett, who wrote his doctoral dissertation on the "potlatch" in 1938 *(The Nature and Function of the Potlatch)*, included Mauss in his bibliography, but ignored his conclusions. As late as 1950 Helen Codere published her well-received study of the Kwakiutl "potlatch" without including Mauss in her bibliography. It remained for Claude Lévi-Strauss (1969) to reestablish Mauss as a guide on the nature of the "potlatch." But at that point in his intellectual history the author of the *Savage Mind* and the series of *mythologiques* was developing a sociology of alliance and did not perceive the relevance of Mauss's ideas on the basically religious character of exchange. A more recent study of the "potlatch" also ignores Mauss on the religious issue, but picks him up on the sociology of status rivalry (Rosman and Rubel 1971).

If Mauss and Lenoir have been almost uniformly ignored by scholars on their most important and original contribution to a theory of primitive exchange, the fault is at least partly their own. In the setting of a powerful anthropological positivism that has been either hostile or indifferent to analysis of religious phenomena, a more substantial exposition of the thesis was needed. Lenoir and Mauss chose rather to present the broad outlines of a general theory of gift exchange. In Mauss's work, Kwakiutl and Northwest Coast were among several examples drawn from around the world. The evidence was not hammered home, although Mauss did bring out a fascinating array of pertinent facts in his voluminous footnotes. At the very least the thesis was provocative and should have led to further exploration. The profession seized rather only upon what it was prepared to believe, namely that primitive exchange was a sociological phenomenon.

In his introduction to the English-language edition Evans-Pritchard wrote of *Essai sur le don*: "It is the first systematic and comparative study of the widespread custom of gift exchange and the first understanding of its function in the articulation of the social order" (1954:ix). Even as he reminds his readers that Mauss had been, above all, a scholar of comparative religions he does not call attention to the religious side of Mauss's thinking about exchange. He converts a truly extraordinary thesis into fashionably bland social anthropology. Thus, finally, Mauss's views on exchange are stripped of their religious significance and made acceptable as a theory that "exchange of goods was not a mechanical but a moral transaction, bringing about and maintaining human, personal, relationships between individuals and groups" (ibid).

If primitive exchange was but one more social device for maintaining the equilibrium of the social order then its import is obvious enough— why struggle with the immense burden of detail George Hunt had so painstakingly assembled? But at the very least a religious theory of exchange has the heuristic value of compelling attention to all details, to the "total system." Yet the "potlatch" as sociology or as socioeconomics soon became so well known that its study in detail seemed even more pointless. "Models" of sociological exchange were easily constructed from Boas's very early and quite tentative general judgments, and later from a general consensus. A distinguished exception is a most perceptive essay that suggests an important connection between Northwest Coast exchanges and a cult of the dead (Wike 1952).

Strictly speaking, the term "potlatch" has no valid place in the vocabulary of professional writing on Kwakiutl simply because it is local jargon and not a Kwakiutl word.[5] Used in place of the real Kwakiutl terms for property distributions it obscures their indigenous meanings. Boas's use of "potlatch" is particularly incomprehensible, not only because it violated his own principles on cultural and historical contexts, but because it did not arise from the texts. George Hunt rarely used "potlatch" in his own translations. And for reasons we may never understand, Boas undiscriminatingly altered Hunt's straightforward "he gave away," to "he gave a potlatch," or "he potlatched."

Boas picked up "potlatch" and bestowed on it an unfortunate professional authenticity by inserting it into his edited versions of the George Hunt texts. "Potlatch" appears so often in the published texts that the reader must assume the word was thoroughly assimilated into the Kwakiutl language. From Boas's Kwakiutl writings, "potlatch" diffused rapidly all along the Northwest coast and finally, through the work of Mauss, around the world.

If "potlatch," as used in the scholarly literature, referred only to gifts, as in Chinook jargon, there would be no problem. Perhaps scholars should enjoy the privilege of using an arcane term in place of such well known words as "give," "gift," "distribute," or "exchange." But the problem exists because around "potlatch" has been constructed the mirage of an institution—The Potlatch.

There never were, at least in precontact days, such events as "potlatches." Rather, there were specific ritual occasions commemorating marriage, death, the construction of a house, investiture of an heir, elevation of young people to new positions, the "sale" of coppers, the giving of Winter Cercmonial dances, the giving of oil feasts in connection with the Winter Ceremonial, and the display of supernatural properties shortly after they had been received. These were not mere occasions for "potlatches," they were ritual occasions in their own right, at which properties were distributed. Occasion and distribution were, however, essential elements of a common ritual unit.

By professional standards of cultural analysis a word as vague and misleading as "potlatch" is an embarrassment at best, and at worst a serious impediment to understanding. Yet scholars who habitually draw razor-sharp distinctions on other subjects have accepted "potlatch," drawing all the associations loosely assembled in its name into a single concept. Thus Lévi-Strauss has described the "potlatch" as a festival during which:

> considerable valuables are transferred . . . sometimes amounting to several tens of thousands of rugs handed over in kind, or in the symbolical form of copper plaques whose face value increases in terms of the importance of the transaction in which they have figured. These ceremonies have a triple purpose, viz. to return gifts previously received, together with an appropriate amount of interest, sometimes as much as 100 percent; to establish publicly the claim of a family or social group to a title or prerogative, or to announce officially a change of status; finally to surpass a rival in generosity, to crush him if possible with future obligations which it is hoped he cannot meet so as to take from him his prerogatives, titles, rank, authority and prestige. (1969:52–53)

Mauss, who was more mindful of the diversity of motive and function of gift giving and exchange on the Northwest Coast, set a more limited but also misleading definition of the "potlatch," as antagonistic exchange. "It is above all," he wrote, "a struggle among nobles to determine their positions in the hierarchy to the ultimate benefit, if they are successful, of their clans. This antagonistic type of total exchange we propose to call the potlatch" (1954:4–5). This definition with its implication of a "war of property" to determine social position leaves open the designation of other forms of gift giving and exchange. But the nature of agonistic relations on the Northwest Coast and especially among the Kwakiutl is too complex a phenomenon to be encompassed under what is usually understood as aristocratic status rivalry, or under a single all-embracing term such as "potlatch." I would prefer not to speak of "potlatch" at all in this chapter, relying instead on the more basic and unequivocal terms such as "gift," "distribution," and "exchange." Kwakiutl have, of course, their own vocabulary which defines these concepts with more precision.

Vocabulary serves only as a guide to native meanings, and surely not as their total explication, which must be derived from all pertinent contexts. But if the term for an action does not describe all its implications it may sometimes lay bare its essentials. The possibility of a deep revelation is particularly strong for Kwakiutl, who utilize a remarkably vivid and evocative vocabulary, especially in ritual relations.[6]

In place of "potlatch," Kwakiutl employed at least four terms. These are: *walasila,* meaning "doing a great thing"; *pasa,* "to flatten"; *yaxwede,* and *maxwede,* both translated by Hunt as "giving away." *Walasila* is a colorful expression for any conspicuous or lavish act of antagonistic distribution. *Pasa* has an ambiguous meaning. In his earliest writings Boas thought it had the aggressive connotation of "flattening the name of a rival" (1897:343). Later, he realized it actually had a more passive significance that referred to the gradual flattening of a soft basket from which objects had been removed (1935b:40). The latter meaning seems correct from the textual contexts, and is also consistent with Boas's belief that the *pasa* distribution was limited to one's own tribe—where, of course, there could be no question of "flattening a rival's name." From a study of the original Hunt manuscript texts, one must conclude rather that *pasa* is actually synonymous with *maxwede* and *yaxwede,* and that all have the general meaning, as translated by Hunt, of giving away. In the texts *pasa* definitely includes intertribal distributions (Boas 1921:901, line 14). Since it occurs most frequently in modern contexts when woolen blankets are given away it may be a more current term. In any case, *pasa* introduces a concept of self-divestment, of emptying out in behalf of a name, the contrary of "flattening" an opponent.

The most commonly used terms are *yaxwede* and *maxwede.* They appear in texts referring to ancient times as well as to more recent occasions. In context they are clear synonyms, though they have distinctive etymologies. Their etymons suggest the deeper meanings of ritual distribution.

Before discussing these, I should add the cautionary note that Boas's vocabularies are phonetic rather than phonemic. Hence phonetic differences in his vocabularies may refer not to real semantic distinctions, but rather to a variety of phonological impressions from different informants and from different texts. For example, in his collected vocabularies Boas wrote *yaq* as the stem for *yaxwede* to mean "potlatch" (before *w* in Kwakiutl, *q* softens to *x*), thus correcting Hunt, who usually wrote *yak.* But if there is a phonemic distinction between *yaq* and *yak* Boas does not call attention to it. Nor does he warn, in general, against confusing the meanings of *q* and *k* sounds. In the absence of such a caveat, one may venture to consider the words given as *yaq* and *yak* in Boas's vocabularies as synonymous. Thus, listed as *yak* are such meanings as "to lie dead," "to vanquish," "bad things," "to talk." Listed as *yaq* is "property." In similar fashion the stem *maq* (*max, mak*) includes a stem meaning of "property," "to cause shame," "to carry off," and "to pursue secretly." *Pasa* is etymologically clear, conveying the definite idea of a distribution as an emptying, an idea that is developed fully and explicitly in the texts. Boxes are emptied, houses are emptied, baskets are emptied. In still another and related sense property is said to be vomited out, another version of emptying, with the powerful significance of a resurrection of life (see Ch. 8).

The connotations from the stem *yaq/yak* include that of property, as that which lies dead, and that which has been vanquished. The allusion is apt for animal skins, which represent killed and vanquished animals. The expression "bad things" refers to the father-in-law's return gifts, a probable allusion to Iakim *(yakim)* the Sea Monster, who distributes blankets to all the tribes (Boas 1897:480, 482). Thus the expression *yaxwede* does, in fact, convey the Kwakiutl concept of ambivalence in distribution, as we see in the course of this and the following chapter. Giving to the tribes is simultaneously benefice and malevolence. The tribes are pleased to receive, but—and this is where *yaxwede* makes its point—they are also swallowed up (killed) and otherwise vanquished. *Yaxwede* states the nature of property and implies its distribution. *Maxwede* states the nature of distribution and implies property. An important clue to the etymology of this term may come from *maxenox*, the killer whale, the deadly and silent pursuer of fish and sea mammals. The killer whale epitomizes supreme hunting powers. Thus *maxenox* links *max* with *yak* in a common concept of killing and vanquishing, and by extension, of shaming. The place of *yak*, "to talk" is unclear in this syndrome of related meanings.

Feasts, commonly considered "potlatches," are *kwelas* (from *kes*, "to eat"). They fall definitely within the general framework of ritual exchange, but with distinctive symbolic meanings.

The replacing of woolen, store-bought blankets by animal skins imposed a powerful, quantitative impression on distribution that obscured for many scholars what had actually been the traditional pattern of a linked regard for both the quantity and the symbolic significance of each item of complementary property. The Hudson's Bay blanket reduced exchange to a single unit; the older exchanges, as the records show, usually included an ensemble of properties—sea mammals, land mammals, human beings (slaves), yellow cedar bark, and an assortment of containers and conveyors, such as boxes, dishes, and canoes. By more contemporary standards of extravagance, when "tens of thousands" of store blankets were given away, the early distributions were quite modest, in keeping with North American Indian conservationism. The

"Dionysian" Kwakiutl were also so noticeably opposed to excess that Benedict, who thought she saw in them a fury of profligate imagination, nevertheless recognized a definite resistance to "overdoing." In Kwakiutl folktales, hunters who have been granted supernatural power to kill animals easily are enjoined against overdoing. In one tale, the set limit was four mountain goats (Boas and Hunt 1905:18). Latter-day Kwakiutl became extravagant with cash; traditional Indians could not be extravagant with the lives of animals to whom they were bound in reciprocal moral and religious respects.

The family histories document carefully all important distributions, and are more reliable guides to quantitative scale than the scattered reports of monumental "potlatches" that have beguiled the anthropological imagination. The histories do not describe extravagantly rivalrous distributions. They deal rather with marriage distributions and with distributions accompanying other phases of the life cycle. Marriage distributions and exchanges are the most fully documented, and are quite typical as to scale. In Appendix 4 I summarize a series of distributions from the major family histories. Including bride price and return payments, the average comes to fewer than 300 "blankets," of which about half were cedar bark robes of little value, given only to commoners. Since all distributions were to lineages and to tribes, depending on the rank of the bride and groom, each person of rank received relatively few skins. The obligation was for at least one skin to each holder of a ranked name. In some instances only 50 animal skins were given to all of a visiting tribe (Boas 1921:841). Even in postcontact distributions of store blankets the scale normally remained moderate. Thus at a Mamaleleqala mourning distribution only 2000 blankets were given for all the men of rank of all the tribes of the Ritual Congregation, a maximum of perhaps five blankets per recipient. At one of the great and more recent distributions, when a new chief was to be installed, only the highest-ranking Eagle chief was given as many as five blankets (Boas 1925:231). At many distributions it was not unusual for several recipients to share a single woolen blanket.

Examples of more lavish giving and of "wasteful" destruction have been reported. But these are clearly exceptional, and have been overemphasized by writers who misunderstood the system, recognizing it only as an example of Veblenian conspicuous consumption. Not only was the normal standard of distribution modest, but it should be remembered that almost all the complementary properties were durable, and were recirculated repeatedly. The most persistent distortion of the Kwakiutl system came from Boas's odd impression—with its implications of spectacular economic expansion—that all gifts had to be returned with 100 percent interest. There are in fact examples of doubling a return, and there are examples of "lending" property at "interest." I discuss these in Chapter 8 to show how specialized and exceptional such forms of exchange were. Ritual distributions and exchanges were mainly general rather than dyadic, nonrivalrous rather than antagonistic, and only in special ritual circumstances were recipients expected to match donors' gifts. As a rule, donors gave according to their own ritual standards. The destruction of property by fire or the throwing of coppers into the sea, forms of ritual sacrifice, were for most chiefs a once in a lifetime event. Considering the lavish resources of the Northwest Coast the ritual economy, as a whole, was hardly burdensome.

The issue of quality in distribution was even more important. Complementary properties were matched with rank—an expression of emblematic property—so that canoes and slaves, and seals and sea otters circulated only among the highest chiefs. Yellow cedar bark robes and sewed mink blankets were given to commoners; all other forest mammal skins went to chiefs of middle rank. If the mink skins, which were in fact quite uncommon, are ignored, the religious principle that relates emblematic and complementary properties becomes reasonably clear. Highest rank is associated with the sea, the primary source of wealth, middle rank with the forest beasts, and lowest rank with a forest tree, whose bark is its "skin." Sea and forest are for Kwakiutl natural oppositions, as we have seen through the metaphoric language of the Winter Ceremonial. The sea, the domain of Qomogwa, the spirit of wealth that overcomes death, opposes the forest, the region of wolves and the maneaters. From another but related perspective, the world of animal life, of hunting and killing, is counterpointed to the bloodless but living character of the yellow cedar.

Yet the pattern is by no means crystalline. Mink skins were given to commoners as well as to nobles, perhaps because they were trapped rather than hunted, and conceivably because of the mythical significance of Mink, a transformer, son of the sun, and overcomer of the wolves in their first Winter Ceremonial. The legendary character of the animal was evidently taken into account. Thus wolf skins were never worn as robes and were not included in exchange, because the Wolf was a sacred medicine animal forbidden to be hunted. The pattern that associates complementary properties and rank is complicated also by the equivalency established by Kwakiutl between sea mammal skins (sea otter was more prominent than seal) and slaves and canoes. In some instances, highest chiefs received seal, sea otter, slaves, and canoes. More commonly, one set substituted for the other. The equivalence may be attributed directly to scarcity value, but from a symbolic perspective, to the maritime association. The slave was a "product" brought in by canoe.

The first ritual distribution, according to Kwakiutl tradition, came from the flesh and hide of a mammal (Boas 1897:382). The son of a tribal founder went by canoe to an island and clubbed seals all day. He returned to feed the people seal flesh and to give away seal skins. Even though this tale is a local tradition, it defines a primary pattern: The original donor is a youth; the animals are conveyed by canoe; the original animal is the seal, a representative of Qomogwa; feast and distribution of skins are united in a single ritual. I would assume that at this formative period only high chiefs were present to receive seals. In later times only the highest-ranking tribes were privileged to partake of a seal feast.

The final pattern of ritual distribution and exchange undoubtedly evolved and gained in complexity over time. New properties were added, and new symbolic meanings were introduced.

Feasts and distributions of durable goods continued to be joined in a single ritual occasion, but were thematically separated. The privilege of giving durable goods was inherited from the paternal lineage, as a rule; that of giving a feast came from the affinal lineage through the father-in-law. The skins have a masculine significance, as we might expect from an assumption they are form soul analogues to masculine crests. The sexual connection is, perhaps, more directly that of the masculine hunter and the female feeder. In the context of marital distributions, animals skins are said to be given for the "weight" of the groom's name, and foodstuffs for the weight of the bride's name (Boas 1921:963). The concept of "weightiness" of a name is presumably that of body mass added to the name soul.

Seal feasts are not commonly described in the texts. At the great ritual feasts, fish oil (oulachen) was served with berries or crabapples. In distributions of fish oil and animal skins the issue of sex gender is set forth. Thus in the context of oil feasts and distributions of durables, especially animal skins, it is the masculine attribute that enters into relatively permanent circulation, and the female attribute that is directly consumed.

[137   ]

The qualities and the quantities of the complementary properties that circulate within the entire Ritual Congregation define only part of the entire system. The mechanics of circulation, the principles that regulate the reciprocal motions of emblematic and of complementary properties, convey other symbolic meanings. Popular writings have left an impression of spontaneous and angry exchanges between ambitious rival chiefs. In reality, emblematic and complementary properties follow laws of motion as carefully regulated as the natural order itself, with which they are indeed enmeshed.

The grand theme is the circulation of lives and of life forces, a circulation like that of an organism, total and fully integrated. When Mauss chose to limit "potlatch" to agonistic exchange he immediately confused the issues. There is but a single system of circulation, albeit divided, like a blood system, into branches serving specialized functions.

One set of functions is associated with "generalized exchange" and another with "restricted exchange" (Lévi-Strauss 1969). Generalized exchange involves distributions among the entire Ritual Congregation, or among a few of its tribes, or among the lineages of a single tribe, which do not require direct return. In accordance with the requirements of the life cycle, each family carries out its own obligations to distribute to all. Its complementary properties are set into general circulation. Restricted exchanges involve mainly the moiety of rival tribes and are then in a ritual setting of antagonism. These include all fish oil feasts and transactions with coppers, as well as animal skin distributions and all ritual destructions of property.

Marital exchanges are more complex. They combine restricted exchanges between the lineages and tribes of bride and groom with a broader pattern of more general distributions. The initial stage in marital exchange is, in fact, dyadic. A "bride price" is given to the father-in-law and an immediate return gift goes to the son-in-law. This stage isolates socially and ritually the groom and his new father-surrogate, identifying them as a newly formed unit. Thereafter distributions precipitated by marriage move outward in successive waves until ultimately the entire Ritual Congregation has been covered. Outside of marriage, restricted and antagonistic exchanges occur only during the Winter Ceremonial. In a broad sense, however, these exchanges are usually the continuation of the marital pattern which includes, as we know, the transfer of Winter Ceremonial privileges.

Since antagonism has major symbolic significance for Kwakiutl, I discuss it in a separate chapter. Accordingly, my treatment of ritual distribution and exchange is divided into two parts, the present chapter dealing mainly with generalized and nonantagonistic exchanges,and the ensuing chapter with exchanges, which if they are antagonistic are simultaneously restricted. Antagonism is of necessity restricted. Both modes of exchange, the general and the restricted, incorporate four basic principles of circulation:

1. *Distribution as a hereditary privilege confined to noble possessions of property and feast-giving names.* A distinction may be drawn between privileged giving or distributing, and nonprivileged giving. The former is an expression of a power; the latter, which concerns only the giving of property to a lineage or tribal chief for further distribution is rather an obligation of kinship or of lineage-tribal affiliation. Chiefs are privileged givers and commoners are obligatory givers. Privileged giving goes outward beyond lineage and tribe; nonprivileged giving is strictly internal. Fundamentally, of course, privileged giving is involved in what I have designated as the primary exchange between emblematic and primary properties. Nonprivileged giving is nothing more than a phase in the assemblage of property for privileged distribution.

Privileged distribution is perhaps everywhere the most highly regarded prerogative of aristocracy. In the terminology of Mauss the privileged donor is *magister,* a master, a superior, a source from whom bounty flows. In Kwakiutl thought, which may stand readily for the general paradigm of distribution in primitive societies, the giver is privileged to be the godlike source of valued treasures and powers. Powers were first granted in the primary (mythical) era to ancestors, who transmitted them to their heirs. Sequentially they distributed animal skins. Thus the common belief fostered by Boas that the distribution of property is the source of rank—actually an order of powers—states the reverse of the true order. The distribution of complementary properties does not initiate, it completes the transaction. In the Kwakiutl phrase the property distribution "fastens on" the name. Since the name represents an ancestral or supernatural incarnate, the distribution stands for one of the consequences of that major event.

2. *Distribution as an intrasexual, and a primarily masculine privilege.*[7] When women inherit men's names and rank they are privileged givers as bearers of a masculine being. Women give to other women, but presum-

ably in unimportant summer exchanges (Boas 1925:111). When a woman gives a female name to her daughter's daughter the distribution of property is made by her son-in-law. The confinement of all principal exchanges to men and among men implies a concept of asexual propagation of vital entities. We may go so far as to say that the incarnation involved in the assumption of a new name is like a birth in two stages. A spirit being is reborn, and animal skins issue from their storage boxes to move into new domains. This analogue of birth is, however, postulated as a spiritualized and desexualized process, one that is the primary prerogative of men. The process takes a parallel asexual form in the primary exchange when a male ancestor sheds his animal form soul, thereby propagating the propatrilineal transmission of the crest. In marriage, transmission is both sexual in the obvious sense and asexual in that marital exchanges initiate a wave of intrasexual distributions.

3. *Distribution as graded by the fixed order of ranking.* In the idea of the eagle who eats first, the Kwakiutl have an image of a natural order of ritual precedence in feasts. Family traditions, however, ignore the natural order, and set forth instead an order lacking an explanatory principle. The real Kwakiutl concern seems to be in the fact of rank and not in the logic of a rank system. The focus is on protocol of ritual precedence. Tally keepers kept accurate note of the rank order and arranged for blankets to be piled in advance, in order of distribution: Skin blankets designated for highest chiefs were on top and for lowest on bottom. The Kwakiutl continued this arrangement even with woolen blankets. The arrangement was not in the interests of stock control. The pile symbolized in its height the loftiness and weightiness of the name of the donor and of his lineage. At the same time, it represented the receivers in their order of rank. Since rank is an expression of emblematic properties, the pile of blankets established a visual and tangible association between names and animal skin complements. In parallel manner the protocol of distribution used the rank order of men, even if derived abstractly from animals, to coordinate a rank order among animals.[8] Religiously, rank as a qualitative order of supernatural powers becomes the practical measure of parallel gradations in the nonhuman world. Even store-bought woolen blankets achieve an order of differentiation by the order in which they are assembled, which has at least a quantitative equivalent to the symbolic distinctions among blankets of sea mammals, of land mammals, and of cedar bark.

The protocol of distribution counteracts the inherent inequality of what Mauss called the magister-minister relationship. If the donor is indeed the masterful benefactor, the fixed order of distribution compels him to acknowledge the actual equality and the near equality of those at his level, and to recognize the superiority of those higher in the order, even when they are recipients.

4. *Distribution in accord with the segmentary order.* Only tribal chiefs of high rank are privileged to distribute property among all the tribes. Lower ranks are restricted to a grouping of tribes—as for example, to the four tribes of Fort Rupert, or to the four tribes of the Mamaleleqala federation—or to a single tribe or to a single lineage. In parallel manner the quality of emblematic property follows similar segmentary gradation. The pertinent religious principle is equivalent to a physical law; namely, it requires a great force to move property in a wide orbit. In myth, the greatest powers move freely around the earth. In general, the powerful move outward, the weak are confined to narrow orbits of motion.

The principle of privileged orbits calibrates personal ranks, and the motions of emblematic properties, with the dimensions of growth of a family tree. The largest and most powerful family line has the capacity to feed the entire Ritual Congregation. It has the inherited powers to which wealth accrues. Its universal orbit defines its high rank and makes it as of special divinity. The ranking tribes transcend the limitations of their own roots to reconstitute on earth through ritual distribution and exchange the presumed unity of peoples that had existed in the mythical past.

A unity of separate lineages-tribes could in principle be achieved through a system of symmetrical exchanges among all. The Kwakiutl system imposes rather a pattern of constant inequality. The high ranks, as great supernatural powers, are universal donors. The low ranks are universal receivers. There is, unfortunately, no empirical documentation of economic flow in this system that might reveal the actual dimensions of inequality in separate and generalized series of distributions. That the burden of replenishing the supply of properties in circulation does in fact fall upon the higher-ranking chiefs can be assumed from family traditions that portray them as recipients of property-acquiring treasures, as though to say that primary accumulation was their special responsibility. Asymmetry is consistent with the principle of chiefs as magister.

The principles of exchange establish a general format for the grand circulation of properties. The complete pattern emerges from the sequential order of distributions as they follow the life histories of chiefs from birth to death. The sociological imagination formulates a concept of exchange as depersonalized, and as moving among generalized social entities. The Kwakiutl imagination dwells on named persons who are simultaneously spirit incarnates, but nonetheless personalized.

Early students of Northwest Coast exchange ("potlatch") insisted on the clans rather than individuals as the active entities (see Mauss, Lenoir). The issue is not whether exchanges are individual or collective; the collective is an entity of named individual beings. However, giving and receiving produces a parallel distinction between the collective and the individual. Distributors of property represent lineage and tribe, receivers represent only themselves.[9] The donor is corporate because magisterial power is considered as inhering in founders of descent lines. The receiver is always a person. But the equation between corporate giver and individual receiver is somewhat more complex. While a chief gives in the name of his lineage or tribe, so that it shares in the giving, he does so as an individualized spirit incarnate as well. Ultimately, then, the general format of circulation is to be visualized as a grand circulation among individuals. The obligation to be a donor, who is after all the energetic initiator of a cycle in the ongoing circulation of properties, rests only on individuals, even as they represent their lineages and tribes.

In his lifetime each chief carries out the fixed obligations for distribution that pertain to his inherited names. As his names are distinctive, so are his particular distributions. There is, of course, a common pattern arising out of limited possibilities. The point of honor is in fulfillment of the obligations. Mourning ritual memorializes the achievements of the deceased in songs that itemize all his distributions and destructions. In the case of Lalakotsa, a Mamaleleqala chief, the mourning song lists the following: (1) that he gave away property at the end of each year, (2) that he gave away property all the time, (3) that he gave away canoes, (4) that he gave feasts, (5) that he destroyed property, (6) that he broke coppers, (7) that he threw property into the sea, (8) that he gave away the roof boards of his house, (9) that he gave property as "striking to kill," (10) that he paid the marriage debt for his daughter, (11) that he broke canoes, and (12) that he completed the course of marriage payments for his daughter. An additional mourning song completes the list with (13) oil feasts, (14) sale of coppers, (15) giving of Winter Ceremonial dances (for which property is distributed) (Boas 1925:77–79).

This listing, certainly not atypical, epitomizes the basic pattern, which includes generalized exchanges, antagonistic and restricted exchanges, marital exchanges, the transmission of coppers, and the destruction of property, a mode of religious sacrifice. There are similar songs in the literature indicating that for a high chief completeness demands this combination of distributions and destructions. Each distribution is listed as a dance and with the distinctive name under which it was carried out. The setting of dance and accompanying song and inherited name marks the occasions as spiritual.

VIII

ANTAGONISM

Strength in opposition to weakness is the primary antagonism. It has for the Kwakiutl the force of a metaphysical proposition that undergoes numerous symbolic and metaphoric transformations to reach into every aspect of the ritual process. Thus ritual events and most mythical contexts are reducible to a single and basic formula: weakness succumbs to strength, and its converse, weakness is convertible to strength. The opposition between weakness and strength appears to the Kwakiutl as a permanent antagonism. In ritual and myth this antagonism appears as a relativistic and dynamic relationship in which, in some contexts, the strong are in conflict with a force that is stronger than they are. In other contexts the balance of power is reversed. Weakness is, indeed, derided. Kwakiutl ritual rhetoric is fluent and inventive in expressing contempt for the lowly flies and mosquitoes, the insignificant sparrows, the trembling dogs with tails between their legs, the frightened adversary with his eyes popping and his tongue protruding with fear.

Nevertheless, it would be a misrepresentation of the power and subtlety of Kwakiutl thought on this subject if we were to reduce their formulation of permanent and necessary antagonism to some paltry doctrine such as "stamp out weakness!" The opposition between strength and weakness is for them not political, and certainly not moralizing: it is, as every study of their texts cannot fail to reveal, a rendering of the natural scene. They have synthesized the natural scene into religious imagery of supernatural powers such as *nawalak,* without obscuring the root biological issues of the cycle of life and death. In this cycle, life and death, vigor and illness, victor and victim, killer and killed, devourer and devoured are permanently bound in restless opposition. The pattern of opposition is permanent, but the figures change position constantly, yielding and then regaining cyclical ascendancy.

The spirit of antagonism is essentially the Kwakiutl Indians' understanding of the nature of that natural vitality which sustains the cycle. Nothing in the Kwakiutl texts even remotely implies a yearning for nirvana, or suggests the death wish of putting an end to contest. Rivals struggle against one another because contest is the most self-evident expression of biological process for hunting peoples. They do not anticipate crushing the rival finally, because such an expression of excess implies an unacceptable extravagance in nature that might destroy the ongoing rhythms and cycles of natural existence.

We must speak of Kwakiutl antagonism as a ritual affair because that is the context in which it appears as a clearly established doctrine. Scholars differ, however, on what is ritual context among Kwakiutl. Boas, for example, thought of the feasts and property distributions associated with the Winter Ceremonial as secular adjuncts, hence as forms of secular ritual. Those who regard the "potlatch" as a mode of economic rivalry for social standing and prestige would also insist on a secular ritual context, and so define the terms and aims of "potlatch" antagonism sociologically. From a Kwakiutl viewpoint, however, the primary context of antagonism is religious, and is related to supernatural powers and cosmic purposes.

Kwakiutl antagonisms also have a genuine life beyond the fields of ritual. Warfare was a sociological reality of hatreds and desires to crush an outside enemy with little evident concern for his ultimate welfare. The ritual rhetoric of ascendancy spilled over into the psychological immediacies of personal ambitions and jealousies (see Boas 1921:862). Myths and their ritual surrogates, however, usually elevated antagonisms to cosmological heights and enveloped them in a mysticism that transcended the personal. Still, if under the ritual mask there was the inescapable person, the grandeur of the modes of ritual antagonism required of the person was not on the human scale. Acting as impersonator, as incarnate of ancestors, of supernatural beings, and of shamans, the person was submerged in the religious performer. But it is also clear, given the evidence of real hatreds and rivalries, that religion and social reality had fused. Ritual behavior and social behavior are differing expressions of the same reality. Yet we would not naively assume an identity. In their ritual and in their ritual rhetoric, the Kwakiutl understood the distinction between their representing spirit beings and their powers, and themselves as human beings. The misunderstanding has been on the side of the academic, whose liberal and understated standards of deportment are easily outraged by the unabashed worship of the domineering forces of nature. Kwakiutl were not meek; neither did they live on the scale of their liturgical rhetoric. Apropos of Ruth Benedict's interesting representation of Kwakiutl as megalomaniacal, Boas once remarked to me, "The words are those of the Kwakiutl, but they have nothing to do with the Indians that I knew."

Myth sets forth the primary conditions that are to be carried out in ritual. When rival chiefs are symbolically at one another's throats, or when a chief is proclaiming his powers, it is said that they are "going back to the beginnings." Kwakiutl tales portray two main arenas of antagonism. One sets forth contests among great spirit beings, the second depicts antagonism between persons and supernatural beings. At bottom, both carry the common message that the treasures of this earth are to be won in battle. Both depict a balance of forces that compels permanent contest and precludes final victory. Two myth cycles illustrate the first arena of contest. One is a narrative of the wars between the birds of earth and their land mammal confederates against the birds of heaven, led by Thunderbird. The Thunderbird forces are defeated, a conclusion establishing once and for all the proper season for thundering. The issue is not, of course, entirely meteorological. As on the Plains, thunder, the attribute of the Thunderbird, heralds the turn from winter to spring and is thus a pivot of the life cycle. The birds and their animal confederates have won the battle in order to impose an order on the life cycle.

In this epic antagonism the chief Thunderbird is killed, but characteristically his infant son, who will replenish the line, survives to live in heaven with his shame. A younger brother, Qolos, thereupon comes down to earth, takes off his Thunderbird mask, and becomes Tsaqame, or Head Winter Dancer. He becomes the father of a man-eater and of Dzonoqwa, and, even more significantly, launches himself into a series of shamanistic contests with Qanekelak, a major creator and transformer, who represents the powers of the summer season. After the earlier defeat of the Thunderbirds, which led to a permanent fixing of the seasons, the battles between Head Winter Dancer and Qanekelak are always standoffs. Qanekelak, the aggressor, cannot overcome the winter season, Tsaqame. Whatever Qanekelak can do to him—cut off his head, rip open his belly, drop him far out to sea—Tsaqame can cure. His is the shamanistic power of the Winter Ceremonial, and Qanekelak's is the shamanistic power of the secular season. Acknowledging their supernatural equality, Qanekelak cries out with admiration: "O friend! It is wonderful. You are really a man of supernatural power" (Boas and Hunt 1905:170). Human "rivals" for whom this myth, among many others, is a ritual model speak in the same vein.

Having withstood Qanekelak's attacks on him, Tsaqame gives his opponent his neck ring and the cross piece from his head ring, which contain the Winter Ceremonial powers. Qanekelak responds by sending frogs that cause illness into the stomach of Tsaqame, who retains them, however, as sorcery powers that he will later use. In short, the epic antagonisms lead to the exchange of supernatural powers. When Qanekelak engages the supernatural being Xatetsen, the outcome is transformation, another expression of powers. Angrily they transform each other successively into stone, fog, and cranes. Throughout his useful career, Qanekelak, the great transformer, acts in anger. Thus antagonism would seem to be the requisite setting for transformations and for exchanges and acquisitions of power, events that are essential to the ongoing vitality of the natural world. Understandably, therefore, contest is, as Boas observed, a principal theme in Kwakiutl mythology (1935b:102).

The grizzly bear is, accordingly, the earthly model of chiefly character. Either as the animal that only chiefs are qualifed to hunt and kill, or as the supernatural associate of Man Eater, the grizzly bear is a supreme symbol of fearlessness and wildness. The chiefly hunter of the grizzly emulates, in effect, the characters in myth. When he meets the bear, he says:

> Be ready friend, that we may try our strength. You dreaded one. I am of the same kind, for I am dreaded also. Listen to me, Supernatural One, now I will take by war your power of not respecting anything, and not being afraid, and your wildness, great, good, Supernatural One.

(Boas 1930:194)

[147]

Antagonism in the Winter Ceremonial. The Winter Ceremonial is the natural setting for antagonism. The chiefs in their grizzly bear mold, as incarnates of aggressive spirits and as shamans are obliged to portray the modes of managing supernatural powers that their patron spirits employ. Impressed by the aggressive tone of the rites, Boas reasoned they "had their origin in methods of warfare" (1940:382). The military association is unmistakable, not only because of the prominence of Winalagilis, but also because the killing of an enemy in battle was likely to initiate Winter Ceremonial dances even in summer. The principal dancers were known as "chief warriors," and when one of these slew his foe he was possessed at once by the dead man's spirit and began to dance. The military connections of the winter rites are no clue to their origins. What is demonstrated, however, is the willingness of the Kwakiutl to fuse ritual with present realities. Since the victor acquires the names, the crests, and the supernatural powers of his victim, combat in war assumes a mythical character. It is the present counterpart of the mythic period when the incarnates of spirits were in combat with one another. Since the transmission of the marriage payments also initiates the rites, the proper context of Winter Ceremonial antagonism is not warfare but shamanism. Within the ceremonial house the participants are not only spirit incarnates, but shamans. The Kwakiutl Winter Ceremonial is not a ritualization of secular warfare but is rather in the tradition of the Algonquian *Midewiwin*, a conclave of shamans who display their powers and engage one another in spirit battles.

While Kwakiutl antagonisms have broader connotations, their most characteristic expression, nevertheless, is in the shamanistic idiom. In the Winter Ceremonial the shamanistic powers of the nobility and the majesty of their spirit sponsors are on trial. All the great displays of ritual antagonism, the oil feasts, the sale and breaking of coppers, the killing of slaves, the destruction of property, the rivalrous and angry distributions of skins are in the context of the Winter Ceremonial. The songs that accompany such antagonistic displays proclaim unabashedly the grandeur of chiefs, who are of course, at the moment, spirits. The expression "fighting with property," for many the paradigm of the "potlatch," is used in property distributions that accompany the Ceremonial.

There are other ritual settings for antagonism: at the taking of a bride; when coppers are broken during the installation of a chief; at mourning rites; when a new house is completed. As at the Winter Ceremonial, these are the times when powers are displayed and the great themes of transformation and exchange are set forth. In killing an enemy, a chief brings the same themes into the present.

Appeasement is another mode of contest. As the *hamatsa* songs proclaim, Man Eater the omnivorous devourer of lives is to be appeased and subdued by being fed property, which is animal lives. It is the *hamatsa* dancer as incarnate who is understood to be the swallower of property. The following statement by the father of a *hamatsa* initiate explains that the property distributed in his behalf is, in this sense, swallowed:

> *This here is my* [hamatsa]. *I sold a copper for 1000 blankets and he swallowed it. I sold a copper for 1200 blankets and he swallowed it. At another time I bought a copper for 1200 blankets and threw it into the fire for the sake of his name. Now look out! I may do the same again this year. I want to make him as heavy as I can on my part.*

(Boas 1897:556)

Appeasement, however, is at the cost of animal lives, and the Kwakiutl in the Winter Ceremonial are engaged in a desperate barter. To avoid the perils and disgrace of sheer passivity against the threat to their own lives, they announce their adherence to the cause of the Man Eater. They become devourers like him. They have, in effect, infiltrated his kingdom to secure their safety. The exchange, nevertheless, is only partial. Nature does not accept unbalanced barter. As Man Eater incarnates, the dancers and their entourage are still omnivorous. They add slaves to the feast, a direct human offering. When chiefs give property in behalf of dancers they also speak of "swallowing the tribes," thus adding a metaphoric offering and simultaneously an exchange that tends to restore the balanced equity between men and animals.[1] In short, the distributions at the Winter Ceremonial pronounce the swallowing of property (animal lives) by *hamatsa*-Man Eater; the swallowing of the tribes by chiefs, who are the Dzonoqwa warrior associates of Man Eater; and the distributions of property to those who are swallowed. In the last case, the equity between men and animals is metaphorically restored. The men are devoured and the animals are given a new life among men.

Ultimately, whatever is devoured is restored to life. The figure of the Cormorant, a minor spirit, conveys the message of resurrection. A speaker asks a bird, "What is in your stomach?" It replies, "The Kwakiutl, the Koskimo, and all the tribes." Another cormorant adds that he had gone around the world swallowing the tribes, that is, as Boas adds in a footnote, giving away blankets. The speaker thanks them for coming to the dance house and says, "I am glad that you are not light cormorants, but that you are heavy with property." Another cormorant pretends to vomit, and the text explains, "This means that he was vomiting the property that was to be distributed that night" (see Boas 1897:558–559). In utter brevity, the cormorant incident portrays the key themes, the resurrection through vomiting, the convertibility of people and property, and the cyclic and eternal nature of the cosmic exchange.

In such contexts, ritual distributions are inevitably antagonistic. The general sociological assumption of the benevolence of this giving is not untrue. It is the special nature of benevolence, at least among Kwakiutl, that needs further exploration. True, the Kwakiutl donor is benevolent in accepting the difficult responsibilities of consorting with dangerous spirits for the sake of sustaining the life cycle. But many images stress the antagonistic mode of distribution. The property given in behalf of the *hamatsa* is said to cascade from his red cedar bark neck ring in a stream that will drown his rivals (ibid:557). The menace in this instance is of excess. Excess, however, in the metaphysical setting of transformation. What is devoured is vomited out alive. Hence the property (lives) that cascades from the life-giving cedar bark conveys the alarming image of death.

Transactions with Coppers.   The Winter Ceremonial season is, as Boas observed, the time for dealing in coppers. They are then sold, broken, and passed on by a man to his son-in-law (1897:346). Boas represented copper transactions as commercial, whereas in fact they are all-important aspects of the winter rites. What has been described as the "sale" of a copper is said by the Kwakiutl to be its "sending down" to a tribe of the rival moiety. The breaking of a copper, an act that impressed Boas and others as an extravagant disregard of valuable property, is described by the Kwakiutl as a solemn ritual act that causes the copper to be "killed" or made to "disappear," as though it too were a Winter Ceremonial initiate (see ibid:564). After a copper has been broken, the pieces are reassembled, and the newly resurrected plaque has an even higher value.

The transfer of the copper to the son-in-law during the winter season carries out the basic theme of marriage, as one of the two ways of acquisition of winter dances (war is the other). The copper, as I have already demonstrated, is not a higher denomination of currency, but a ritual entity closely associated with the major themes of the Winter Ceremonial, as is, of course, wealth. Copper shields may even have been post-European introductions to the Northwest Coast. If so, they very quickly became powerful symbols of wealth in the sensate meaning of property as a form of life that, unlike the supernatural beings, must die and be reborn. All other forms of property have for the Kwakiutl a concrete connection to a living creature. The copper plaques alone are relatively pure symbols and abstract representations. The name of the copper *(tlaq,* "red"), conveys the abstract idea of an essence of life, perhaps as blood and as light. More likely, the copper in its positive identification with salmon stands, more narrowly, for the wealth of the sea. It is in its connotation as light, however, that it achieves genuine abstractness. When the copper is turned face down in the sea, the Kwakiutl say, it becomes night. Turned face up, it restores daylight (Boas and Hunt 1905:145). Since day and night are equated with summer and winter, the copper symbolism joins together the dual themes of the Winter Ceremonial.

The life of a copper moves through four stages: (1) it goes from a man to his son-in-law as companion to the bride, (2) it goes from the son-in-law to a local chief as a means of assembling animal skin blankets, (3) it is "passed down" to a rival tribe, and (4) it is "killed," or made to "disappear." These stages represent, I believe, a formal sequence that is parallel to marriage. Copper is depicted as a child, carried on the back of a woman as a gift to her husband. If the copper does indeed symbolize a child, its implications for the Kwakiutl view of kinship are then quite extraordinary, for this type of "child" cannot remain within the lineage of its "father." It is passed on at once to a chief of a neighboring lineage in exchange for animal skin blankets, which are then distributed among the tribes in acknowledgment of the receipt of treasures in marriage.

The metaphoric theme of these two stages may be stated as follows. The arrival of a bride provokes a flow of wealth to the tribes, a beneficent event with no intimations of antagonism. The tribes are thus all beneficiaries of a marriage. The first transfer of the copper is to a non-rival chief, and the distribution of wealth that follows is to the "tribes." Antagonism enters at the third stage when the copper is "sold" during the winter to a rival tribe. That is to say, it is made to cross a gap, to enter a new social realm that is a counterpart of the one to which it had been assgined.

Within the ritual order, rivals are conceived of on the model of Tsaqame and Qanakelak, carefully balanced representatives of two cosmological orders and sets of powers. If the movements of a copper parallel those of a marriage, its third stage sets forth the idea that when a bride has moved across an exogamy gap, the copper, her counterpart, moves across a corresponding gap, but not in direct exchange. The geometry of motion of the exchange is tripolar. The bride moves from A to B, the copper moves from A to B to C, with a side excursion to a nonrivalrous tribe related to B. Marriage rites are not, as I have shown, necessarily antagonistic in particular cases. Nevertheless, such expressions as "making war against all the daughters of all the chiefs," and the linkage of war and marriage as equivalent ways of acquiring winter dances set it within the antagonistic mode. For that matter, not all copper transmissions across the gap are notably antagonistic either. The actual parallel is between marriages with tribes who own the prerogatives of ritual antagonism, and transfers of coppers between tribes who also have special privileges of ritual antagonism.

Sale of a Copper. Boas described the sale of a copper he evidently witnessed in the winter of 1894 (see 1897:346ff). Although a postcontact transaction with store blankets, it was conducted along traditional lines and is a valuable account of such a proceeding. Unfortunately, Boas was unaware then of the ritual significance of copper "sales" and omitted vital information on the setting in which it took place. He describes it only as an economic challenge to a rival, allowing the reader to assume another case of "fighting with property." If the copper that has been brought by a Mamaleleqala chief to the high chief of the Gwetela "is not accepted," he writes, "it is an acknowledgment that nobody in the tribe has money enough to buy it, and the name of the tribe or clan would consequently lose in weight" (ibid:345). Even as presented, out of context, this account of an exchange of blankets for the copper One of Whom All Are Afraid (Maxtsolem) is not quite as Boas understood it.

A Mamaleleqala chief declares at once that the exchange follows established tradition.

Our ways are not new ways. They were made by our chief (the deity) and marked out for us when he made our ancestors men. We try to imitate what our ancestors were told to do by the creator. Keep in your old ways Kwakiutl; keep in the ways of your grandfathers, who laid down the custom for you.

(ibid:346)

The chiefs declare their friendship. A Mamaleleqala says to his hosts, "I have nothing against the way, Kwakiutl, in which you treat me and my tribe." The guests distribute blankets among all their Kwakiutl hosts, and are promised a feast. The rivalrous tone emerges only later. After the exchange of copper and blankets has taken place, the chief who brought the copper speaks:

This Kwakiutl, is the strength of the [Mamaleleqala]. *These whom you see here are your rivals. These are the ones who have the great coppers which have names, and therefore it is hard work for you to rival them. Look out!* [he adds, turning to his own people] *in case they should bring us the copper* [Maxtsolem], *which we now sold that one of you may take it up at once, or else we must be ashamed.*

(ibid:352)

In this speech, as Boas observed, there is a note of concern that the seller should have the economic competency to repurchase the copper; but the rather common assumption (see, for example, Benedict 1934) that the rapid escalation in value of the copper after each exchange would render a rival incompetent is, in fact, quite exaggerated. The fear of being shamed is part of an antagonistic rhetoric. There are no examples in any of the texts of a tribe shamed for its inability to purchase a proferred copper. Moreover, neither in this example nor in many others described in the texts is there evidence of repeated increases in value. The copper Maxtsolem, it is said, had been bought by the Mamaleleqala for 4000 blankets (Boas 1897:350), and was offered to the Kwakiutl tribes for the same amount (ibid:352). The Kwakiutl purchaser, however, added 200 blankets to the price, saying:

You take the price too soon; you must think poorly of me. Chief! I am a Kwakiutl. I am one of those from whom all your tribes over the world took their names. Now you give up before I finish trading with you, [Mamaleleqala]. *You must always stand beneath us, wa, wa!*

(ibid:353)

[153   ]

There is no record in the texts of a return sale. Nor is there substantial reason to assume that if there were a return offer of the copper that Mamaleleqala would have to pay more than the price they had already received. The Kwakiutl statement of superiority was, in this instance, a true reflection of their higher rank, and not mere boastfulness. When the Kwakiutl chief Owaxalagilis declares as he sets down the blankets for the purchase price: "Now you have seen my name; this is the weight of my name. This mountain of blankets rises through our heaven. My name is the name of the Kwakiutl, and you cannot do as we do, tribes" (ibid:349), the Mamaleleqala chief replies:

> "Yes, Chief, your speech is true, your word is true. Who is like you, Kwakiutl, who buy coppers and who give away blankets. Long life to all of you, chiefs of the Kwakiutl. I can not attain to your high name, great tribes." But then turning to his own tribe he adds, "That is what I said, chiefs of the [Mamaleleqala] that we may beat these Kwakiutl. They are like a large mountain with a steep precipice."

(ibid:350)

The challenging taunt is taken in a friendly manner; the superiority of the Kwakiutl is acknowledged. The expression, "that we may beat these Kwakiutl," is standard Kwakiutl ritual rhetoric. Each side must proclaim its uniqueness, its superiority over all others, and its proud record of never having been beaten in such ritual competition. This exchange of oratory is unusual in that the Mamaleleqala concede the higher rank of the Kwakiutl tribes. The real concern, nevertheless, is not to reduce a rival, but to engage in a mutual display of powers. In their religious objectives the tribes benefit by demonstrating their great capabilities rather then their possible weaknesses. Having acknowledged the superiority of the Kwakiutl, the Mamaleleqala turn to their own chief, whom they address as Dzonoqwa (the provisioner of the Man Eater): "You cannot be equaled by anybody. You great mountain from which wealth is rolling down, wa, wa!" (ibid:350). He replies by uttering the Dzonoqwa cry, and pretends to lift the copper as though it were very heavy. He recites his family tradition and reveals his descent from Hoxhoq, of the Man Eater retinue. His Kwakiutl host adds his praise saying, "Yes, yes, you are feared by all, Great Chief. Do not show mercy in your speech" (ibid).

The Dzonoqwa reference implies that the great weight of copper is being transmitted as an offering to Man Eater. The "seller" of the copper is the merciless donor, the benefactor, and the antagonist partner of the purchaser, who is also a benefactor.

Breaking a Copper.   Boas made the important observation that the destruction of property, as described in myth, occurs only during the Winter Ceremonial, when Man Eater devours his own slaves or is given slaves to eat (1935b:68). In real life also, coppers and other property are destroyed during the course of the winter rites. As a rule, a copper is broken at the same time that grease feasts are given, and slaves are killed and eaten. The Winter Ceremonial is the standard occasion for breaking a copper. But there are other events, thematically related to the Winter Ceremonial, when it is appropriate to "kill" a copper, and to cause it to "disappear." These are the completion of a new lineage house, and the elevation of the heir to the chiefship. In the Winter Ceremonial, the copper as wealth in salmon and as symbol of heavenly light is evidently an offering to Man Eater. In connection with the installation of a chief and the appearance of a new house, the killing of the copper is also in the service of the same theme, namely, a death for a life, and finally, a resurrection. A new chief appears; his father disappears as a chief. The old lineage house has died; a new one replaces it. The copper shares an analogous death and resurrection.

The texts give many accounts of the breaking of a copper. But these accounts are mainly isolated narratives. An event as important as that of causing the copper to disappear must be seen in the context of related rituals and within the long-range ritual cycle. Thus the most significant account is from the Lasotiwalas history (Boas 1925:215–229), which, though it has the demerit of being postcontact, is valuable for relative completeness. The copper is broken at the installation of a new Kwakiutl chief and involves the rivalrous Kwakiutl and Mamalcleqala moieties. In advance of this event, the Kwakiutl father of the chief-to-be sells a copper to the Tlawitsis of the opposite moiety for 1500 blankets, which he will distribute to "fasten on" the new name. That is, the opposite moiety contributes in behalf of the new chief. The copper that will be broken is the gift of the maternal grandfather, a donation equivalent to the gift of Winter Ceremonial privileges. The accompanying songs connect the breaking of a copper to the initiation of a Winter Ceremonial novice.

The copper, which has the name Cause of Fear, is represented as

Dzonoqwa, the fearsome antogatonist of all rival chiefs. The breaking of this copper is equated with striking the people, the traditional role of Dzonoqwa, the warrior of Man Eater:

> *Make way and let him have this with which I am always trying to strike my rival chiefs among the tribes.*

The second stanza develops the theme:

> *Do not ask in vain for mercy, putting out your tongues and pressing back your hands. Am I not going to become excited and am I not going to cause to disappear the one who has the great name the Great-Cause-of-Fear the great property, the great one that causes people to lose their senses, the great one that makes people unmerciful, the* [Dzonoqwa] *among the chiefs of the tribes.*

(ibid:169)

The final stanza calls out the names of the chief-to-be and reveals his descent from an ancestor who shared the Dzonoqwa wildness.

Before the copper is broken the rival tribes exchange grease feasts. The feasts, which I discuss later, are also in the name of Dzonoqwa and carry forward the mythic theme of menace. The grease feast and the breaking of a copper are thematically joined as Dzonoqwa-Man Eater analogues in this case, and as counterparts of other Winter Ceremonial themes, depending on the name of the copper. Like a person, the copper has its own spirit identity; hence the precise ritual meaning of its being "killed," which is after all equivalent to the condition of *laxsa*, depends, evidently, on its name. The accompanying grease feasts, however, seem to be centered on the constant theme of devouring, in the spirit if not in the literal image of Man Eater.

The guests offer the first of the grease feasts. Their feasting song speaks of "the great terrifying Dzonoqwa," in counterpoint to the copper that will be broken. The rival chief declares his fear of the copper:

> *Already I was scared; I was afraid of the Cause–of–Fear, the Great Chief, tribes, as he was about to strike with that which hurts that has the great name* [Dentalayu], *the property of my chief, tribes.*

(ibid:181)

When the Kwakiutl tribes promise a return feast they mention in their feasting songs all the coppers their chiefs have given away, and how many have been broken. Other tribes are taunted (not by name) for not having matched their accomplishments with coppers. The meaning of rivalry is to be judged, however, by such remarks as (in a reference to eight coppers) "broken by my ancestors for you, tribes" (ibid:195), and by a Mamaleleqala chief in reference to all the Kwakiutl songs:

Indeed it is true what was said by our ancestors who first spoke in the way we speak in the various ways we are now doing. I mean there is nothing new in what we are saying.

(ibid:205)

There is, as I have already suggested, a logical connection between coppers sold and coppers broken. In the ritual of breaking a copper the two events are sequential. First a copper is sold and the proceeds in animal skins are distributed to the rival tribes just before another copper is to be broken. The connection suggests the events in marriage. The father-in-law brings coppers as a gift to his son-in-law, and when he brings a second copper he inaugurates a winter dance, and the initiation of his son-in-law and of his grandchildren. As in the Winter Ceremonial, when an initiate is transformed into a spirit being, the heir being elevated to chiefship is asked, "Will you now become an extravagant chief?" He replies, "Now I have been made unmerciful" (ibid:217). That is to say, the Dzonoqwa copper, another form of spirit, is his patron; its initiation, in an analogous ceremony, transforms the heir into a Dzonoqwa figure.

The copper may be broken only by those who are privileged by heredity to do so. They break off carefully marked segments from the body of the copper and give the pieces to the new chief. He then awards the pieces to chiefs of the rival moiety, who have assembled not in animosity or status rivalry but to join in the elevation to chiefship, or in the ritual sense, to participate in the transfer of a founding ancestor from one corpus to another. The recipient replies gratefully, "Thank you chief Lasotiwalas, that you do not think me too small to give this that comes from the copper that has a name, [Dentalayu]" (ibid). The donor says to the rival tribes, "I have danced to pieces [Dentalayu] for you, three tribes" (ibid).

The copper appears to us as an overloaded and hence elusive symbol. As person, as salmon, as light, as a Dzonoqwa associate, as a commodity interchangeable with animal form souls, as a property of sea and of the sky, as the companion of the bride and of the Winter Ceremonial,

[157   ]

as a healing substance, and as a life-giver it presents itself, finally, as the synthesis of all forms and realms of life. The tribes that exchange coppers are carrying out a ritual that is symbolically equivalent to the transfer of a bride and her accompanying cargo of spiritual treasures. The tribes that are breaking or "killing" coppers are conducting a ritual that is parallel to the Winter Ceremonial theme of death and renewal. When the copper is "danced to death" for the tribes it is in some respect, like the Winter Ceremonial initiate. But since it is evidently a symbol of fusion of all forms of life, its death implies the death of human beings as well. When the copper is broken, human beings are broken. When it is killed, the tribes of the rival moiety are killed. But as the copper is later reassembled to have even greater value so are, in effect, the tribes. The atmosphere of menace that accompanies the breaking of the copper is not final, but a phase in a process for the welfare of the entire community. When chiefs rival one another in breaking coppers they are exerting their powers for the common spiritual good.

The Grease Feast. For Boas, the grease feast, when the clear oil of the *oulachen* was consumed, burned in flames, and otherwise "wasted," was the climactic scene of hostile chiefly rivalry. His writing on this subject left so vivid an impression of extravagant antagonisms on future generations of Northwest Coast scholars that I take the liberty of quoting him in full on it. This passage from his early work sets forth the Kwakiutl ethos more articulately than anything else he wrote, and has contributed more than anything else to the misunderstanding of the true quality of Kwakiutl life.

> The rivalry between chiefs, when carried so far that coppers are destroyed and that grease feasts are given in order to destroy the prestige of the rival, often develop into open enmity. When a person gives a grease feast, a great fire is lighted in the center of the house. The flames leap up to the roof and the guests are almost scorched by the heat. Still the etiquette demands that they do not stir, else the host's fire has conquered them. Even when the roof begins to burn and the fire attacks the rafters, they must appear unconcerned. The host alone has the right to send a man up to the roof to put out the fire. While the feast is in progress the host sings a scathing song ridiculing his rival and praising his own clan, the feats of his forefathers and his own. Then the grease is filled in large spoons and passed to the rival chief first. If a person thinks he has given a greater grease feast than that offered by the host, he refuses

the spoon. Then he runs out of the house to fetch his copper to squelch with it the fire. The host proceeds at once to tie a copper to each of his house posts. If he should not do so, the person who refused the spoon would, on returning, strike the posts with the copper, which is considered equal to striking the chief's face. Then the man who went to fetch his copper breaks it and gives it to the host. This is called, 'squelching the host's fire.'[2] The host retaliates as described above. (1897:355)

The source of Boas's own misunderstanding of the nature of Kwa-kiutl ritual antagonisms comes from his original failure to recognize the religious elements and the religious contexts of ritual behavior concerning copper, fire, and *oulachen* oil.

Perhaps the strongest evidence for Boas's impression of angry person-al antagonisms carried out through grease feasts and other forms of destruction comes from a brief and isolated text collected by Hunt (1906). In introductory remarks to the text, Hunt emphasizes the issue of personal antagonism when he says, "This is the true story of the two chiefs who were true friends in the beginning, and turned out to be the worst enemies at the end," (ibid:110). A synopsis that accompanies the text also depicts it as an example of spontaneous rivalry and animosi-ty in a ritual setting. Benedict later drew on this narrative as illustrative of the Kwakiutl ethos (1934). But read in the light of Kwakiutl religious conceptions, Hunt's text leads to a different interpretation. The text is unquestionably important as a guide to Kwakiutl religious thought. First, it is set in an ancient period when the Kwakiutl tribes were still residing at Crooked Beach, an original ancestral site. Thus, it would seem to deal with very early customs. Second, it concerns rivalry between chiefs of the same tribe rather than the usual antagonisms between op-posing moieties.

The two friends are Throw Away, a chief of the Gwetela, and Fast Runner, a chief of a lower-ranking lineage of the same tribe. At a salmon berry feast Throw Away serves his guest, Fast Runner, in a dirty dish (actually a small canoe). Fast Runner shows his displeasure by lying prone on his back. He then asks to have his copper, Sea Monster, brought in to "extinguish" the fire of his host. When Throw Away counters by placing his own copper into the fire, Fast Runner has a second copper brought in, and the fire is "put out" again. On the third round, Throw Away concedes defeat. As the text says, "Well then was beaten Throw-Away in that way. Well then was extinguished the past-feasting place fire of his house" (ibid:116).

[159   ]

Some time later, Fast Runner, "wishing to find out the thinking of his friend Throw Away," invites him to a feast of crabapples and *oulachen* oil, a traditional occasion for antagonistic display. Now it is he who serves his guest in a dirty dish. Throw Away responds by "putting out" his host's fire with his copper, Day Face. Whereupon Fast Runner gets "excited" into his *nutlmatl* dance. At this point his father-in-law gives him four canoes, which are broken up and thrown into the fire. Throw Away meets the challenge of the raging blaze coolly, wrapping himself in his bearskin robe and calmly proceeding to eat his crabapples. The text explains, that despite what was done to him he did not get sick. (ibid:121) His courage and coolness wins the praise of his host's attendants.

After this, the two friends announce winter dances for their children to "be equal to the rival," a traditional obligation among established rivals. They display their hereditary powers. Fast Runner has the privilege of killing a slave to be eaten by *hamatsa* dancers, and of Toxwid dances which permit two female slaves to be burned alive. Throw Away cannot match such powers and is beaten again. He joins a war party against the Nootka and loses his life. The text concludes, "Well, then was beaten Throw Away after that" (ibid:136). This final remark reveals the point of view. In ritual and in war, Throw Away owned the weaker powers. The matches were not a contest, but a demonstration. In this context the affront to the rival by serving him in a dirty dish must be seen as part of the ritual display. In the "defeat" of the higher-ranking chief, the ritual demonstrates the analagous defeat of spirit powers by men who begin with lower powers. The theme of lower overcoming the higher in rank is not uncommon in primitive aristocracies. No system may be so rigid as to deny altogether a reversal of its main principles.

Without knowledge of Kwakiutl thinking about food, feasts, and fire, the entire episode is inexplicable. The privileges of feasting the tribes are as firmly controlled as are those of property distributions. Both privileges are associated with a name, that is, with the incarnation of a being, and both represent supernatural powers. They are in complementary relationship in that one is a gift from the paternal lineage, and the other, the "feast name," is given by the father-in-law. Thus the feast name is comparable in ritual significance to Winter Ceremonial privileges. Men who lack the privilege of feeding the tribes are said to be "clay face" (Boas 1921:787). It is implied they are metaphorically dead, and an angry chief would break (kill) a copper if he met a colleague who could not give a feast. In this controversial setting the killing of a copper is analogous to killing the culprit who suffers from an incompleteness of powers. But since broken or killed coppers are resurrected, the angry act is finally transmuted into a shamanistic endeavor to revive a moribund colleague.[3]

The feast differs thematically from a property distribution. It evokes directly the Man Eater image of devouring and consuming. Distribution implies that the form souls of what has been devoured are returned to circulate among men. Thus the feast has a special connotation, when considered in the setting of ritual. There is an important distinction between the hospitality of the repast when guests are fed fresh meat or dried salmon, and the prescribed antagonisms of the grease feasts. Although Boas does not draw such a distinction, the texts suggest that the feasts with ritual significance are not the repasts, which every hospitable host may offer, but those that serve the *oulachen* oil. The seal feast, however, is in a ritual category, although its significance escapes me, partly because there are so few accounts of it in the texts. Seal feasts are involved in marital exchanges, and they are confined to tribes of highest rank, presumably because the first distribution of property followed such a feast.

The great Kwakiutl interest is in the grease feast, always a major ritual event and, as in the narrative just discussed, always disturbing and menacing to the guests. Oil is sloshed over the guests; it is poured so freely they must swim in it; it is fed to the fire so that the guests are scorched and threatened with a massive conflagration. At the very least, they are made nauseous by the quantity they are expected to swallow. In the Kwakiutl dialectic each unpleasant experience implies a benefit. Thus what seems to the outside observer to be a festival designed to alarm and humiliate the guests is rather a ritual of hope on the order of the Winter Ceremonial. And, as a rule, grease feasts are part of the winter rites.

The *oulachen* oil feeds the fire around which guests are seated from a "vomiter beam" close to the ceiling. This is a hollowed log with a man's head and mouth through which the oil is "vomited" onto the fire. The configuration of vomited oil, consumed by flames that blaze wildly and threaten to burn down the house, the form soul of the lineage, presents a fairly transparent set of ideas that echo the central theme of the Winter Ceremonial.

For Kwakiutl, as for much of mankind, vomiting is a sensately ambivalent image of rebirth, unpleasant for the person, but useful for all. In Kwakiutl traditions there are many examples of persons swallowed by animals, vomited out and restored to life. Vomited oil feeds the flames in the manner in which property vomited by the cormorants will feed the voracity of Man Eater. Like Man Eater, the flames threaten life, property, and the soul of the lineage. But such a threat is controlled by coppers, which can both nourish and quench flames. The fire is potentially destructive, but its spirit is associated with the ghosts of the underworld, and has the power to cure illness (see Boas 1921:1298). What is destroyed in the fire goes to the ghosts, and then returns to the community, because ghosts, like the animals of the sea, are bringers of wealth. The guests who suffer nausea and flames and the affront of being sloshed with oil are the dauntless men who have entered dangerous territory to deal with great powers.

Kwakiutl consider candlefish oil to be a female substance. The oil, they say, is given in marriage in behalf of the weight of the name of the bride, whereas animal skins are given in behalf of the weight of the groom's name. There is reason then to consider fish oil as sexual, as analogous to amniotic or perhaps to seminal fluid, even though Kwakiutl themselves to do not make that direct an association. In line though with such hypothetical connection, vomiting would be seen as analogous to birth, actually a rather obvious association for the Kwakiutl. The oil as adding to the spiritual weight of a bride would refer to her reproductive value. In ritual, the birth-vomiting association would have the effect of giving to men a metaphoric sexual part in the reproduction of lives. Why, however, should rites of rebirth convey antagonistic menace? Presumably, one may reply, because in this analogue of birth through vomiting there is generally, as in distribution, a prior condition of having been swallowed, that is, killed. In other words, vomiting does not, in Kwakiutl imagery, merely replicate the idea of birth. It transforms the idea of birth into the masculine process of killing, and then of restoring to life.

The great antagonistic feast of the Kwakiutl is of crabapples and *salal* berries, always given by an angry chief to chiefs of the rival moiety. They call such a feast "making satiated," a rather transparent reference to feeding a devouring spirit. In this setting, the host pours oil on the fire and says to it, "Now, spirit of the fire, open your mouth son, so that you get enough to eat" (Boas 1921:774). The symbolic meaning of *salal* berries, the food of birds, is obscure. But crabapples are represented in myth as the eyes of men. In the light of such an association, those taking part in the sacraments of feeding the flames are joined for the moment with the spirits who devour the eyes of men. The angry chief is not of the human world, and neither for the ritual period are his guests. Host and guests are locked in reciprocal ritual roles. As the exponent of the devouring spirits, the host feeds the flames. The rival, the exponent of regulation and control, is the quencher of the flames. The regulator is the copper. Set in the fire by the host, it feeds the flames. Set in the fire by the guest, it puts it out, an analogue to another property of the copper: Placed on one side it brings light, on the other, darkness.

Repayment with Interest.   Though Boas himself was the source of the common belief that Kwakiutl exchanges escalated successively through high interest rates, we must consider this view as misleading. As I have already indicated, and as I demonstrate shortly from the record of the texts, the Kwakiutl regarded "interest" payments as very special, and they returned double only in particular circumstances. In evaluating Boas's remarks on the "potlatch," it must be remembered that these were made very early in his work (1897), well before the great bulk of his textual data were in hand. He wrote then from only partial evidence and without having carried out all of the corroborative field work that might elucidate so complex and uncharted a subject as ritual exchange. It is a tribute to Boas's extraordinary reputation for accuracy that even his first impressions were taken by fellow scholars as flat truths. Boas, unfortunately, never corrected his early impressions of the "potlatch." They appear again in his posthumous work (1966) taken verbatim from the 1897 publication. Of course, since Boas evidently left no testament concerning this last work we do not really know what he thought of it nor what he intended to do with it. Had Boas felt that this manuscript really reflected his considered retrospective views on Kwakiutl and their "potlatch," he would probably have submitted the work for publication himself.

   To clarify the widespread impression of "potlatches" at which rival chiefs supposedly were obliged to return double what they had received or face humiliation and loss of rank, I shall quote Boas's original remarks on the subject and then compare them with the evidence of the texts. In 1897 (see also 1966:81) Boas wrote:

[163   ]

I referred several times to the distribution of blankets. The recipient in such a distribution is not at liberty to refuse the gift, although according to what I have said it is nothing but an interest-bearing loan that must be refunded at some future time with 100 per cent interest. This festival is called p'ása, literally, flattening something (for instance a basket). This means that by the amount of property given the name of the rival is flattened.

Continuing his exposition of the "potlatch," Boas refers to *dapeno*. He writes:

There is still another method of rising in the social scale, namely, by showing one's self superior to the rival. This may be done by inviting the rival and his clan or tribe to a festival and giving him a considerable number of blankets. He is compelled to accept these, but is not allowed to do so until after he has placed an equal number of blankets on top of the pile offered to him. This is called [dapentgala] and the blankets placed on top of the first pile are called [da'peno]. Then he receives the whole pile and becomes debtor to that amount, i.e., he must repay the gift with 100 per cent interest.

I have read all the published and available unpublished texts on Kwakiutl distributions and exchanges and have found no supporting data for these observations. On these points the texts are either ambiguous or they reveal quite a different concept of exchange. Boas's statements are clear enough as to their meaning, but are actually dubious as to interpretation. Since these two paragraphs have become central to standard models of "potlatch" theory they merit close examination.

I shall start with the apparent confusion in Boas's mind between interest loans and the custom of doubling, called by the Kwakiutl *dapentgala*. The confusion comes from Boas's use of the same concept for a loan and for a ritual gift to a rival. The Kwakiutl, as I show shortly, made the distinction, calling a loan *dlekomas* (Hunt: "to make a lend" ms. 14:1468) and the interest *dlekoyo*. The entire transaction of lending at interest is called *dedamasaqek* (vocabulary from an unpublished Hunt manuscript titled "Solidarity of the Numaym").

For Boas doubling was simply the charge of 100 percent interest, in keeping, of course, with his definition of the "potlatch" as the "interest-bearing investment of property." Boas must have known that the Kwakiutl distinguished clearly between lending at interest and ritual doubling, but seems not to have grasped the significance of the distinction at the time he first wrote about it (1897:341–344). In this early work, the original source of "potlatch" theory, he begins his discussion of the "potlatch" by describing internal borrowing of blankets for a youth who is preparing to distribute property at an intertribal gathering. In this discussion based on texts, he lists the correct Kwakiutl terminology. The purpose of these internal loans, which Boas understood to be some form of debt-hiking, is to allow the youth "to amass a fortune" (ibid:342). However, I have found no record in the published texts, especially those dealing with elevation of a youth by stages, to substantiate Boas's account of escalation of loans in the course of which the youth borrows at 100 percent, and lends out at 100 percent until the entire accumulation comes his way.

Along with the common concept of "potlatch" as interest-bearing investment, Boas brought within the same framework the helpfulness of lineage mates toward a youth aspiring to chiefship, and the "flattening" of a rival's name. The two motifs are opposite even for Kwakiutl, who characteristically transform some events into their opposite. However, in this instance the assumption that in the *pasa* the rival's name is flattened is dubious. In the first place, Boas's later gloss of *pasa* brought out rather the emptying of a basket. And, second, the image of persons crushed in an avalanche of property appeared in the special context of the Winter Ceremonial, and not as the consequence of giving gifts with the expectation of return with 100 percent interest.

Boas's final example of the return with interest through doubling is not confirmed by the texts in the manner in which he has presented it. As Boas understood the system, the rival was indebted to his host for the joint sum of blankets both had put together. That is, having received 100 plus 100 blankets he was subsequently indebted for 400. According to the texts, the point is rather that the blankets to be distributed on the occasion of the elevation of a chief are, in fact, a joint enterprise that is spoken of as "pressing together" the advanced blankets (given by the guests) and the blankets really given away (see Boas 1925:209). The obligation on this, as upon almost all other ritual occasions, is for the guest merely to match the largesse of the host; the guest is, after all, the recipient of this largesse. As I have said before, the texts do not speak of escalation or of obligations to return specific amounts at a future date. The only bona fide examples of ritual gifts that are returned double or more concern the affinal relationship. The father-in-law always returns far more than he receives, in some instances double.

The view that the interest-bearing loan is distinct from the ritual gift is a clarification of Boas's impressions, which Curtis had published in 1915 (p. 143). Curtis's information came from Hunt but did not receive due attention, partly because his work on Kwakiutl was not easily accessible. Curtis considered loans at interest as a postcontact commercial development. Perhaps it was that. Information from an unpublished text sent to Boas by Hunt indicates rather that the interest-bearing loan had, in fact, been given a ritual setting. As its title, "Solidarity of the Numaym," stresses, the document is not a study of usurious practices but of the obligations of a lineage to support even its commoner members (see Hunt ms. 14:1461–1492). It describes two related events to which Hunt was a witness and participant. These events concern a commoner who needed to put up 100 blankets in a "fight in talk" (qalapeda) with a rival from another lineage. Later, the same man on his death bed needed 50 blankets for a mortuary distribution. In both instances, the chief assembled the lineage and urged its members to help a needy kinsman. In both instances the debtor pledged to repay with "interest." The term for interest is dlekoyo, which is unrelated to the usual expressions for interlineage or intertribal distributions and exchanges. The stem dlek appears in dlekomas, a "loan," with omas, the suffix, standing for classes of things, that is, a collective (ibid:332). The suffix oyo means "the middle," or "half" (ibid). The etymology is difficult to render other than as a "middle loan," referring perhaps to the obligation of repayment of the principal, that is, the other half of the transaction.

Hunt, a talented field worker, introduces the examples of loans and interest indebtedness by explaining how they differ from contributions to a lineage chief who is preparing to make a ritual distribution. In the latter case, he says, there is no repayment. Property is due him as chief. If he were to repay, it would be said of the lineage, "they eat their own property" (literally, "eat up themselves their property") (ibid:1461), in a form of incestuous exchange that, as Hunt adds, would disgrace their name.

In the example of "fight talk" or rivalrous exchange, the lineage mate promised to match the 100 blankets put up by his rival even though, as he later admitted, he had not a single blanket in the house. This text, incidentally, states explicitly that in this rivalrous exchange, at least, the obligation is to equal and not surpass the rival. In the words of Hunt, a man is defeated (yakawe) "when he don't come up to the counting of the other one." He then becomes a "wet eye" (kunxsla). He can redeem himself by promising to give away an equal amount of blankets to the lineage of his rival. It was in such straits that he appealed for a loan.

The chief assembled his lineage, and asked each member to offer one or several pairs of blankets. The debtor handed over 300 cedar sticks as his pledge of repayment. In addition, he pawned his daughter (to be "taken by the foot") as a "slave." Hunt explains that it is the man who will be the slave of the chief, saying:

> it is just the same as sold himself his own man body for him to go and slave of the chief there as long as he has not pay for the one hundred blankets that take hold of the feet by the chief to the only one woman daughter of his with the three hundred will be blankets will be.

(ibid:1948)

In the second example of lending at interest this common man needed 50 blankets. He was dying of consumption, and his daughter had just died. His lineage mates who had arrived to comfort him offered the loan. Each man in giving his share of the collective loan spoke of "buying a slave" (ibid:1473). Having no daughter to pawn, the debtor offered one side of his body as "slave" to the chief. His sister, at his side, submitted cedar sticks as a pledge to return 150 blankets for the loan.

Even if lending at interest were a postcontact innovation, the setting of these transactions follows traditional forms. The transactions are special only insofar as they represent a distinctive ritual occasion, specifically, the indebtedness of a commoner to his lineage. As a debtor the commoner has publicly acknowledged his inferiority, but at the same time he has put in question the honor of his chief and the good name of his lineage. They redeem him and themselves by assuming his obligations. In return, he enters into dual and contrasting relationships with them. By giving his daughter (or niece, or his own body) into "slavery" he completes his own degradation. But by offering to pay double interest, which is the equivalent of an internal distribution twice over, he redeems his own honor, not in the ordinary commercial manner of repaying a debt, but by acquiring the honorable status of giver of property to his own lineage. Involvement of the commoner debtor's own sense of honor is revealed when he adds an additional 50 blankets to the required 100 on the loan of 50. Such overgiving is characteristic of transactions with coppers. As donor to his lineage the commoner debtor asserts status analogous to a chief's. But in accepting the obligation to pawn his daughter or his name, he concedes his true commoner status.

The second example, borrowing for a mortuary distribution, reveals the ritual emphasis of the transaction even more clearly. The borrower, a commoner (ibid:1476), was actually a wealthy man. He owned, according to Hunt, much property and many high-priced coppers (ibid) and did not need to borrow. Thus it appears from these examples that borrowing and repayment with interest serve all participants. The transaction was really an ingenious arrangement for involving commoners— honorably for all concerned—in honorific exchange.

Status Rivalry.   The public rivalries and antagonisms are real, we must conclude, only as they relate men to the supernatural world—for Kwakiutl, the "real" world. Personal animus may penetrate the masks that cover the human being, but the mask wearer and the bearer of the name has the higher obligation to represent his spirits rather than himself. Ritual occasions are not the proper forum for secular status rivalry, and ritual is simply not the cultural means for conducting covert and personal rivalry. Personal jealousies, hatreds, and rivalries must find other than established ritual outlets, and they do. In Polynesia, by contrast, personal status rivalry was official; it followed established, even ritualized forms. There, the official tradition and the main religious precepts of power encompassed economic production and the everyday life of the community. Power, always the focus of status rivalry, had become political. Political rivalry, no matter how formal, demands skill in dealing with shifting balances of forces, and calls forth qualities of spontaneity, of tactical improvisation. Contenders calculate the possibilities of changing balances of power, and of holding and expanding powers they have. Polynesian status rivalry was politically energetic. Kwakiutl status rivalry projected an atmosphere of rivalry and antagonism that achieved its heights in imagery and symbolic actions, and yet, by Polynesian standards, left the political economy relatively undisturbed.

In the public sphere it is antagonism that is central among Kwakiutl. Through antagonism they display their powers and, like their heroic figures in myth, battle their opponents to a standstill. Rivalry is a secondary form of antagonism. It concerns the obligation to be unique, to be first and most powerful among men. Primary antagonism is essentially cosmological, pitting men against spirits and men as spirits against other men as spirits. Rivalry is more fully a social concern. In the religious sphere, cosmic antagonism and social rivalry are, in effect, joined through the Kwakiutl concept of the champion, the shaman supreme. It is assumed that the most powerful in the human community is the privileged and most effective contender against the most powerful of spirits. In this respect, of course, Kwakiutl fall within the classical tradition of aristocracy. Primacy achieves the aristocratic aim of establishing the unassailable criteria for centricity and for uniqueness. The center, the locus of the first-ranking tribe, lineage, or chief, is the focal point of powers. The unique status represents nothing less than the sanctity of the individual organic being in nature, the ultimate container of spirit and powers. Rank immediately grants uniqueness; primacy brings the quality of uniqueness to its highest level. Thus status rivalry is in the service of cosmological antagonism. Though the language of rivalry is social and at times personal, the sphere of its real action is, to all intents and purposes, still cosmological. From my knowledge of the texts, I can say that the secular social rivalries belong to the postcontact era when chiefs joined in common action to put down commoner pretenders, who in the past would not have presumed to enter the higher caste. I have found no record in the texts of an actual reduction in rank of a chief through acceptable forms of contest. As I have already explained, there were opportunities through marriage and war to supplement basic rank. We may properly regard the war party and the contest for a bride as forms of status rivalry for supplementary ranks directly, and for basic rank only indirectly. There are examples of jealousies and rivalries that result in murder. But internal homicide is a criminal act. What is definite is that property distributions were not an economic mode of pursuing a social form of status rivalry. Hunt's example of "fight talk" among commoners, previously cited, was not in the mainstream of traditional property distributions. It is undeniable, of course, that status rivalry was a prominent theme in traditional songs and orations. In the setting of religious ritual, the assertion of supremacy and of disdain for rivals is to be understood as part of the broader pattern of cosmological antagonism. The songs, the oratory, the refrains in the family traditions authenticate the right of the chief to be a champion.

The Kwakiutl term for rival is *hayot.* To understand its meaning in the light of Kwakiutl associations we turn to terms listed by Boas as cognates (see Boas 1921:1297). These are *hayaqa,* "to pass," *hayegi,* "to imitate," *hayosela,* "to go across," and *hayotlala,* "to bring out of the woods." From these associative terms the meaning of "rival" appears close to our own. The rival is one who seeks to pass or to emulate. The phrase going across or coming out of the woods suggests the religious idea of leaving one realm to enter another. There is an implication here of a rival as one who seeks to enter a terrain that is not rightfully his. A common refrain in the traditional texts is, "they try only to imitate us." In the social universe of the Kwakiutl, imitation is challenging. Imitation defies the perceived law of nature that two centers of power cannot occupy the same space. To pass a chief is to challenge traditional primacy. If the rhetoric of rivalry has, as it would seem, no genuine sociological significance, it must still have for the Kwakiutl a genuine reality. Rivalry is real in that it corresponds to Kwakiutl perceptions of the natural scene. They understand envy, anger, and the jostling for supremacy and uniqueness as natural among human beings. In their religious imagination they give full reign to the desires and feelings of rivalry that the Polynesians, a politically developed people, have brought openly into the social arena.

Fighting with Property.   Describing a Winter Ceremonial he had observed at Fort Rupert during the 1895–96 season, Boas quotes several participants who speak of "fighting with property" in place of weapons of war. In one instance, a Koskimo dancer who is carrying a copper says:

> *Oh friends! turn your faces this way. Look at me! Treat me and my cedar bark ornaments in the right manner. In former times I and my people have suffered at your hands, Kwakiutl. We used to fight with bows and arrows, with spears and guns. We robbed each other's blood. But now we fight with this here* (pointing at the copper which he was holding in his hands), *and if we have no coppers, we fight with canoes or blankets. That is all.*

To this the speaker, Qoalxala, replies:

> *True is your word, friend* [Gasa]. *When I was young, I have seen streams of blood shed in war. But since that time the white man came and stopped up that stream of blood with wealth. Now we are fighting with our wealth. That is all.*

$$(1897:571)$$

Boas picked this note as a paradigm of the "potlatch," saying: "Formerly feats of bravery counted as well as distributions of property, but nowadays, as the Indians say, 'rivals fight with property only.' The clans are thus traditionally pitted against each other according to their rank" (ibid:343). Codere's study takes the more provocative position that the "potlatch" became a substitute for war. Echoing Boas's own conclusion, she adds:

> The Kwakiutl potlatch, throughout the historical record, was always a form of rivalry and fighting and it could absorb and command anything in warfare that would add to its impressiveness. It was ridden with the imagery and drama and meaning of Kwakiutl warfare and it was empty of physical violence and destructiveness except occasionally toward property. (1950:129)

At this stage in our analysis of property and antagonism the issue is no longer whether the "potlatch" is a form of warfare, or whether "potlatching" has become a moral alternative to war, but rather what the Kwakiutl meant by the expression "fighting with property." The expression, it should be said, does not occur in the traditional Kwakiutl texts. It is mentioned by implication in Hunt's text on commoners engaging in "fight talk," and appears directly only in Boas's cited description. At this dance, however, the phrase occurs several times, so that even if it had not been a traditional sentiment it might have become so by 1897. It occurred in the special context of the Winter Ceremonial and its powers, and in the more exceptional circumstances of Kwakiutl rivalry with the Koskimo, who speak a different dialect and were not part of the traditional congregation. Conceivably, it was the Koskimo who had crystallized aphoristically the connection between warfare and the uses of property. On this matter we merely speculate. What is reasonably clear is that "fighting with property" is associated specifically with the Winter Ceremonial, and not with exchange and distribution in general. In this connection, a Gapenox, a member of a tribe allied to the Koskimo, says at this same Winter Ceremonial in reference to an ancestor's death bringer treasure: "But instead of fighting our enemies with his death bringer we fight with these blankets and other kinds of property" (Boas 1897:577). A Kwakiutl fool dancer, the Warrior, makes a similar point when he says: "The time of fighting has passed. The fool dancer represents the warriors, but we do not fight now with weapons; we fight with property" (ibid:602).

While the historical implications of these remarks must remain ambiguous, they do establish a conceptual continuity between warfare, the Winter Ceremonial, and certain of its property distributions. We have already discussed the mythological concept underlying such unity. War is conceived of as a means of satiating Man Eater through lives and property, including coppers. In this pattern—considered synchronically—myth expresses the theme at the deepest level of comprehension; ritual expresses it symbolically as between persons—spirit representations. Warfare converts the theme to a more concrete but still symbolic form. In their final structural integration, however, warfare and Winter Ceremonial rituals formed a coextensive unity. The rituals actually carried out every military theme: the killing of enemies, the destruction of property, the burning of a house, the breaking of canoes. They portrayed the ambience of menace, the aspect of chiefly terror, the image of host and guest in confrontation as hostile warriors. In the killing and eating of slaves and in destructions of property, ritual and warfare achieved a genuine fusion of mythological subject matter. But the personal antagonisms remained frozen as purely symbolic projections of the myth. Thus, in the Koskimo-Kwakiutl Winter Ceremonial confrontation the formal rhetoric is of vanquishing. In fact no one is vanquished in any sense, and by their own statements neither antagonist has been vanquished by the other. A Kwakiutl lavishly praising the rival Koskimo as "a vast mountain of wealth, from which rocks are rolling all the time" then warns his own people "if we do not open our eyes and awake, we shall lose our high rank. Remember Kwakiutl we have never been vanquished by another tribe" (ibid:576). The reply, which comes later during the dances, states: "We are the Koskimo, who have never been vanquished by any tribe, neither in wars of blood, nor in wars of property" (ibid:580). Obviously, we have here an example of standard rhetoric that imposes on all ritual antagonists the absolute qualities of invincibility and uniqueness. Only the imagery is warlike; the consequences are not.

Even a chief of the very low-ranking Nakwaxdax is able to boast against the Kwakiutl: "No other can equal mine; no chief can equal me. I always distribute all my property" (ibid:551). Then this Nakwaxdax chief turns to a Koskimo and says: "Let both our tribes strive against the Kwakiutl, so that we may take off two finger widths of their highness" (ibid). In this remark we gain new insight on intertribal rivalries. Boas explains that since the Kwakiutl of Fort Rupert consist of four tribes they are counted as four fingers high. Other tribes are only one finger-width high (ibid). Here the rivalrous tone has a militaristic edge in suggesting a reduction in population. The Koskimo deride their rivals for being few in number. "Look out!" their spokesman says. "Do not let the Kwakiutl vanquish you, for they are few only. . . . The Kwakiutl could not fill one-half the seats in this house, therefore, they cannot vanquish us" (ibid:589–590).

Perhaps numbers are, in fact, economic data: Large tribes assemble more property and so overcome smaller tribes. Images of rivals drowned in a sea of property, or buried under an avalanche of property, are in the same key as the demographic portrayal. The explanation most congenial to our own logical sensibilities is that whatever the metaphoric meanings of fighting with property may be, the resolution of all questions of intertribal superiority should be an answer to the single question: Who gave the most property? As I have said repeatedly, nowhere is this question answered in the texts. Our hope for an answer from Boas, who witnessed a major part of a Winter Ceremonial and recorded it in reasonably close detail, is disappointed. Boas does not mention the outcome of any property fight, although he does speak of distributions accompanying dances. If there was indeed a public summation and decision, or any manifestation of victory or defeat, Boas failed to notice it. Strange that in a society world-renowned for its excesses in the service of status rivalry there should not be a single bona fide example of one particular chief reducing the rank of another in a contest over who has more wealth—and that in a published literature covering several thousand printed pages! In the literature on Polynesian societies, by contrast, the most fragmentary ethnographies document specific cases of chiefs vanquishing their rivals.

Warfare. One must agree with Codere that Kwakiutl warfare had no economic or political rationale (1950:127–28). Since her study explicitly steered clear of religion and ritual, her alternative rationale is of warfare as an instrument for status and prestige.

Following a religious perspective, we have seen war as an extension of the Winter Ceremonial. "Now I wish to go and make war again on all the tribes, that you may give your winter dance, says Dzonoqwa (the Warrior) to his eldest brother" (Boas and Hunt 1905:240). Therein is established the mythical foundation. Boas learned that Winter Ceremonial dances acquired in war, that is by killing the owners and seizing their boxes of dance paraphernalia, were more valued than those received in marriage. Connecting this general observation with Dzonoqwa's specific statement, we come again to the familiar Kwakiutl dialectic: To live one must kill.

The ritual significance of warfare is to be ascertained from our knowledge of the total ritual conception, which includes a variety of religious themes. A major theme concerns the relation between human beings and animals. Coordinate with this theme is that of relations among human beings. If animals are hunted, humans are to be hunted. If animals are killed, humans are to be killed. If animals are eaten, humans are to be eaten. For Kwakiutl, warfare is indeed an extension of hunting, with this important distinction: Animals give of themselves freely, humans do not. Consequently, the human victim of war is degraded, while the animal is not.

The relations between humans are also coordinate with those between humans and supernatural beings, in that great supernatural treasures are acquired from each. Again, an important distinction: Supernatural beings are an original source; humans are a secondary source of powers. However, the secondary source is the only relevant source in the post-mythical era. If among the secondary acquisitions of powers warfare is even more significant than marriage, as Boas said, it is probably because it is the most explicit statement of Winter Ceremonial themes. Warfare expresses the basic ceremonial ideas. Marriage stands for the means of their conveyance.

Warfare completes the ritual cycle by giving concrete substance to religious ideas of feeding Man Eater, of destroying property, and of seizing supernatural powers by force. Warfare restores the primal realities and rescues ritual from sheer symbolism. An incident related by Curtis (1915) when a chief shot and killed a guest as a manifestation of his power to terrorize is another example of a feeling for the real breaking through the barriers of sheer symbolism. That extravagant action is analogous to warfare.

In the sense that both served religious purposes, Kwakiutl and Plains Indian warfare were similar. The Plains Indians emphasized the aspect of chivalric courage, while the Kwakiutl chose rather to represent in war the antagonisms of supernatural beings and the animal ferocity of the grizzly bear. The Western tradition giving chivalry the edge over animal ferocity would magnify the distinction between Kwakiutl and, let us say, Crow Indians. From the North American Indian perspective the distinction narrows. Kwakiutl ferocity allowing savage and unprovoked surprise attacks at minimum personal risk depicted, nevertheless, the hunter vis-à-vis his prey. Since human beings were the victims of an unprovoked and surprise attack by death, human war exploits served the ritual purpose of giving them equity with the higher powers. The

Kwakiutl took scalps and stored them in boxes the way they took and stored animal skins.

The status of the warrior derives from his traditional position as the next younger brother of a chief, a position in precise parallel to that of Dzonoqwa and his older brother, Man Eater. In this relationship the warrior is the feeder of the chief, the bringer of powers. The warrior is not apparently a direct giver of powers to the chief. The names and ceremonial privileges he has taken from his victim are evidently his, although our information on this point and on the related matter of ownership of the slaves is not very clear. What is clear, though, is that the seizures of war are fed to the lineages and the tribes, adding to their substance and forcefulness. The warrior, finally, appears to have the position of rival to his older brother by virtue of his prowess as a killer and as one who adds substance. According to Boas, the younger brother is the traditional rival of the elder. The position of rival, I would suggest, may arise from the quality of a warrior, who has a means outside of pedigree and marriage to approximate and even to surpass the senior.

The most detailed information on warfare, evidently small-scale attacks on undefended villages or more often quick ambushes of small parties or solitary fishermen, is from Curtis. The Kwakiutl fought, he wrote, not only for the renown and wealth brought by taking booty and heads, but also to alleviate the grief of mourning. Kwakiutl, characteristically, did not seek directed vengeance. Any victim helped balance the books. The warriors were professionals, ritually prepared from childhood to acquire the fierceness of the grizzly bear. The term *papaqa*, "warrior," means "merciless man" (Curtis 1915:99). The war party followed ritual precautions of bathing in a river, and gashing their thighs and calves. Curtis describes a war party of the Lekwiltok, the fiercest of the Kwakiutl tribes. One Indian said of them: "They were like a great mouth always open to swallow whatever attempted to pass" (ibid:105). The ritual character of the warpath, from initial preparations to the carefully staged approach to the enemy and the return home, is more than faintly reminiscent of the Plains. During the Winter Ceremonial the warriors recounted their exploits. The principal chief applauded the "winner" and chastised the men with the poorest record.

The texts do not indicate who were traditional enemies. The Lekwiltok fought against all Salishan tribes, and the Kwakiutl associated with the Fort Rupert tribes fought Bella Coola. In one war they seized a great quantity of property: 400 marten, 400 lynx, 100 bear, 100 grizzly bear, 200 caribou, 40 marmot, 4 rattles, 10 bark boxes of hemlock bark, and 10 boxes of cinquefoil (Boas and Hunt 1905:223). Such a haul leads one to suspect that in the early days wars were an important if not a necessary adjunct to ritual distribution and exchange. In all probability "fighting with property" did not substitute for war; rather war financed "fighting" with property.

In other instances, fighting meshed directly into the Winter Ceremonical, as though killing in battle and the *hamatsa* ritual were coordinate events. Hunt tells of a Nakwaxdax chief who went to arrange a mock marriage with the Bella Coola that would give him valuable prerogatives, though not the woman herself. Perhaps because of the unusual nature of such a wedding the party was never invited into the Bella Coola house. On the way home the party brooded over this insult and decided to attack a neighboring tribe, the Dawildex. They took the village by surprise in the dead of night, set it on fire, and killed the men. They took away nine heads, a woman as a slave, and a large box containing Winter Ceremonial adornments. Arriving home, the Nakwaxdax chief, on learning that he had killed the Dawildex chief and had acquired his man-eater spirit, "disappeared" that winter and gave a *hamatsa* dance. The woman slave, in an act reminiscent of the rooted woman in the Man Eater tradition, instructed him in his new privileges. Hunt remarks: "Indeed, why should they not learn the songs of the cannibal-dancer? because they obtained it by killing in war, for it is more valuable when obtained in war than when obtained in marriage." The narrative continues:

> *When* [Laqwagila] *had learned the ways in which the cannibal's dance was danced by the* [Dalwidex]*, and the songs, he got excited in his cannibal-dance. Then they killed the woman slave, and he ate her, and* [Laqwagila] *himself ate the whole slave. Then he changed his name, because he had swallowed the whole woman-slave.*

(Boas 1921:1017)

IX

SYNTHESIS

The Kwakiutl see each community as an incomplete segment of a wider universe. No part, no person, no tribe, no species, no body of supernatural beings is self-sufficient. Each possesses a portion of the sum of all powers and properties of the cosmos; each must share with all or the entire system of nature would die. The Kwakiutl human community places itself at the center of the cosmic system only because it has no choice but to assert its own special perspective, to cherish its own special qualities, and to assure its own continued existence. At the same time, and as genuine naturalists, the Indians accept the parity and the indestructible uniqueness of all other members of the common universe. Kwakiutl religion represents the concern of the people to occupy their own proper place within the total system of life, and to act responsibly within it, so as to acquire and control the powers that sustain life.

The total community of life includes human beings, animals, vegetable life, and supernatural beings, a sacred tetrad of dependent and interactive realms. Each realm is subdivided in its own fashion: human beings, animals, and supernatural beings by family, by hierarchy, and by antag-

onistic opposition; the vegetable realm, represented by trees and mainly by the cedar and the hemlock, is less differentiated. The copper,
a form of life, stands for still a fifth element, distinct from the others
in having no specific locus in the natural world. Unlike supernatural
beings, who are either zoomorphic or anthropomorphic and in either
form energetic activists, the copper exists as a symbolic property connected with sky, sea, and salmon. The members of the tetrad interlace
through systems of exchanges and transformations; the place of the copper is as an instrument of these exchanges.

The organizational structure of this basic tetrad is symmetrical rather
than hierarchical and is based on interdependence. When Hunt asked
elders about the Creator he provoked only disagreement (see Boas
1930:178). One man insisted the Sun had created mankind. Others dis-
puted him, arguing that each lineage had its own creator. Another
thought that human beings had created themselves. Those who proposed Qanekelak as the creator were reminded that he was but a transformer. The tetrad as a supercommunity evidently transcends hierarchy,
which is, for Kwakiutl, primarily a mode of interior order.

A cosmological hierarchy may not be formally established, but neither
for that matter do the Kwakiutl formally declare a principle of equality
among the four realms. The issue is left open and formally unresolved,
compelling us, and of course the Indians, to acknowledge the subtle
hand of nature for whom relationships are often sometimes this way
and sometimes that way. There is much in Kwakiutl religious thought
that seems to imply the superiority of the human to the animal. Men,
for example, were the original form of both. All animals were originally
human beings, and when human beings were animals it was only by
wearing the animal form as a removable mask. And yet it is only when
humans resume their animal forms as Sparrows and as Seals in the Winter Ceremonial that they regain access to the primary sources of immortality. Animals are obliged to give their bodies for the benefit of humans.
Humans for their part provide for the immortality of the animals. Thus
it is only at a chosen and fixed point in time that one or the other
appears superior. This is far from the Judeo-Christian subordination
of the animal, but it is certainly of human origin, that of the Kwakiutl
who is telling the story, and tilting the scale on his side. At the same
time, his naturalistic realism does not allow him to regard the animal
as nothing but food or emblem of personal prestige.

From the Kwakiutl point of view, the realms of animals, trees, and supernatural beings are sources of power. They are primary and external realms, and thus authentic sources of power. Within the Kwakiutl universe, primary acquisitions of power demand relationships of equity. Even within the human sphere, which is formally hierarchical, transferences of powers require some equalization between the two parties. The heir is built up to the level of rank of his father, the son-in-law demonstrates his parity with his father-in-law before receiving his wife and her associated treasures. And for the passing over of coppers, the normal hierarchy of the Ritual Congregation converts to a moiety of formal oppositions, the ritual equivalent of internal-external for an interior system.

With respect to the movement of powers, hierarchy and opposition have their distinct and formal roles. Primary acquisitions of power move across opposing sections. The secondary allocation of what has been received moves down the interior hierarchy. In short, the organization of the cosmos follows a more complex set of rules than simple repetition of social hierarchy. Within each of the four realms of nature, some hierarchical arrangement prevails. Human ranking has already been discussed. In the animal world there is no formal rank order, but the idea of rank is present among birds, where Eagle eats first, and in an imputed early social organization, where Deer, Wolf, and Mink were chiefs. Among salmon, Spring Salmon is the chief. Within the framework of the Winter Ceremonial the spirit world is as precisely ranked as the human. In the vegetable realm the red cedar is evidently the highest, but there is no suggestion of a complete system of formal rank.

The tetradic order has a double significance in the religious sense. In the first place it establishes the basic topography of life, of its unity in diversity, and hence of the incompleteness of each realm. Given the topography, the means is devised of overcoming their separateness, of crossing the boundaries between each realm and the others. Boundaries are crossed for the specific purpose of acquiring powers. I turn shortly to a discussion of the three realms other than the human, and then to the modes of crossing boundaries, of acquiring powers, and of exchanging qualities of being. Our immediate and prior concern is with the concept of supernatural powers, the central issue in Kwakiutl religion.

Nawalak has been translated by both Hunt and Boas as "supernatural power." Its ultimate source is in the realm of spirits, and its possession allows people to transcend what Kwakiutl call the ordinary human conditions. Two terms define the negative condition, *baxus*, a state of being ordinary (secular), and *aoms*, "not having *nawalak*." There are other such terms in the Kwakiutl vocabulary, but it is not clear whether they actually imply different concepts. *Nawalak* is unquestionably the basic concept. Although the supernatural power with which a shaman cures is called *helika*, and his state of being a source of shamanistic power is *paxa*, he would not be a shaman without *nawalak*. The terms *helika* and *paxa* are also evidently specialized forms of *nawalak*. So is *hayatliligas*, translated by Boas as "supernatural means by which people are protected or harmed." Finally, *tlogwe*, the "treasures" acquired from supernatural beings, are the specified forms of *nawalak*. When the shaman sings, "I was taken away far inland to the edge of the world by the magical power of heaven, the treasure *(naxnaualagwets tlogwala)*" (Boas 1930:47), he is describing the *nawalak* of heaven as the treasure.

Nawalak, like Oceanic *mana*, Algonquian *manitou*, Siouan *wakanda*, and Iroquoian *orenda*, denotes a general power, characteristically impersonal, but capable of implying a supreme power as a being. *Nawalakwene* has been translated as "supernaturalness" (Boas 1927:386), and *nawalakume* as the Great Supernatural Power (Boas 1930:47). A common reference in the religious texts is to the *nawalak* of the Great Supernatural Power, a definite allusion to the impersonal power as the essential attribute of whatever has power.

Nawalak is widespread, though not universal. Some beings are naturally endowed with it, but humans must acquire it from an outer realm, either by primary search as did original ancestors, or by secondary means, as contemporary people do through the Winter Ceremonial and general adherence to ritual rules. The primary acquisition had laid the foundation for secondary access through ritual observance. Among beings naturally endowed with *nawalak*, Boas mentions the salmon, twins, the skylark, the cedar and other trees, and all supernatural beings who appear in dreams (1927:387). The latter category, comparable to myth narratives of encounters with animals and spirits, encompasses a large section of the animal realm. Thus three of the tetrad are donors of *nawalak* to mankind. Dependent mankind preserves itself and arranges, therefore, for its own immortality and that of the animals, thus bringing these two species of existence on to a level with the immortality of the spirits. The status of trees in this respect is unclear. Existing symmetry in Kwakiutl cosmological thought would lead one to expect trees to be equated with spirits. The Kwakiutl do not, however, seek symmetry in that direction. Men and animals were paired from the beginning.

Among human beings, only twins have natural or inherent *nawalak*. Twins are regarded as human manifestations of salmon. In contrast to Polynesia, where *mana* is an inherent attribute of rank, Kwakiutl supernatural powers must be acquired and are not therefore distributed according to a methodical rank order. In Polynesia, rank and sanctity *(tapu)*, the counterpart of *mana*, are givens. But rank then becomes variable, and sanctity remains stable. Among the Kwakiutl it is rank that is stable and *nawalak* that is variable. What observers have usually taken to be rivalry over rank are, in fact, invidious demonstrations of supernatural powers—of *nawalak*. The demonstrations do not, however, affect the possession of powers; they are intended only to portray actual states of being. They manifest aggressive hostility against rivals to demonstrate that the capability of destroying is one of the attributes of *nawalak*.

Unlike *mana*, *nawalak* is not quantitatively graded against a comparative standard like genealogical rank. Kwakiutl grading is much coarser. Persons have or do not have *nawalak*. In the concept of *tlogwe*, of special powers, *nawalak* becomes a qualitative property; persons may then possess many or few, or major or minor supernatural treasures. Their supernatural wealth is related to their rank, but is not a quantitative governor of it, since there is no standard of measurement. Nevertheless, the highest chiefs have the richest genealogical heritage of powers as well as the richest prospects for further acquisition through marriages. On the principle that powers attract more powers, Kwakiutl may contemplate monopoly even if they cannot, in fact, achieve it.

Rank and *nawalak* relate from either side. Chiefs acquire *nawalak*, and those who acquire *nawalak* are said to become chiefs (see Boas 1921:820). The seeming contradiction is resolved in the basic idea of a connection with the supernatural powers who grant their gifts. The founders of lineages (and of tribes) had primary and initial grants. Lesser chiefs—not original founders—received later or secondary grants.

The pattern of distinctions and similarities between chiefs and shamans points to parallel differentiations in the common concept of *nawalak*. It seems unlikely, for example, that commoners become chiefs only through obtaining *nawalak,* because the texts never portray a clear case of this sort. Commoners, however, acquire *nawalak* to become *paxala*. Having become shamans, they acquire a counterpart status to the real chiefs, as chiefs become counterpart shamans during the Winter Ceremonial. Shamanism has been described as a "back door" to social position among the Kwakiutl. It is so only partially. The counterpart position permits participation in property distributions on the principle that an acquired power must be accompanied by fomenting circulation of wealth. It does not, insofar as I have been able to discover, insert the shaman directly into the official order of rank. The shaman without basic rank acquires perquisites of rank, not the seat of rank. Slaves can acquire *nawalak*, but are not allowed its social benefits.

Finally, we distinguish between *nawalak* granted as a personal *tlogwe*—the truly honorific power of chiefs and shamans—and *nawalak* acquired through more general means. *Tlogwe* are specific and demonstrable powers, which establish through song, dance, and name, an identification with the granting spirit. General *nawalak*, expressed more diffusely, is available to all persons and acquired from the Winter Ceremonial, from prayers and requests, and from obedience to ritual injunction. Chiefs and shamans among Kwakiutl are equivalent to visionaries and religious society members among Woodland and Plains Indians. The common folk are also looked after, but less intimately, by the spirits. Women—apart from their *tlogwe* possession—are said to have more *nawalak* than men because they are the most punctilious in ritual observance (see Boas, 1932a:228–229). The key to the distinction between ordinary *nawalak* and *tlogwe nawalak* is in the concept of transformation. With *tlogwe* the person is transformed into a representative of the donor. With general *nawalak* he is not. By becoming a spirit representative the recipient becomes, in turn, a potential donor of *nawalak* associated with his *tlogwe*.

Realm of Animals.   Of the tetrad, animals and humans are linked in the intimacy of having been a single being in the beginning. The removal of the animal mask that initiated the cycle of human development, implies, as I have already suggested, a metaphoric concept of asexual birth, the full-grown ancestor having come forth from within the animal form. As between parent and child, the physical separation is considered complete, while the social and spiritual ties are never to be severed. It is in the light principally of this analogy of birth, in effect the essence of the totemic relationship, that the pairing of animal and human may be visualized as true kinship.

Animals declare themselves to be people wearing animal clothing (Boas 1895:169). Thus they are kin to mankind generically, as well as specific and totemic founders of lineages. Though linked by a common humanness, animals and humans are apart in their domains and the connections between them are not intended to be self-evident. Mountain goats find it necessary to tell a hunter they are people. Other animals, who habitually remove their animal clothing when at home, are embarrassed to have people come upon them in undress. In either case they identify their humanness as alien to true mankind. By removing their masks to found human lineages they declare the necessity for going separate ways. Subsequently, as in wealth exchanges, animals and men share their distinctive qualities with one another. In the religious sense animals remain ambiguous beings. Their animal existence resides in their removable outer surface, their covering. A mountain goat gives a man his skin with which he can then successfully hunt the species, another version of animals giving themselves to men. And as I observed earlier, animals remove their skins when they seek supernatural power by diving into deep, fresh water, implying that the animal nature is not a power acquirer.

From the mythical position, the outer covering of animals is their form and their treasure, although animals are also givers of their own flesh. But if the substance of animals is human, the flesh that men eat is by analogy human also. In this curious respect the consumption of animal food becomes a form of spiritual cannibalism. Hence the killing of an animal is also like an act of war. Ritual cannibalism, therefore, brings into the open what is a standard, implicit understanding of what animal flesh really is. Perhaps because it is as though human, animal flesh becomes subordinate in ritual to the skins, which are the genuinely animal. When the great Man Eater spirit devours property, he consumes actual human flesh but only animal skins. He keeps his categories distinct.

In earlier chapters, I considered the animal mask and the animal skin as alike. Looking more closely, we may now distinguish between what is a real part of a real animal, and the symbolic skin of a mythical animal. Made of wood and stylized, masks are transcendent, having left the animal kingdom. In contrast to skins, which are generic representatives of their species and stand for animals killed, the masks are incarnations of specific beings who met a human ancestor and gave him specific powers. Animal skins and masks are in a common category of animal form souls. But the skins are a common form, in themselves depersonalized, and only in distribution arriving at categorization. The masks, on the other hand, being associated with human pedigrees and being themselves energetic, are equivalent to chiefs among their kind. Skins represent actual lives that have been taken; masks are only visualized as alive. Masks get "excited" during winter dances as do real participants, but skins remain inert.

The skins, however, are the quantitative wealth of the Kwakiutl, the numerical expression of natural bounty.[1] The masks invoke mythical beginnings, the skins perpetuate rhythmically the many faceted nature of wealth. As a great benefactor, the animal corresponds to a father-in-law, the great source of wealth within the human sphere. As a donor it is the animal who excels, for, in the final analysis, he is a major source of powers and virtues. The animal skins are but the complements of power. All powers, and all treasures from the supernatural sphere find their measure in the ceaseless dialectic of the transformations of life into death and back.

Through its skin the animal is, of course, the fastener on of the name, the endlessly repetitive paradigm of the primal theme: The human name soul is in exchange for the animal form, which is sent away. Animal skins are the substance for spiritual weight. Distributions in their behalf make the young "heavy"—not necessarily corpulent, although body mass on the Northwest Coast as in Polynesia was a physical accessory to social status. Among Kwakiutl, weight, most clearly expressed in the bride, implies immovability. It calls up the image of a mountain, down whose flanks property would fall in a deadly avalanche, or in the case of the woman, of a monumental mass to be moved with great effort. Piles of skins measured against "potlatch poles" suggest an ascension to the sky by association with the pole, the earth-sky bridge. Weight as a mountain may convey a similar idea, since mountains rising out of the sea are also bridges—between sea, land, and sky—in Kwakiutl thought.

In more general terms, wealth in animal skins serves three functions. The first is constructive, contributing to human identity, building weight, opening access to the sky, to a bride, to general human growth. The second is antagonistically defensive as is metaphysically revealed in feeding the voraciousness of Man Eater. The third is antagonistically offensive as in references to swallowing the tribes or engulfing them in an avalanche of property. The third category with its implication of the destruction of the tribes calls attention, it would seem, to the menace of excess, to the threat of a vast and rapidly burgeoning species overcoming and devouring the weaker. Since natural excess in mammalian species was not a Northwest Coast problem, one must imagine its invocation as a potentiality, associated probably with the basic idea of animal skins as stimulators of natural increase (see Boas 1935a:57). The great giver of wealth gives in proportion to his powers. Hence he is simultaneously a powerful giver, a powerful promoter of animal life, and even a more powerful promoter of animal life that is, at the same time, predatory and devouring and, in excess, menacing.

The relations between men and animals may be visualized as two strands, coiled helix-wise around each other, touching at some points, separated at others, but always symmetrically positioned. When they touch they exchange powers; when they are separate they reflect each other—humans appear as animals and animals as humans. Myth portrays the animals in their houses, holding winter dances or seeking supernatural powers by diving into deep waters in the guise of humans. Humans are portrayed in ritual in the guise of animals as they seek and portray powers. In another mode of parallel reflection humans are represented as metaphoric animals, chiefs as eagles and guests as salmon. Literary metaphor is merely suggestive; religious metaphor moves toward positing, if not genuine identity, a mystical connection. The Eagle chief is not a true eagle; he has, however, certain powers and privileges of the eagle. When the guests are visualized as salmon, drawn inexorably by the power of the host to his house, they enter into a relationship with him within which their animal characteristics set some of the patterns of social intercourse. As salmon they are the wealth of the host. They are supernatural representatives of the wealth of the sea, bringers of blessings. Logically, they might be expected to bring the *nawalak* of the salmon into the house. At the same time, salmon are devoured. Hence the host is analogous to the Great Devourer, as indeed the songs say when they speak of the chief "swallowing" his guests.

The relationship between host and guests qua salmon is, of course, more complex. He attracts "salmon" because he has powers achieved from animals, and because he has wealth in animal skins to distribute. Thus a double and parallel set of relations appears: Humans draw humans to themselves by their great powers, and then engage each other in exchanges. Simultaneously, animals, through the medium of humans, draw to themselves and engage in their own exchanges. The coming of the "salmon" sets off the circulation of the form souls of mammals.

Supernatural Beings. The animals the Kwakiutl encounter in myth and in ritual, and who are either sources or representations of powers are, broadly speaking, also supernatural beings. They are not ordinary animals, who by Kwakiutl definition do not wear their outer covering as a mask or garment. In the evolution of forms of life, according to myth, many animals emerged from beneath animal coverings as natural animals. Others, retaining their original masks and not releasing humans, remained as dual beings, animal on the outside, nonanimal or human on the inside. The animals whose skins circulate as wealth are of the ordinary species. Those who deal in *nawalak* or *tlogwe* are supernatural beings. They may be thought of as animal spirits and, possibly, as links between the worlds of ordinary animals and of the anthropomorphic supernatural beings.

Since animals, as depicted in myth, have a social and ritual existence parallel to that of human beings, living in villages and houses, celebrating winter dances, and diving for power, it would be logical to assume that they, like humans, are also connected to a supernatural world from which they get powers. An expectation of cosmological symmetry would lead us to seek a parallel between ordinary animals and spirit animals on the one hand, and ordinary people and supernatural beings on the other. There is in fact no such simple symmetry. In Kwakiutl thought humans are the principal receivers of powers *(nawalak)* and animals and their spirit counterparts are the principal donors.

Quite naturally the Kwakiutl are interested in how humans get their powers and not in how the animals get theirs. Wolves, for example, are said to possess the great supernatural treasures men seek, but it is not said how they got them. Myth allows the Kwakiutl to believe that the spirit animals are all primary owners of powers. There is no explicit higher source or original dispenser. They have their independent world in which they contest with one another, and from time to time deal with human ancestors. What their connections may be with the ordinary members of their species remains an unanswered question. However, from context we surmise this basic distinction between spirit and ordinary animals: Mask-wearing spirit animals (Raven, Mink, Deer, Wolf, Grizzly Bear, Killer Whale, etc.) are like human chiefs, activists, contenders, power centers. Ordinary animals, like the common people, are in a different and lesser category of generalized beings.

A third and separate realm includes supernatural beings whose forms are either undefined, or merge different orders of species. Four major spirits dominate this realm. The great Man Eater, Baxbakualanuxsiwae; Qomogwa, the guardian spirit of the seas and custodian of its animal wealth and copper; Qanekelak, the transformer; and Thunderbird, chief of the birds of heaven. Their forms are diverse, just as their powers are. Mink and Raven are also transformers like Qanekelak, but as specialized representatives of their species. Animal spirits are of the earth; the generalized spirits cover the cosmic zones, the forest depths, the inhabited shoreline, the sea, and the sky. Their powers embrace the major cycles of life renewal, the production of wealth, transformation, and death and resurrection. The interdependence of vital processes is in accord with that of the cosmic zones, each of which is a natural contributor of forces sustaining life. In Qanekelak, who comes close to being a creator, the Kwakiutl find the central and essential paradigm for natural continuity. Transformation is a genuinely natural process, whereas creation is a philosophical abstraction. Transformation acknowledges continuity, creation invokes an unreal concept of discontinuity, which is alien to Kwakiutl naturalistic thought.

The four spiritual parties of this realm form, characteristically, two pairs: Man Eater and Thunderbird are linked as powers of the winter season; Qanakelak and Qomogwa are antithetical powers of the summer. Myth portrays their antagonism. Qanekelak battles Thunderbird in his guise as Head Winter Dancer, Thunderbird is in combat with the Whale. The sea counteracts the powers of the Winter Ceremonial spirits. Copper, like men, is an antagonist of the winter spirits, as are the Seals. In further distinguishing between animal supernaturals and generalized supernaturals, we note that the former, like the natural species they are, constitute a mosaic structure, each a distinct but interdependent portion of the totality. The generalized supernaturals representing not species but processes constitute a dualistic structure in accordance with the clear principle that life processes fall naturally into sets of oppositions, of light and darkness, summer and winter, life and death, health and illness, and so on. The resolution of opposition is through transformation. I would assume that it is in deference to the logic of transformation that the generalized supernaturals are themselves intermediate forms, though they themselves were arrested in a state of metamorphosis. Man Eater is humanoid, but covered with mouths all over his body and stupid, unlike animals or humans. The major members of his entourage are grotesquely animal or humanoid. The monstrous Hoxhoq and the monstrous Dzonoqwa are respectively birds and humanoid verging into more abstract forms.

I have not included the spirit of war, Winalagilis, among the four major generalized supernaturals, not out of excess of respect for Kwakiutl tetradism, but because in myth the warrior is the adjutant of Man Eater. Thus Man Eater and War are paired spirits. Even though Boas regarded Winalagilis as the leading spirit of the Winter Ceremonial among the Fort Rupert tribes, I prefer to accept the myth version that sets forth the idea of a man-eater–warrior fraternal pair. The war spirit is never represented in graphic imagery either by mask, carving, or painting. In myth, the figure is visualized as associated with a canoe, but not in physical form. The canoe, which is in itself an image associated with the transport of a bride and of wealth from the sea, is thus the only tangible image of the warrior, and reasonably clear evidence of the principle that imported wealth feeds and appeases Man Eater.

As it recreates its own community of supernatural beings, the Winter Ceremonial simultaneously sets forth their individual properties and their interrelatedness. The pattern of fixed relations reveals further a deeper structure of religious meanings. The winter spirits are the most numerous and perhaps the most important. But they represent a subdomain among supernatural beings with the specialized tasks of overcoming death and darkness. The *hamatsa* dancers hold highest rank because Baxbakualanuxsiwae, their guardian spirit, is the central figure, and all others have roles pertinent to him, either as antagonists, as cohorts, or as parallel figures. As I have already suggested, the spiritual organization of the Winter Ceremonial is elementary in its central theme, but intricately complex in presentation. The complexity of the *tsetseqa* results, in the first place, from a process of accretion, by adding new dances acquired by war or by marriage. In time the ceremonial of each important tribe would coalesce into a single conceptual framework of all the separate rituals of the entire region. Insofar as the entire Northwest Coast shares a common religion, the totality of its ritual elements is readily shared. The desire to assemble within one tribe all the genealogical attributes of surrounding peoples through intermarriage is also realized through accompanying ritual interchange. In other words, the increasing elaboration through acquisition of the Winter Ceremonial is inherent in its religious character and is not to be explained away as a historical idiosyncrasy. In any case, the ritual concept of the Winter Ceremonial is as general in its adherence to processes of nature as is nature itself.

The complexity of spiritual heterogenity notwithstanding, the Winter Ceremonial coheres around four categories of supernatural beings. Boas has listed these as: (1) War, (2) "Cannibal" (Man Eater), (3) *matem*, and (4) ghosts. Like all Kwakiutl spiritual tetrads, these fall into opposing pairs: War and Man Eater are linked as killer-devourer, and *matem* (who are birds) and ghosts are a life-restoring pair. Ghosts are specifically described as giving powers to restore the dead to life. *Matem* are described in explanatory myth as birds that intercept a youth bent on suicide, and give him the power of flight, which saves his life. Although a specialized group, the four categories of spirit beings also represent four distinct cosmic zones. The canoe-traveling Winalagilis is of the sea, the Man Eater is of the forested mountain interior, the *matem* bird is of the mountain tops—an access to the sky—and the ghosts are of the underworld. In this pattern, the pairing of spirits represents a constant, but the zones, which enter into a variety of thematic associations with spirits, do not. What is interesting about the *tsetseqa* pattern is that in the winter season the two zones most directly associated with human activity are represented by death-bringing spirits; the nonhuman zones are restorative. In other settings the cosmic zones shift and they are then represented by opposite sets of spirits. In all instances a tetradic order of spirits divided into opposing pairs poses a fundamental law of the containment of forces. No powerful spirit or supernatural being enjoys an exclusive option. Each is paired, as though to demonstrate that it does not act on its own; and each is opposed to show it cannot have the field to itself. In the special case of Man Eater, there is a secret opponent in the rooted woman, who betrays him to his youthful adversary. War and Man Eater each command a community of cohort spirits. But *matem* and ghosts are solitary.

Winalagilis (Making War All Over the Earth) has three spirit associates: the Toxwid, a spirit of general invulnerability, the Mamaqa, a spirit of sorcery, and Hawinalatl (War Dancer) who cannot die of wounds. The spirit associates may be viewed as the components of the broader principle of death-dealing. These portray the two modes of killing (war and sorcery) and their inherent antithesis. The Toxwid, danced by a woman, is a female spirit who controls the double-headed serpent— a deadly killer in his live form as a blazing salmon, or an armor of invulnerability when girdled around the body.

The Sisiutl is a powerful example of intermediate form among supernatural beings. He is a serpent, a species of the land, but also appears as a salmon, and as a blazing light. He has serpent heads at each extremity and a human head at his center. He kills by converting human and animal victims to stone, or protects by making skin stony. I shall suggest now, in advance of later discussion, that the power of the Sisiutl is indeed a property of its intermediate character. In the Kwakiutl scheme, categorical purity is a defect. I also reserve for later discussion the special connection between women and intermediate forms.

Baxbakualanuxsiwae, Man Eater at the Mouth of the River, has been designated "cannibal" by Boas. Since this designation is appropriate only if the creature is himself human, which in fact he is not, I have accepted the literal translation as given by George Hunt. The *hamatsa* who portray Baxbakualanuxsiwae are actual cannibals, but their guardian spirit, who is of another realm, is specifically a man-eater, occupying in the carnivorous scheme a relation to human beings parallel to that of human beings to animals. However, when we take into account all the qualities of Man Eater we see him, in fact, as the complete carnivore, an attribute that humans share with him when they become cannibalistic.

Boas has interpreted the phrase "at the mouth of the river" as a reference to the north, explaining that Kwakiutl consider the ocean a stream running northward. Since I have found no corroboration of such an interpretation in the texts, I fall back on the literal interpretation: Man Eater is in symbolic parallel with the river mouths, which swallow the salmon. This interpretation is supported by many textual references, perhaps the most striking being that of guests who as salmon are swallowed by the host. All supernatural beings of the Kwakiutl cosmos are represented in association with other and parallel phenomena so as to assert their abstract character. The tenor of Kwakiutl imagery is consistently concrete—except for *nawalak*—but when several concrete images are brought into relationship the effect is to generalize. The multiplication of images is, as it were, a rhetorical device for indicating abstractness, but without yielding concreteness. This imagery relies on the mosaic type of vision, like the eye of an insect.

The constant model for Kwakiutl imagery is nature, which endlessly reveals its basic and profound processes through an almost infinite multiplicity of forms. The idea of death as a devourer may be crystallized in Baxbakualanuxsiwae, but is also portrayed in the raven, the crane, the wolf, the grizzly bear, the killer whale, the Dzonoqwas, rivers, humans, and in heaven itself, whose great mouth swallows the sun. Because he is the crystallized form, Man Eater demands the quality of abstractness which a diverseness of portrayal gives to him. Man Eater is unmistakably masculine. He alone is the Great Devourer. His women only procure for him, they do not share in his feast, according to the descriptions. In the Kwakiutl scheme, women are lesser man eaters. The female Dzonoqwa, for example, eats only human children, a minor matter morally, but an important contrast nevertheless to the all-devouring Man Eater. When the *hamatsa* cult came among Kwakiutl the *hamshamtses*, a mere fleshbiter, was relegated to the women. Among dancers, the women do not partake fully of human flesh. Man Eater is always an intermediate being, depicted in myth and in visual arts as hawklike, beastlike, and as humanoid.

While Man Eater is not, and of course cannot be a cannibal (does death consume itself?) he lives within the Kwakiutl imagination as a creator of cannibals. As the personification of devouring, he also provides for the completion of the carnivorous cycle over which he presides. It is doubtful that the Kwakiutl concern is merely with the aesthetics of a completed equation. The ultimate concern of religion is power. When the people have become man-eaters they have risen to the level of Man Eater. They are no longer as sparrow to eagle. Having dissolved the natural hierarchy, so to speak, they are immune from one-sidedness. In all respects, as myth and ritual reveal, men and the Man Eater arrive on the equivalent plane as contenders. One might add that the people transcend the natural hierarchy between supernatural and human beings by an adversary relationship such as exists between the antagonistic moieties of the tribes.

The human beings who have encountered Man Eater and have acquired his powers are also part of his retinue. They represent him and his household on earth, but in a dual capacity, as protagonists and as antagonists. As protagonists, the *hamatsa* dancers complete the carnivorous cycle by becoming genuine cannibals. They also complete the configuration, which finally includes supernatural beings, men and women, earth and sky, monsters or transitional beings, the modalities of devouring and the modalities of antidevouring. Devouring is neither generalized nor focalized. Man Eater and the grizzly bear share human flesh, and the birds of heaven feed on the head, the source of the human spirit. Man Eater pursues men on his own. But that does not suffice. Two women, Qominoqa, and Kinqalatlala procure live human victims for him, as well as corpses. Within his own household he feasts on human flesh. But as incarnated in dancers he is also a devourer of property, that is, animals. He is ultimately the universal devourer.[3] The natural human concern is that he spare people by exercising restraint. But that is no problem, since the restraints of counteractions are imposed by his configuration, as well as by the dual-sidedness of his nature.

Trees and Wood Products. The arboreal world is a third realm of being beyond men. Trees and bushes are not only alive but are considered to be human beings, whose spirits are represented in the Winter Ceremonial (Boas 1921:1220). Trees, cedar and hemlock in particular, have special significance because they are sacred in their own right, and because they are the materials of houses, canoes, boxes, masks, and ceremonial poles. Bark of the red cedar is a direct source of *nawalak* and has been a source of human life as well. If trees are human and alive they belong in a broad category with animals, but of an independent order. As if alive and human, trees cannot be treated as though they were mere materials or substances. They are forms of life that undergo transformations, becoming all other forms. From this point of view, one does not speak of images carved in wood, but of wood transformed. The Kwakiutl concept of the material is somewhat different, however, from that of the Eskimo who speak of discovering the being within a stone. The Kwakiutl do not speak of bringing out what is already there; they convert the wood into desired form. Thus all carvings are presumed to be alive, and many are expressly described as speaking and as snapping their jaws. In myth, houses, carved posts, and other figures of wood always appear as living creatures but, like trees, are rooted in place. The house posts come alive but cannot move. The doorways snap their angry jaws at guests but are stationary like devouring plants. The mythical image remains true to a concept of transformation by fusion. Animals and trees join their forms and qualities. Myth yields to the imagination what reality cannot; myth is always in the background to supplement the impoverished vision of the naked eye. Even so, Kwakiutl graphic art is extraordinarily dynamic and restlessly animate. Masks, lending themselves to such clever manipulation, are made with movable jaws and with outer faces that open to reveal an inner visage.

The tree consists of three vital parts, its outer bark, its planks, and its body or pole. The growing tree in the forest is perhaps a fourth entity. The bark of the yellow cedar is woven into blankets for circulation among commoners. The bark blanket has equivalence with animal skins as the outer covering or "form soul" of the tree. Bark of the red cedar represents a new and indeed a cosmic dimension. The red cedar bark is fashioned into ropes that stand for wealth, and into neck rings that suggest to the Kwakiutl celestial phenonomena. The rings shrink and expand like the moon. Forms of life hang from them and cascade from them. They are the most potent carriers of *nawalak*. The red of the cedar is seen as blood, in the ultimate sense as human blood, but human blood rendered powerful by being in associative form, by being associated with the most remote branch of a generalized human kind, and by its association with a ring, the celestial symbol.

The plank from which almost all of Kwakiutl material culture is derived is considered a gift of the tree. It is formally requested, and then taken from the standing tree. Whatever is fashioned from it—canoes, boxes, houses—is alive, a transformation. The trunk stripped of its bark is converted into pure being, that is into images that are represented in myth as being alive. The planks, which are segments of the whole, also represent beings, but in the aspect of containers, which are the housing of vital properties on the analogy of the body as the "house of the soul." The trunk is transformed into posts and poles, the former as components of a house, as its supports. As wooden posts hold up a house, they also hold up the world (Post of the World) or the heaven. The pole is visualized in still another aspect, the aspect of reaching upward, presumably as a bridge to the sky.

The so-called "cannibal pole,"[4] the insignia of Baxbakualanuxsiwae, the Man Eater, is a smooth mast of cedar some 40 feet tall that projects through the roof of the house. It is wrapped in red cedar bark, the great *nawalak* source, and is fittingly called Healing Woman and Long Life Maker (Boas 1930:105). The names with their obvious shamanistic references, and the red cedar bark wrapping convey the general theme of the Winter Ceremonial as shamanistic ritual. By piercing the roof of the house (container) the pole introduces the ancillary concept of connecting two spatial realms—the Winter Ceremonial house, the temporary locus of spirits who have arrived from another world, and the outside realm from which they have come. I suspect that the Kwakiutl recognize a parallel between the living tree as a repository for corpses and the cannibal pole. The cannibal pole as a passage is explicitly represented in the legend of a boy who is led by a mouse to a cedar tree.

Other mythical elaborations of the cannibal pole represent it as carved with such devourer images as Dzonoqwa, Raven, Hoxhoq, and men. It is also depicted as a rainbow (ibid). The latter depiction establishes the link with the copper poles that are explicitly described as means of passage between heaven and earth. The copper pole is the beam of light down which the sun, moon, and chief of the stars descend. But when the wooden cannibal pole is also described as the Milky Way (Boas 1897:346), a conceptual link has been established between trees and light as bridges between distinct realms.

[193   ]

The potlatch pole *(maxpeq)* is still another form of pole, smaller and contained within the house, but characterized by weight and height as the dimensions of property to be distributed. Legend describes the primordial *maxpeq* as the gift of supernatural beings to humans. Originally it arises out of the sea, that other realm of great gifts for humans, then it is transmitted in marriage as a symbol of the increase of wealth. It makes "property swell in the house," the Kwakiutl say (Boas 1935b:108). Thus when animal skins or even wool blankets are measured against the height of a potlatch pole, the point of view is not that of the shipping clerk. As an increaser of wealth the potlatch pole is to the cannibal pole as wealth itself is to Man Eater.

The Celestial Realm. A fourth realm of beings beyond men is the celestial. The sky realm is a great source of supernatural power. But the celestial beings, the sun, the moon, the stars, and Abalone of the World, a representative of light, are distant and relatively uninvolved with men or with the animal worlds. In their exterior relations the sky beings are represented by mediating spirits, the Thunderbirds and the supernatural avians known collectively as the "birds of heaven." These avians are not, however, autochthonous heaven-dwellers. An interesting concept of interchange places Thunderbird and associated avians as original earth-dwellers who retreated to the sky after a defeat. Animals and humans, who had lived in the upper world, descended to earth. Such interchanges are the very essence of relations among the spatial realms.

The Chief of the Sky has two names, Going from One End of the World to the Other, and Covered with Abalone Shell. He is the father of Sun and Moon, who are of either sex. The abalone shell is also the insignia of the sun. Having no definite form, the Chief of the Sky is one of the few relatively abstract figures in a remarkably concrete and personified universe. He has, of course, the concreteness of gender, chiefship, and fatherhood, but not of form. His abstract qualities are those of moving about the world, a manifestation of energy shared by all the great supernatural beings, and of light as conveyed by the abalone shell image—an interesting conception since the abalone shell is also of the sea and acknowledged as such by the Kwakiutl. Copper, also of the sky and sea, is only indirectly associated with the Sky Chief. The white light of abalone and the red light of copper are components of the spectrum that unites sky and sea.

[194]

In representing the realms of beings we have referred to spatial realms. Each form of being is located either by origin or by conventional habitat within its own spiritual realm. The spatial realms are, of course, fixed, but their inhabitants are mobile, exchanging habitats or, in any case, moving among them. The spatial realms correspond to a natural geography at least in their broad topography. Boas properly warns his readers of inconsistencies in Kwakiutl cosmology. But on the proposition that the world is divided into five parts there is substantial agreement (Boas 1935b:125). Boas's classification derived from all these myths comprises: (1) an upper world, (2) the earth, (3) the world beyond the ocean, (4) the bottom of the sea, and (5) the underworld of the ghosts. The concern of myth is less with topography than with means of access and with acquisitions of treasures. Each spatial realm is a source of treasures and of supernatural powers, which are in some respects distinctive as appropriate to their realm, but are for the most part generalized. Each realm has its own products, and all share common products.

The upper world, Boas tells us, is a country like our own. It has villages and its inhabitants perform the Winter Ceremonial. Much thought has gone into imagining entrances and exits from the upper world. There are the familiar pan-Indian accesses by way of a chain of arrows or by ladder, and there is the egress by a spider thread. A local means of egress is the copper pole. A more decidedly Northwest Coast type of entry is the complex idea of a passage under the sea that leads under a mountain that reaches into the sky. The sea passage requires the ability to dive deep and to stay under water for a long time. It is the shamanistic test of coming to the verge of death to win the reward of a more vigorous life. With respect to the geographic relations of the different realms, the point is made that access to the upper world is also by sea. Entry is through a snapping door, a celestial mouth, a feature incorporated in ceremonial houses that come down from the sky.

The World Beyond the Ocean and the World Under the Ocean are coextensive domains occupied by the same beings. The World Beyond, the far west, is evidently distinguished as the gateway to the sky (ibid:128), presumably the far horizon where sea meets sky. It is also the location of the Post of Heaven, a gathering place for seals, sea lions, whales, and killer whales, as well as for salmon and herring. Both oceanic regions are dominated by Qomogwa (Wealthy), a sea deity reminiscent of the Eskimo Sedna and guardian of wealth. Like the Chief of the

Sky, Qomogwa is also associated with light. He is the maker of copper, which represents simultaneously his salmon and the connecting red light beams between copper and lower worlds. Copper has its place in the sky, but its true locus is the sea. Similarly, the abalone has its place in the sea, while its true locus is in the sky.

There is a certain symmetry between the upper world and the two oceanic worlds. The most striking parallel relationship is in the counterpoint of red copper and white abalone. Each world has also its houses, its snapping doors, its resident beings from other worlds, its own winter ceremonials, its gifts of life and death to those who can enter and go back. Symmetry breaks at one important point: Celestial beings are distant from human beings. Qomogwa kills seal hunters and eats the eyes of human beings the way human beings eat crabapples. The symmetry of feature is incomplete because the sea is conceived of as a transitional zone between upper and lower worlds and thus is seen as closer to humans. Although it is a zone of *nawalak,* and hence an other worldly realm, it is for a maritime people their special zone of active engagement. The symbolic associations between abalone and copper illustrate most succinctly the pattern of relationship between the sky world and the two ocean realms. In the active life of ritual and of ritual exchange, only the copper is fully active. It is only the copper that ramifies richly into diverse and living images. Abalone is, by contrast, both remote and stable, appropriate to the distant figure of a formless Chief of the Sky.

The oceanic worlds and the world of humans and animals are understandably kin, as the prime zones of energetic living beings. By comparison, the underworld of the ghosts is cognate in abstractness with the sky. The sky was a habitat before people became human. The underworld is their habitat after they have left their humanness. In a similar pattern of opposition, in their primordial state in the sky, human beings had human substance but no human form.

In their postprimordial state in the underworld, the ghosts of humans have human form but not human substance. The underworld is generally a region of reversal. Its day, for example, is the human night. It is a linear world, conceivably imagined on the lines of a river whose source is a place both of powers and of dangers. A journey up a river has the mystical equivalence of the deep dive into a lake; each leads to an ultimate divide. In the underworld are four villages spaced in a line from the boundaries of the world of living mortals. The underworld may be safely visited, but whoever reaches the fourth village cannot return. Thus, only the underworld is a terminus where substance is lost and only form remains.

Nevertheless, like the rest of the world it is a zone of wealth. The Chief of the Ghosts is apparently a counterpart of the Chief of the Sea. He is called Wealth Coming Up (ibid:131). The wealth of the sea is obvious, but not that of the underworld. Yet the text of a ghost song of the Winter Ceremonial says:

> Now ghosts go all to that upper world
> For great is your wealth in the ground ghosts
> For great is your fire and many your hot stoves, ghosts.

(Boas 1897:409)

While there is no self-evident explanation in the Kwakiutl texts of the nature of ghostly wealth, the meaning of the song is clear enough: Wealth and fire are the means for the restoration of life. The wealth of the ghosts seems to be nothing more nor less than their gift of returning the dead to life. The fire is for Kwakiutl a property destroyer and a death bringer. For ghosts, however, fire is the source of wealth and nourishment, for they live only on what is ritually consumed in fire, hence the ritual destruction of property and fish oil. The ritual principle is clear: Ghosts and human beings also live by interchange. If humans give of their wealth to the ghosts who share their banquets, the ghosts must have wealth to sustain their equity in the religious transaction. By the logic of exchange, ghostly wealth is the gift of resurrection, and thus analogous to all Kwakiutl wealth as a form of life and renewal.

Finally, what Kwakiutl call "Our World" is also zoned. The beaches are the human zone and became so after humans had divested themselves of their animal masks. Before, the primordial animals possessed the beaches. As humans and animals exchanged their forms they also exchanged their habitats. The forested mountain interior is of our world, but a distinct zone of it, a magical realm of animal and intermediate form spirits.

The Kwakiutl concept of cosmological worlds and of realms of beings serves to define the distribution of *nawalak*, and poses the problems of its acquisition. Supernatural power, to repeat an earlier observation, must come from an outside realm, from an outer cosmological zone or from another type of being. This principle of acquisition is pervasive and fundamental. It lies at the foundation of Kwakiutl lineage exogamy, of ritual exchange and antagonism, and it lies at the heart of the shamanistic Winter Ceremonial. I speak of this principle of acquisition as Kwakiutl only out of regard for the circumscribed focus of this book. In fact, we are dealing with a Kwakiutl version of a universal principle of acquisition of powers.

To state the principle more concretely, for Kwakiutl the available supernatural powers are both specific and general. Animals, for example, give a power that is inherent in their own nature: beavers give their industriousness, grizzly bears their fierceness. Animals offer themselves as a comprehensive gift; they give their flesh, their form, their specific nature. Spirit beings cannot give their flesh, but they can give their specific natures.

Transfers of power. Powers link donor and receiver, and ultimately interlace all classes of beings and all cosmological zones. If the Kwakiutl have indeed in mind a grand conception of linking together all the disparate parts of their universe, the responsibility for carrying out the plan falls on their chiefs. In the religious sense, the chiefs are the assemblers, the concentrators, and the managers of supernatural powers. Their first ancestors began the task and each generation repeats it. We can appreciate the concrete significance of their accomplishment by means of one especially meaningful example—salmon fishing. The salmon, a Winter Ceremonial song says, come ashore for the *nawalak* of the house: "You have supernatural power. Therefore the chief of the salmon came from beyond the ocean" (Boas 1897:475). This expressive text brings out the cyclical character of the power quest. The human chiefs go out into alien realms and deal with alien beings to accumulate *nawalak*, and to concentrate it in the ceremonial house. When they have become centers of *nawalak* the salmon come to them. The power to draw the salmon to one's house is equated with the power to draw people.[5] The power to attract derives from *nawalak* and demonstrates its possession. Some supernatural beings in the oceanic worlds originally gave *nawalak* to humans. When the Salmon Chief arrives, the exchange, we are led to assume, is completed. In exchanges of *nawalak* and in the collections of the treasures that promote the increase of life and property, the human being is the actively energetic agent. He is the primary intruder into other worlds—though not the only one—the primary collector, and ultimately the central unifier or perhaps the only reunifier of the universe of life. The great chief who can assemble the tribes into his own house has corresponding powers and responsibilities on a cosmic scale.

In mythical time all powers, general and specific, were transmitted through a personal encounter with the supernatural owner. Later, by recapitulating the original encounter, ritual sustains, though surely on a reduced level, these original powers. In myth, the encounter is with a true being from another realm. In ritual, the simulated encounter is with other human beings who assume the roles of the original supernatural protagonists. People cannot, and probably do not, hope to recapture or to reinstate the pristine events that are described in myth. Nor will religious believers allow their rituals to degenerate into mere symbolism or metaphor. Religion can be reduced neither to aesthetic experience nor to formal logic. It is either a belief in the reality of powers, beings, and forces that constitute the nature of the universe, or it is nothing. Thus religious ritual is not so real as that which happened in the beginning, but within a firmly held concept of gradation it has its own reality. The ritual actors are not Baxbakualanuxsiwae, but neither are they ordinary people. The ritual encounters transform the human actors in a manner parallel to the original encounters in myth time, but they do so on a lower level. Transformation is the means of transmitting supernatural powers both at the pristine levels of myth and at the secondary levels of current ritual.

Nawalak and *tlogwe* are actual powers, and one might imagine a mode of mechanical transmission from donor to receiver. The Kwakiutl idea, in anticipation of Martin Buber, is that important transactions transform the participants. Receivers of powers become new beings; they become like their patron, the donor who gives them simultaneously the powers, name, and crest which is their form soul. The vision quest of North American Indians is predicated on a similar principle of transformation. The visionary enters the world of the supernatural protector and is adopted as a child. The adopted son of Eagle is not a true eagle, but he is of the eagle category, and is entitled to the privileges and powers pertaining to eagle kinship. Kwakiutl do not visualize the relationship in terms of blood kinship, but insofar as a name and crest accompany the powers a kinship concept in the broad sense is involved. The Kwakiutl stress is on affinal kinship, so that donor and receiver are in the position of in-laws, if not literally then figuratively. Boas was struck by the characteristic transmission of names and rights in myth through marriage rather than through linear descent. The 23-generation Gwasela genealogy, like other family histories, is a record of marriages. And the record of marriages is a record of acquisitions and transmissions of powers. Hence, the relationship between a man and his father-in-law is, among Kwakiutl, parallel to that between a seeker and his donor of supernatural powers.

Transformation. Powers are not altogether independent of beings, but are attributes of beings. To receive the attribute one must also become in some measure the source being. In all Kwakiutl rituals the persons who display their powers present themselves simultaneously as their supernatural donors. Thus they have become dual beings, as indeed they were at the beginning. They retain their human and their lineage substance, and by means of mask, song, and dance, the new substance and attributes of the original donor add to it. What occurs is not a total transformation, but a masking transformation; it is always known that another human being is beneath the mask. For the supernatural donor, the benefit is as for all beings in the universe, the privilege of entering and being received in an outer realm. The privilege of being in another's house is, so to speak, like the privilege of a tree to broaden and deepen its roots.

As does all mankind, Kwakiutl recognize transformation as a fundamental natural process. They have gone beyond direct empirical observations—eggs transformed into birds and fish, for example—to the profound comprehension common to religious and scientific thinkers of an underlying unity of organic life. Kwakiutl call the common substance human, an anthropocentrism, no doubt, but still a statement of consubstantiality. To visualize speciated form as mask or covering is not to underestimate its significance, but in the finest Darwinian tradition, to assert motion and change. The Kwakiutl tradition, however, unlike that of Indians of the Southwest or of Mexico, is not evolutionary in the linear sense. Their thought has moved in another direction, to demonstrate that the unity of life is both given from the beginning and sustained by human action. The common substance is the given. The interchangeability of forms—implying an ultimate sharing of all properties—is the product of active agencies. Active agents, who are human, animal, and supernatural, but not vegetable, are represented as acting by will, by choice, even to the point of going against the rules, as when youths seeking supernatural powers invariably ignore parental warnings. But even as the Kwakiutl impute conscious will and choice to their protagonists they leave no doubt as to the imperatives of transformation and interchange.

Transformation within a configuration that includes exchanges and circulation of forms and powers is perhaps the central idea of Kwakiutl religious thought. It is the leading motif in myth. Even when the point of the narrative is acquisition of *nawalak* or *tlogwe,* its content is transformation. Transformation is central to the Winter Ceremonial and to rituals of marriage, of distribution and exchange, and finally to the life cycle from birth to death. Rank is, for the Kwakiutl, also a transformational phenomenon.

The great Kwakiutl theme of devouring is also in a transformational setting. Man Eater embodies the ultimate transformation, represented as a double transformation, in the Kwakiutl tradition that killers are life-givers. The perpetrators of the injury have the remedy. The transformation is double in a double sense. The beings are transformed from life to death and back to life, and the destroyer of lives is transformed into a giver of life. The continuity of life depends on the reliability of this ultimate transformation. It is not difficult to imagine, following Kwakiutl lines of thought, how in the absence of a dialectic of transformation into opposites the universe of life would soon drain away. I venture the belief that forebodings of entropy underlie Kwakiutl religious philosophy. In the concept of transformation generally, and in its ultimate version as transformation into opposites, they have achieved as have all religions a credible and optimistic answer.

The metaphor of the devourer as life-giver has received spectacular artistic elaboration in Kwakiutl imagination. The devouring mouth is a reasonable image for hunters, but none to my knowledge have gone so far with it as the Indians of the Northwest Coast. In Kwakiutl thought, the sky itself appears as the great mouth of heaven that swallows the sun. At eclipse it is asked to disgorge its mouthful with cries of Vomit! Vomit! The imagery of devouring as a phase of a cycle that is always dual is most intimately connected with the inevitable observation that one form of life devours other forms of life, but life is always restored. In scientific thought the life cycle is formulated as multiphasic and complex. In Kwakiutl religious thought, the cycle is compressed to its absolute fundamentals. The imagery is at once concrete, vividly affective, and in its compression generalized and abstract enough to

[201   ]

stand for a cosmic principle. But the principle that devourer is life-giver introduces its own complexity, thus avoiding a simplified and unreal equation of devouring being offset by sexual reproduction. The ideas of interchange, of circulation, of transformation into diverse forms as well as into opposites, imply a general concept of ecological balances, which includes sexual reproduction.

By associating marriage with the transmission of spirit names of the Winter Ceremonial, and with such valuable complementary properties as coppers, canoes, boxes, and dishes, the Kwakiutl have established a conceptual configuration that sets forth sharply and distinctly their ecological metaphysics. The essential idea behind marriage, for Kwakiutl and for all of traditionalist mankind, is that sexual reproduction should not be isolated as a mode of life renewal but set within an accurate context that reveals the issues of renewal more completely and more realistically. Hence, marriages are accompanied by exchanges, not of goods in the bourgeois mercantile sense of wealth, but of forms and attributes of life. They are accompanied by kinship structures that must bind together root systems that were originally separate. The Kwakiutl system of marriage is unusual in the primitive world only in its comprehensiveness; the acquisition of a bride is comparable to the primary acquisition of powers in myth time. The Winter Ceremonial is the post of Kwakiutl religion. And in the Winter Ceremonial, the shamanistic cult reaches beyond the immediacies of healing to the more metaphysical realms of social resurrections. It is difficult to name another cultural tradition in which a bride brings to her husband a greater cargo of treasures. The bride is progenetrix as a woman, and is simultaneously the means by which the metaphysics of transformation is put to work for mankind.

The transmission of religious cargoes is actually a complex process within which the bride is a crucial but not necessarily a paramount component. Again we remind ourselves that Kwakiutl religious thought is never simplistically reductive. Each active element is clearly revealed within its context, within its organic matrix. The contextual intricacy of marriage is typical of all Kwakiutl religious institutions. To recapitulate in compressed form:

1. The groom is elevated through a series of transformations to a status or state of being at which he has the necessary power to acquire new powers.

2. His father, his lineage, and his tribesmen contribute the sum of their supernatural powers.
3. The bride has correspondingly been elevated.
4. The father-in-law and his lineage and tribesmen assemble their powers.
5. The bride is "moved" by supernatural powers from her fixed place in her father's house.
6. Through his son a man has acquired treasures from an outer realm.
7. Through his daughter a man has acquired entrance into another realm for his lineage.
8. The children of the marriage are linked to twin channels for names and powers.

Transmission is indeed through the bride who symbolizes the totality of powers. No transmission would be possible, however, without all other participants (see, for example, the purely secular marriages of commoners). Nor does the Winter Ceremonial operate without lineage and rank.

Sexuality.   The sexual factor is acknowledged biologically. Eroticism, judging by the texts, has no evident role in public ritual. It is a factor, though, in hunting. Coitus is a helpful preliminary in ordinary hunting, but interdicted in hunting or fishing for sacred animals. Sexual intercourse, in other words, is an intensely human act. It can attract animals who ordinarily enter into the human realm; it will prevent humans from entering into other realms. Entrance into a nonhuman realm demands "purity," a condition of being appropriate to the nonhuman world. For Kwakiutl, purity is largely the hunter's awareness of how shy animals are of human odor. Since purification generally calls for elimination of the human odor through bathing and anointing with the smell of hemlock, there may be reason to imagine that it is the odors of sex, of body sweat and sexual secretions, that disturb the supernatural kingdoms. However, there is an explicit antagonism between sexual intercourse and Winalagilis, the spirit of war, which suggests a more fundamental incompatibility—that is, a conviction as to the utter separateness of actions that conceive life and actions that cause death. All mankind shares this conviction, and in all rites of death and mourning there is at some point an interdiction of sexual intercourse. Sexual intercourse is forbidden during the Winter Ceremonial specifically because the participants are living with and as supernatural beings. Thus the concept of life renewal or of resurrection in these rites is defined as asexual. As it is the bride who is the source of the Winter Ceremonial, we encounter again the familiar Kwakiutl dialectic. In this instance, the woman is associated with both modes of renewal, the sexual and the asexual.

By quantitative standards, the Winter Ceremonial would be described as a male cult. Women impersonated certain leading spirits, the Toxwid, the *hamshamtses,* or Man Eater of the Woods, and they were part of the *hamatsa* ensemble. Nevertheless, men were so preeminent, as Boas noticed, that we may view the ceremonial order as designed around a masculine center, just as the lineage order was structured around a patrilineal core. It is characteristic of Kwakiutl structures that they avoid the sociologist's dream of clear-cut binary oppositions in favor of the naturalist's perceptions of rough edges in the organic world. The maleness of the female-brought Winter Ceremonial reflects the outward orientation of masculine activity. In most instances it is the men who go out into outer realms, to bring back powers and wives. The Winter Ceremonial is a close model of this double going out. Thus in the balance between masculine and feminine roles in the Winter Ceremonial, the female as focal in introducing the ceremonial is set on one side, the male as focal in impersonating the spirits on the other.

It is a fair assumption that as biological nature is largely bisexual, all cultures constructed on natural models will sustain a symbolic balance between the sexes. The balances being conceptual rather than mechanical are not obvious by standards of an alien culture. By what criteria then does one weigh the relative importance of each sex to a culture? There is no reason to assume the Kwakiutl weigh the sexes in a balance. They are meticulous in pairing and in setting forth their complementary equivalent characteristics.

As in nature, the sexes are opposed complements in limited respects only. As mothers, as wives, and as sisters, women have roles equivalent to the male partner. The mother is a name giver to her children, the sister acquires rank at her first menses, the wife is a property giver to other women, as her husband is to men. Women have position as Sparrows and as Seals in the Winter Ceremonial. Symbolic gender oppositions relate mainly to fundamental ideas about the separation between sexual and asexual powers. Death and resurrection, as I have observed repeatedly, must be disassociated from sexual intercourse, perhaps because they represent movements in opposite directions: birth as a movement into the human world; death as movement out. Thus the *hamatsa* dancer who, as cannibal, devours persons cannot be a woman who emits persons. She has two symbolically important roles, one as feeder or procuress for Man Eater, and another as tamer, a role shared with male shamans. "Taming" is for Kwakiutl a ritual act of restoring a person to the human realm after that person had been transformed into an other-worldy supernatural being. In the special case of the *hamatsa,* who is the farthest out, "taming" requires a tandem force. It requires the force of the shaman, an expert in the orphic voyage, and of a woman, whose sexual nature as progenetrix and as partner in coitus introduces and also restores persons to the secular world.

Kwakiutl myth insists on recognizing parallels between men and women; there are examples of women going out into the supernatural world like men. The focus is on complementary relations. Women are an initial source of coppers, men transmit them secondarily. The man sings the ancestral song, his sister dances it. His is the ancestral voice, hers an invocation of the ancestral form. Finally, the men as authentic chiefs stand for the core of a lineage. Women as wives and as chieftainesses stand for their equally essential collateral lineages.

Shamanism.   The shamanistic is that aspect of chiefs that reaches through the Winter Ceremonial into the worlds of spirits and brings back *nawalak* to sustain the lineage, again by collateral powers. The shaman is the winter guise of chiefs. As winter is the sacred season, the shaman image completes the total image of sanctity of chiefs. Chiefs have initial sanctity as primary figures and as incarnations of ancestors. Initial sanctity is no more complete than is bachelorhood. One recognizes a triangular concept of a chief's sanctity: his lineage sources, his sources in marriage, his sources in shamanism. In the history of the male these three sources develop in chronological sequence. He reaches chiefly stature, he marries, and he acquires for himself and for his children Winter Ceremonial rights. Thus, if we consider Kwakiutl religion, as in fact we must, as a branch of those North American Indian religions absorbed in the shamanistic cult, we might think of all ritual elevation events preceding that stage of the Winter Ceremonial when a chief is an initiator of the young as an elaborate set of preliminaries to becoming a shaman on a cosmic scale. A structural parallel exists between the sequence of events leading to shamanism on a cosmic scale among the

Kwakiutl and the *Midewiwin* of the Ojibwa. Among Kwakiutl, however, marriage is a crucial stage in the graded initiations into the highest realms of power.

As I have said before, the cosmic shaman and the curing shaman share the same generic term *(paxala)*, but are distinct socially as well as functionally. Unless he has been born to a noble family, the ordinary curing shaman is only a lower-order mystic. His powers, however, allow him to "give potlatches" (Boas 1935b:40). The privilege accorded a commoner shaman to distribute wealth demonstrates rather conclusively that the issue in ritual exchange is not rank as such, but supernatural powers.

Historically, the Kwakiutl shamanistic cult with its triple links to curing, chiefship, and life renewal belongs to the widespread shamanistic configuration reaching from eastern Siberia down to the American Southwest (Eliade 1964). Many tribes have extended the powers of the shaman from curing, divining, and weather control into broader reaches. Among Eskimo the shaman dealt with global matters by taming storms, by inducing the goddess of the sea to release the sea mammals, and by restoring natural balances interrupted by breaches of the supernatural order. On the Plains the shamanic cult entered into and evolved along with the integrated religious complex of vision quest, sun dance, and warfare. In breadth and complexity of integration, the Plains pattern was comparable to that of the Kwakiutl.

Conceivably the entire religious complex of the Kwakiutl grew out of a more elementary core of arctic and subarctic shamanism. But even if Kwakiutl religion was assembled from heterogeneous sources, the final configuration achieved masterful integration—an extraordinary intellectual feat of synthesis on the part of the Indian savants. The central ideas of shamanism have been identified by Eliade (ibid). They include mystical ecstasy, the approach to death, journeys into other cosmic realms, spirit combats (antagonism), transformations, and the designation of the shamans as a chosen elite. Shamanism is characteristically involved in the animal world, especially among North American Indians. The animal is the source of connection with other worlds, a necessary intermediary in the language of Lévi-Straussian structuralism, between men and their sources.

The animal links have been brilliantly formulated by the Indians of the Northwest Coast. On the Plains, among Eskimo, and in the Northeaster Woodlands the basic and primary connection with the animal is through the vision. If Kwakiutl began with this elementary mystical experience, they finally transformed it into a more massive structure within which the elements of personal ecstasy were coordinated with and, I believe, subordinated to a metaphysics of endless interchanges among men, animals, and generalized supernatural beings. Among Kwakiutl, the primary animal connection was with the ancestor, the source of initial powers with which the outward journeys, the supernatural encounters and antagonisms, the sequential accumulation of powers from other sources, the transformation of death to life, and the circulation of animal form souls was begun. The ecstasy of the Winter Ceremonial dancer was for the Kwakiutl a climactic act, the initial experience with the animal intermediaries. Boas recognized how profoundly the Kwakiutl had modified the vision quest from an achieved to an inherited experience. The distinction is subjectively important. The religious principle remains constant. Either way, the shaman is a member of a chosen elite. Even among relatively egalitarian Eskimo the shaman is the elementary model of aristocracy.

Nature and Culture.   Kwakiutl savants share with the academic world an enthusiasm for discovering first principles. Like ourselves they proceed by analogy so as to explain all in terms of one manageable part. Academics, who have shaped their thought to the mechanical imagery of an industrial age, start from the premise that they can explain the organic by analogy with the inorganic. Kwakiutl, like all "savages" reared in the organic world of living things, start from the opposite premise. They seek to explain nature by analogy with the organic. When their analogies go beyond the organic world they play them false, just as ours do when we "explain" persons and cultures by the inappropriate imagery of mechanical processes. When Kwakiutl portray the sun as a living being, like a human, they are in the same intellectual trap of doctrinaire monism as the anthropologists who describe culture as though it were a mechanical system, a computer regulating a machine.

Regardless of the pits into which they may sooner or later fall, all serious thinkers search for the deeper and pervasive realities. Kwakiutl thought, which is as critically self-conscious as our own, seeks its reality in the natural world—in the life of animals and plants, in seasonal periodicities, in the growth and life cycle of individuals, in sensory phenomena, in the continuity of species, in the regularities of transformations, in the hierarchies of weakness and strength, in antagonisms and friendships, in gender, in birth and death, in the complexities of life renewal. The Kwakiutl have represented all natural phenomena as interconnected in obedience to preordained law. They have also allowed for will, for human agency, and they have not ignored the unpredictable, the indeterminate, and the apparently chaotic in life.

Kwakiutl seek to know the laws of their world for the same reasons we do: to know how to live within it. To a Durkheim, reared in the anthropocentric tradition of the Old Testament, it was easy to imagine that "primitive" people projected their own natures onto the rest of nature. It is far more likely that Homo sapiens sought to understand himself and all other realms of nature through a dialectic of interchange, of understanding the outer world in terms of his own nature and his own nature in terms of the outer. If Kwakiutl attribute human qualities to the grizzly bear, they have also learned to define and to regulate their own qualities of physical strength and fearlessness in terms of their knowledge of the bear. In the outer world, each segment of life is a portion of the totality of existence. Each portion is a vital property and a segment of the totality of vital powers, vital to know and vital to possess or control. Kwakiutl do not merely project themselves on the outer world. They seek to incorporate it. Durkheimian anthropocentrism must imagine all religious thought concerning animals and other nonhuman forms of life as symbol and metaphor for human affairs, as though nothing outside of the human could have weighty existence on its own.

Kwakiutl consider the human substance the standard for all life. In postulating a human-based consubstantiality they do not however convert the animal world into a Disneyland of mock characters. They attribute to animals speech, concern for interchange, and Winter Ceremonials—but also distinct and secret lives. What the Kwakiutl project upon animals is not by any means their whole being or their whole social character. They project upon them only human speech and susceptibility to social intercourse, without which their theory of interdependence through a certain mutuality of interests would be difficult to sustain. In turn, they use the animals' songs, dances, whistles, masks, and other devices to make themselves intelligible to them.

How cultures achieve shape and conceptual coherence is still in the realm of unanswered questions. Ruth Benedict (1934) who asked the question about Kwakiutl, answered it in the familiar anthropocentric tradition of the Western academic: Each culture unconsciously selects for elaboration some segment of the arc of human nature. Benedict's view of culture and its intellectual elaborations is in the Freudian tradition, which views religion, in particular, as a system of unconscious projections of psychic ambivalence. In the positivist tradition of functionalism, religious thought has been regarded as little more than a curiosity, once its "function" as adaptive or maladaptive, as the case may be, has been set forth. The content and the architecture of religious thought strikes functionalists as irrelevant to the grand design of adaptation. Even Lévi-Strauss, who more than anyone has brought the "savage mind" onto the exalted heights of the philosopher's Parnassus, has been preoccupied with the innate structures of the human mind to the neglect of the majestic integrative achievements of any particular "savage" tradition. Thus we as students are left with the impression that cultures and their great traditions are shaped by forces beyond direct access to the human intellect and outside of human will.

Can the anthropological theorist justifiably deny theoretical insight to his subjects? Kwakiutl, like all other tribesmen, are also theorists. They have constructed a culture on their perception of natural phenomena and on their understanding of how the natural order works. Not unlike professional theorists they have also drawn upon the unconscious resources of the mind, and upon its innate structures. In their desire to know the natural order and to understand their place within it, they are indeed the architects of their own destiny, and their culture is a personal and collective creation.

APPENDICES

APPENDIX 1   TRIBAL CENSUS: 1836–1841

TRIBE	POPULATION	SLAVES	HOUSES
Gwasela	117	n.a.	6
Kwakiutl	1370	60	40
Mamaleleqala	1990	40	40
Tlawitsis	2450	40	50
Matilpe	2450	40	50
Nimkish	1990	40	40
Qomkyutis	320	20	10
Dzawadenox	950	50	20
Qweqsotenox	950	50	20
Haxuamis	950	50	20
Nakwaxdax	1990	40	40
Denaxdax	950	40	20

Source: Adapted from Curtis 1915:304.

APPENDIX 2   GWASELA FAMILY HISTORY

The narrative is chanted by a Gwasela woman.

Haha hana ne! Now that I come to think of my forefathers, the passed, and also my great grandfathers. Now I will sing the stories that I was a chief in the beginning of this our world. (Hunt ms.)

Haha hana ne! [Yaqatlenala Property on Body] *went about spouting. He was my chief in the beginning of the world. He travelled about in his canoe, a whale; for he was a whale, the ancestor of my people, the Gwasela; and he went in to* [Negetl an inlet]. *He saw that there was a good beach, and he went ashore there; and* [Yaqatlenala] *built a house and came out of his whale-body. Now the whale-canoe of* [Yaqatlenala] *lay crosswise on the beach. Then* [Yaqatlenlis] *gave a name to the village, and called it* [Gweqelis].

Yaqatlenala travels southward and comes to Padzo, where the whale lands in the middle of the beach. He builds a house 10 steps deep, and closes the mouth of the river. Then he changes his name to Stranded Whale (Tsextsexulis). A canoe with a man, his wife, and a pretty girl arrive. The visitor introduces himself as Sentle, explaining that his village is in the world above, and introduces his wife and daughter. At once Stranded Whale asks to marry the girl "so that our names may be really together" (Boas 1921:837). They are married at once, and Sentle gives his son-in-law two names. "And this," says the narrator, "was the first name obtained in marriage by my ancestor the chief" (ibid:838).

A son is born and receives a name from his mother's father, and from his own father another name and the 10-step house.

Yaqatlenala (bearing now the new name received from his father-in-law) travels south, leaving behind his wife and child. Before leaving he gives the whale canoe to his father-in-law as food. When the latter cuts blubber from the whale he acquires a new name for himself and for his daughter.

Yaqatlenala arrives among the Nimkish and marries the chief's daughter, giving his traveling canoe as bride-price. His father-in-law gives him the following: speaking posts of the house, name of the house, a personal name, four house dishes—Seal, Wolf, Dzonoqwa, Beaver—10 sea otter

Source: Adapted from Boas 1921:836–891 and from Hunt's original manuscript.

blankets, 25 marten blankets, 20 black bear blankets, and 50 seals with which to feed a guest tribe, the Nenelkenox, at the wedding feast. After the feast all the blankets are given away and the narrator says, "This was the first time that property was given away with a feast of seals in house-dishes, and this was the first time that the Gwasela made a potlatch at the time of a feast" (ibid:841).

Haha hanane! Therefore I feel like laughing at what the lower chiefs say when they try to claim higher rank than what I have—I, who had in the beginning an ancestor who was a chief who gave away property at a feast.

A daughter is born, and the child's maternal grandmother, giving the marriage gift, invites the Nenelkenox to receive animal skin blankets. The maternal grandfather gives a name, and the father matches with a name from his side. The narrator comments: "Therefore I am Nimkish on one side, an account of my ancestor the chief who had married among the Kwakiutl" (ibid:842).

Haha hanane! Therefore I am known by all the tribes all over this world, and only the chief my ancestor gave away property in a great feast, and therefore they only try to imitate me. They try to imitate the chief, my grandfather, who is the root of my family. (ibid)

The Gwasela history covers 23 generations of marriages and of acquisitions through marriage of names and privileges. It registers virtually all property distributions associated with marriage gifts and the presentation of names. The common refrain after each notable accomplishment is like the following:

Therefore I am full of names and of privileges. And therefore I have many chiefs as ancestors all over the world; and therefore I feel like laughing at what is said by the lower chiefs, when they claim to belong to the chief, my ancestor. (ibid:844)

Although the viewpoint is unabashedly invidious, there are no examples in the history of rivalrous exchange or of shifts in rank. The concern is mainly with the firstborn; other children are mentioned only as they receive names.

APPENDIX 3   TEXTS ON COMMONERS

These are rare texts concering commoner families and lineages. Although recorded by Hunt after 1916, they unquestionably reveal traditional Kwakiutl opinions on social class. The first is a history of the Laxsa, a lineage of the Qomoyaye tribe. For the full text see Boas 1921:1093–1104.

> I shall begin with [Tlotlotsa] *the poor one who helped* [i.e., worked for Omaxtalatle] *when they lived in the village* [Kaga]. *Nobody knows where* [Tlotlotsa] *came from. He would have been chief on account of his supernatural treasure, the canoe found on the river* [Geyox]*, but he just gave it to* [Omaxtalatle] *when he first came home sitting in the hunting-canoe, which he obtained as a supernatural treasure from Blue-Grouse. Then* [Tlotlotsa] *was foolish, and he was only the steersman of* [Omaxtalatle]. *He never became rich, for he was made unlucky by the hunting-canoe which he obtained as a supernatural treasure. He only continued skinning sea otters which were speared by* [Omaxtalatle] *and only was looking on when* [Omaxtalatle] *invited all the villages in the bay of* [Tsaxis] (Fort Rupert).

The narrative continues with Tlotlotsa's courtship of a slave woman, Tsetle, and their marriage after her pregnancy. The narrator says:

> *and* [Tlotlotsa] *did not marry his wife* [Tsetle] *in the formal way. This is called an illegitimate marriage* [sticking together]. *Now* [Tsetle] *gave birth to a boy, and* [Tlalaxsendayo] *was ashamed of what had been done by his slave Tsetle. He thought about the name which he was to give to* [Tlotlotsa]. *Then he gave him* [Nenologeme] *as a marriage name for* [Tlotlotsa] *and also* [Tlespegaak] *for the name of his child.* [Tlalaxsendayo] *just invented these two names. Now* [Nenologeme] *wished to remain with* [Tlalaxsendayo]. (ibid:1094)

The two live with their new master, Tlalaxsendayo, who names their new children with invented names and gives a new name, also made up, to the slave woman. The eldest child, the son Tlespegaak, grows up prudent and has property. He wishes to distribute property to the chiefs at Kaqa. The text resumes:

> *As soon as they came into the house of* [Tlalaxsendayo,] [walas Kwaxilanokume] *felt sick at heart when he saw* [Tlotlotsa,] *who had now the name* [Nenologeme]*, who formed now a great tribe with his children; for* [walas Kwaxilanokume] *had given* [Nenologeme] *to* [Tlalaxsendayo] *to be his slave. And then* [Tlalaxsen-

dayo] *said that* [Nenologeme] *and his children should now form another tribe. And the name of that tribe was* [Elgunwe] *beginning that day. . . . Now* [Tlespegaak] *gave away property to his guests. And then* [Tlespegaak] *said that he would change his name, and he said his name would be* [Gexkenis]. *He did not get the name* [Gexkenis] *from any place. He only thought that he was a chief because he invited the tribe from* [Kaqa]. *But they cannot wipe off their ancestors: his father* [Tlotlotsa] *and his mother Tsetle had been slaves . . . It is a great disgrace to the numaym* [Elgunwe] *that both were slaves.* (ibid:1095–1096)

The narrative shifts to a sister of Gexkenis, who becomes the sweetheart of Tsagilak, the fifth son of the chief of the Haayalikawe lineage. Of this young man the narrator says: "for the youngest one is never taken care of by his father, there being five sons and he was like a slave and a dog" (ibid:1097–1098). These never marry. They bear an illegitimate son and found a new lineage called Laxsa. "And therefore the people of the numaym are ashamed of the name Laxsa, for Tsagilak was the youngest of the children of Haxoyoseme, the head chief of the numaym Haayalikawe of the Qomoyaye" (ibid:1099).

The final incident in this doleful history is in the tragic mode for the aristocrats, but a triumph, though small, for the aspiring commoner. It concerns the unwitting marriage of a lineage chief to a woman of no rank. The daughter of Tsagilak, now grown, is wed to her uncle, her father's eldest brother, chief of his lineage, and innocently ignorant of his new wife's antecedents. When their son is born he gives him a chiefly name. But Tsagilak knows and is "happy because he had fooled his eldest brother, and because he had obtained the true name . . . for his grandchild" (ibid:1099–1100). When the facts come out the old chief, the father of Tsagilak, dies of shame. The transfer of the chiefly name, a real name, is irreversible, however, and enters the roster as the name of the head chief of the Laxsa. The narrator concludes about Laxsa:

They have no privileges because nobody allowed the sons (of the Laxsa) to marry the princesses of the chiefs of the tribes; for only that way do the chiefs of the tribes obtain privileges. The [Laxsa] *are called "slaves-born-from-the-youngest-one," and here the one who told me the story stopped. He said that he was ashamed to talk about the clan* [Laxsa] *because* [Tsagilak] *just made up the names.* (ibid:1104)

The second text is called "The Elgunwe" (ibid:1104–1117) and concerns a lineage of the Gwetela. Some of the persons of low ancestry mentioned in the Laxsa history are in this narrative shown to be the ancestors of the Elgunwe. Gexkenis, the son of Tlotlotsa the "slave," is stated to be the head chief of Elgunwe. According to the previous text, his sister's son was founder of the Laxsa. The two low lineages are related as, of course, are all lineages and tribes. Like the other, this is a history of illegitimate children, of bad marriages, of invented names, but also of aspirations to rank that do not work out.

The period is postcontact; and the incidents in this brief family history are set in the social confusions of a changing order. A man of low rank tries to acquire rank by giving an oil feast to chiefs financed by earnings from Franz Boas. And the chiefs put him down. The history enlightens us on the new social prospects for those without rank in the postcontact period. Unlike the Gwasela narrative, a fully traditional chant, this family record reveals domestic intricacies. The daughter of a chief falls in love with a commoner, and overcomes opposition to marry him.

The Elgunwe lineage, beginning with slave and commoner ancestry, and growing in population through illegitimate marriages, finally achieves a genuine name through the marriage of a chief's daughter to the commoner Hayatlkin. The marriage takes place after her father's death. Since she is the only child, she assumes her father's name and becomes the lineage chief. She gave a chief's name to her husband along with her father's copper. The narrator remarks:

> *Now* [Hayatlkin] *had obtained a chief's name, and he was no longer called* [Hayatl-kin], *because he obtained by good luck the real name* [Wanuk]. *And now he had the name* [Wanuk]; *for now he invited all the tribes with the price of the copper* [Lobetlila]. *Now it was just as though* [Wanuk] *had taken away the copper from the father of his wife . . .* (ibid:1112)

Later Wanuk inherits a copper from a deceased prostitute, a Kwa-kiutl woman, and sells it for 5000 woolen blankets. With these he invites the tribes and takes the name of her father, Wagides. "Then the heart of Wagides was proud because he was spoken to as a chief by all the chiefs of all the tribes. And in the feast his seat was among the real chiefs" (ibid). His luck continues. He befriends an ailing chief, and immediately inherits from him another copper, which he sells, and invites the tribes. He even sits among all the chiefs of the tribes when they are invited for the chief's feast. At this point he has gone too far.

[217   ]

Then the chief [walas Kwaxilanokume] *became angry. Then the chief* [walas Kwaxilanokume] *said that he would put him back into the place of the slaves his forefathers. Thus he said. Then he took the expensive copper named* [Qemtsaxsde] *and broke it, and he asked one man to throw the copper into the sea outside the village* [Qalogwis]. (ibid:1115)

He breaks three coppers and throws them into the sea, to a value of 39,000 blankets.

Then [Wagides] *became a slave again after this. He could not get three large coppers to meet the other three; and he thought it best not to go with his tribe when they were invited by the tribes, because he was really ashamed. Now* [Maxulayugwa] [his wife] *never became a true chieftainess.* (ibid:1116)

To put this narrative in perspective, since it indicates a rise in status for the former commoner, I quote the narrator's comments. When a child is born to his marriage with the chief's daughter:

Now [Maxulayugwa] *herself caused her name to be disgraced and to become a bad name, because she had a common man for a husband, for* [Hayatlkin] *had no chiefs among his ancestors. Now* [Maxulayugwa] *was called a fool on account of what she had done, and so all her children will be bad on their father's side, and they will be in vain good on their mother's side.* (ibid:1112)

In an aside to Boas the narrator says, after relating how the former Hayatlkin sat in feasts among chiefs:

Now, you, chief Dr. Boas, you must have been surprised when I went to Chicago with Johnny Wanuk [Hayatlkin] *and his wife* [Doqwayis]—*that is,* [Maxaluygwa]—*when I called* [Maxaluygwa] *a queen, but Johnny Wanuk was just like a slave of his wife* [Maxaluyugwa]. (ibid:1113)

The Elgunwe text is the only source I have found in reading all the published Kwakiutl texts in which coppers are destroyed and thrown into the sea in order to put down a chief. Ruth Benedict's citation of this case (1934) may have given an unwarranted impression of typical angry status rivalry. The example is not merely the only of its kind, it depicts an event at a period of cultural ambiguity, when commoners

[218]

could aspire to chiefly rank. In other examples of this sort reported by Hunt to Boas, the true chiefs threaten open violence against the pretender. What seems clear, nevertheless, is the sanctity of the name, which is an incarnation after all and hence cannot be ignored; and distributing property does not "buy" a name. The distribution demonstrates only the inherent prerogative of the name.

APPENDIX 4   PROPERTY EXCHANGES IN MARRIAGE[a]

	M		C		C		M		M		C		C		M		M		C		C		M		C
	G	B	G	B	G	B	G	B	G	B	G	B	G	B	G	B	G	B	G	B
Slaves	2	1							2						2		2		2	4
Canoes															4		4		4	4
Sea otter	10	50	10	30	4		2	2	8	5									20	50
Seal	50		20	50																
Marten	25		30	35			40	50			10		4				7		7	10
Mink			50				10	50	10								4	25	20	25
Bear	20		10	7											24					
Deer			50				70	80	10	80										
Elk							54	104	50		25		50	100	100		100		100	100
Mountain goat									100				100		40		40			50
Grizzly bear									9						4					100
Lynx									24	4	24	4	6		4		40		40	50
Marmot									11						30					30
Skin blankets													100							
Cedar bark			100				150	200												
Woolen blankets																				
Mats							60													

[220]

	M		C		M		C		M		C		M		C		M		C			
	G	B	G	B	G	B	G	B	G	B	G	B	G	B	G	B	G	B	G	B	Number	Total	Average
Slaves	4		4		6		4		4		6		4		6		4		6	7	13	53	4
Canoes	6		4		4		8		4		6		4		4		4		6	8	14	61	4
Sea otter	60		42								20										9	79	9
Seal																					2	100	50
Marten																					8	130	16
Mink	40				40		20				10				40					20	8	285	36
Bear							20														10	171	17
Deer																					6	500	83
Elk																					7	373	53
Mountain goat							40		20				100				200				8	700	87
Grizzly bear									6										20		4	39	10
Lynx															20				40		8	188	24
Marmot																					3	71	23
Skin blankets																					1	100	100
Cedar bark	120		120		200		200		100		120		100								10	1410	141
Woolen blankets						10[b]	20										20				2	30	15
Mats																					1	60	60
Mountain goat spoons													200		200				250		2	450	225

Source: From Gwasela and Nakwaxdax histories, Boas 1921: 840–891.

[a]Only variable items included. Excluded are emblematic properties: house, speaking posts, dishes, names, privileges, and copper. Columns follow order of appearance in text. B = bride's side; G = groom's; M = distribution at marriage; C = distribution at birth of child.

[b]Informant notes from white man.

These texts establish structural and thematic parallels between the two classes of shamans. The first text is called "Talk about the Great Shaman of the Nakwaxdax Called Fool" (Boas 1930:41–45), and is a personal statement from a practising healer. The time is about 1870.

He speaks of having been a seal hunter and a nonbeliever in shamans. Paddling along the shore one day he sees a wolf with a deer bone embedded in its mouth. He says to it:

> *You are in trouble, friend. Now I shall be like a great shaman and cure you, friend. I will take out your great trouble and set you right, friend. Now reward me, friend, that I may be able, like you, to get everything easily, all that is taken by you, on account of your fame as a harpooner and of your supernatural power* (ibid:42)

He removes the bone, and the wolf goes into the woods.

That night he dreams of a man who says to him:

> *Take care, friend, I am Harpooner-Body, on whom you took pity today, and now I reward you for your kindness to me, friend. There is nothing hereafter that you will not obtain ... This also, do not lie down with your wife for four years, to pass through all that you will have to do.* (ibid)

Thereafter, he always caught many seals and other animals.

Two years later he goes to Victoria with his nephews and they all contract smallpox. His nephews die, and he imagines he is lying dead among them.

> *Then I thought I also was dead. I was as in a sleep and I awoke on account of many wolves who came whining and others howling. Two of them were licking my body and I saw two wolves vomit up foam and putting it on my body* (ibid:43).

He is treated with wolf vomit for four days. Harpooner-Body appears before him and vomits the magic power into him. Then he dreams of the wolf as a man saying to him:

> *now this shaman-maker has gone into you. Now you will cure the sick and you will catch the souls of the sick and you will throw sickness into anyone whom you wish to die among your tribe. Now they will be afraid of you.*

He awakens, his body trembling and his mind, as he says, different. He says he went about "like drunk" and very happy, and every evening sang the four sacred songs of the wolf.

The Nakwaxdax hear of him and ask him to heal their chief with his "water of life." Four resident shamans go to assemble all the people to see the curing. When he enters, the four shamans are beating fast time. Then his body and belly begin to tremble and he sings his sacred song.

The second text is called [Tlebid] the Real Shaman of the [Gwasela] (ibid:46–50). The narrator tells of Tlebid's long illness and finally of his death in winter. Because of the cold and a heavy snow storm they cannot bury him. One night they hear howling wolves and fear they will eat the corpse. Then they hear Tlebid sing his sacred song, and know he has become a shaman. Tlebid joins the wolves in the forest. The shamans of the Gwasela instruct the Nakwaxdax to purify themselves by washing. Two days later they hear Tlebid singing. Tlebid's wife, his daughters, and sisters clean his house. A fire is started and the Gwasela prepare "to beat time for the new shaman who had come back to life" (ibid:47). The Nakwaxdax shaman instructs them to beat fast time. As they beat they hear the song approaching. At the fourth round of beating, Tlebid enters the house naked, with only hemlock around his head and neck. They beat fast time, and he goes around the fire singing his sacred song:

> *I was taken far away inland to the edge of the world by the magical power of heaven, the treasure. . . . Only then was I cured by it, when it was really thrown into me, the past life bringer of* [Naualakume], *the treasure. . . . I come to cure with this means of healing of* [Naualakume] *the treasure. . . . Therefore I shall be a life bringer. . . . I come with the water of life given into my hand by* [Naualakume], *the means of bringing to life, the treasures. . . .* (ibid)

All who are not shamans leave the house. Those who remain have their faces blackened, and wear on their heads and necks the red cedar rings of the shaman. Only the novice is still adorned in hemlock. The shamans ask him to tell how he had come to life again.

His story is that a man appeared before him, beckoning him to follow. As he did so he was aware he had left his body behind. He was brought to a house in the woods and introduced to Naualakume, the great shaman, who gave him his name and announced he would send him back to be a great shaman among his people. Naualakume took possession of Tlebid's breath, which is the owner of the soul, and replaced it with a quartz crystal he had vomited. The crystal is his shamanistic power. That evening he observed Naualakume's dance among the wolves, who are now men. The great shaman cured him. The men in the house

put on their wolf masks and accompanied Tlebid to his corpse. Naualakume restored the soul to the corpse and it came to life. He denies
he can throw sickness, but Gwasela insist he can, since he has the name
Naualakume.

As in the Winter Ceremonial all acquisitions of shamanistic powers
are personal and therefore distinctive. Each shaman has his own origins.
Some, as these texts reveal, were initiated by wolves who have a traditional role as healers, others by the killer whales, the so-called wolves
of the sea. But many animals are shaman tutelaries. The constant elements are: (1) acquisition from a nonhuman supernatural power; (2)
being at the point of death in order to receive; (3) acquiring the name
and songs of the tutelary; (4) acquiring a vomited quartz crystal; (5)
holding a curing ceremony in a purified house; (6) wearing sacred paraphernalia, such as eagle down, and red cedar bark, repositories of supernatural power; and (7) blackening the face with soot, the symbol of
fearlessness among warriors. The shaman who shows his powers has
the right, like a chief, to distribute property.

This assembly of statements around principal religious ideas should aid the reader to form independent judgments on characteristics of Kwakiutl religious thought. It is a guide to patterns of mental associations rather than a glossary of religious symbolism and imagery. At a certain level of generalization each symbol and image may be reduced to a single concept. In the religious thought of the Kwakiutl, however, the process of symbolization is refractive rather than reductive. That is to say, each symbol, each image, each metaphoric concept is intended to link up with all the many realms of nature and the many zones of the natural order from which powers are obtained, and with which social relations are to be established. The requirements of such mystical linkages break up the symbols, images, and metaphors—all of which I encompass for convenience under the general heading of themes—into related but discrete entities on the analogy of light through a prism. The notion that a symbolic entity, such as a copper, might stand for a single idea, as light or salmon, does not take account of the relentless necessity for religious expansion and elaboration. Like the social system, which demands ceaseless interlacings and interpretations, not to mention transformations, the religious structure, which is the integrative center for the total culture, is restlessly dynamic. After all, persons are also visualized as multiple refractions of an original image, and there is a common denominator to all their identities. But we cannot comprehend that common center except through awareness of its multiple refractions.

Copper.   The use of copper in plaques and ornaments may be posthistoric. Curtis learned that the first coppers were purchased from the Haida, and that the northern tribes got their sheet copper originally from the Russians (1915:144–145). The thoroughness with which copper was subsequently integrated within the total cultural system testifies to the exuberant state of religious elaboration among the Kwakiutl. Its color, its odor, its remarkable metal qualities, its scarcity, and its provenance from an outer realm established its dominance as a major symbol that perhaps replaced earlier ones.

Copper brings light into the world (Boas and Hunt 1905:145). In the Nimkish myth the Sun descends to earth on a copper pole (ibid:352). The chief of the stars descends to earth on a copper pole, which is referred to as the Post of Heaven (ibid:401). Ancestors came down from the upper world on copper ladders, on copper "potlatch" poles, or by mountains that move up and reach the sky (Boas 1935b:47, 107, 108, 126). When Nomas came down to the world as an eagle-sized butterfly he had a copper. He gave a feast and put the copper under a mountain, which was then named Copper Under It (Boas 1910:486). When a copper is laid face down in the water darkness falls on the earth. When it is turned right side up again light returns (Boas 1935b:101, 168); or light returns to the world when a copper is put into the sea (Boas and Hunt 1905:145). Thunderbird has a house of copper (ibid:98).

Qomogwa, the spirit of the sea, is a source of giving away coppers all over the world, and is a source of the Winter Ceremonial (ibid:85). Qomogwa is known as Wealthy, and as Copper-Maker (Boas 1935b:127ff). The walls and roof boards of his house are of copper. His daughter is Copper-Maker Woman, who marries an ancestor of Dzawadenox. Qomogwa lives under the sea beyond the land of the dead (Boas and Hunt:60ff). He eats human eyes in the way human beings eat crabapples (Boas 1935b:130). Copper-Maker's house is filled with seals and other sea mammals. He is the source of sea otters on the beach (Boas 1935a:216–217). He has a copper canoe that is self-propelling (Boas and Hunt 1905:81). He gives seal feasts (Boas 1935a:203). In his house is a pond of water which is "the water of life" (Boas 1935b:109).

The canoe of Raven is the double-headed serpent (Sisiutl); but it is of copper and must be fed seals (Boas 1935b:108). Copper is also the salmon and must be fed salmon and fish oil, and be treated like a guest. A piece of salmon is placed at the center of the copper's face and then thrown into the fire with this prayer: "O Sitter-on-the-Fire now you will help me to come and be the stomach of this great copper that has a name" (Boas 1930:185–186). (Note that through the figure of Sisiutl, copper is devourer of seals, who are devourers of salmon, and as salmon is thus a cannibalistic self-devourer).

A man goes to the place where his children have drowned and finds a stick with a copper attached. He makes a copper plate from it, sells it and distributes the property (Boas 1910:485). Coppers are stored in flat boxes on layers of cedar bark and eagle down. They are fed. They are called steel-head salmons "The Great Supernatural One." A prayer to it asks it to protect the chief, and to invite coppers of its size to come to the chief (Boas 1930:185).

Coppers are used in curing (Boas 1932a:182). They are used to cure a woman who spits blood. Blood and saliva are placed between thin copper sheets that are driven into a crabapple tree (Boas 1930:238–9). They are a means of putting an end to both lucky and unlucky events. They can stay the run of fish, disease, and life. Some claim the effect of the copper is due to its smell, which is like that of salmon. By putting up coppers at the side of a boy, he will be protected against the bad words of other chiefs (Boas 1932a:228).

The transfer of a copper inaugurates the Winter Ceremonial (Boas 1921:903, 970). The copper is sold always to a rival (Boas 1897:346). Coppers are broken for a Winter Ceremonial (Boas 1921:861), usually for the *hamatsa* initiations. The copper in the house groans because it is not broken (Boas 1897:622). Coppers are broken at investiture of a new chief (Boas 1925:217). When a guest has no feast name an angry host breaks coppers to extinguish the fire (i.e., a man without a feast name is "clay face" or dead). A copper is put to death to match his being dead, and the fire, the source of connection with ghosts, is also killed. But since the "death" of a copper is equivalent to the "death" *(laxsa)* of a *hamatsa* initiate, a resurrection is implied.

The coppers the bride brings to her husband at marriage are the masts of her canoe (Boas 1921:777). (The mast is not a sail support, but the post connecting her canoe to the upper world).

Coverings (Blankets, Animal Skins, Bark Robes).   Animals live in village of their own, inland. When at home they take off their skins and appear as human beings (Boas 1935b:133). Mountain goats say they are people and their skins are their clothing. They give a man their skin, and tell a hunter he can always catch mountain goats with it (Boas 1895:169). The blanket of Thunderbird produces lightning (Boas and Hunt 1905:211). Grizzly Bear removes his skin which is his "food producing mask" when he dives under water in a test of ability to obtain supernatural powers (ibid:25ff). A hunter steals the mask of Grizzly Bear and is given a winter dance privilege for its return (Boas 1935b:80). A dressed deerskin is obtained as a supernatural treasure which is inexhaustible. One side will always bring other deerskins, the other side is a "death-bringer" (Boas 1935a:57). After acquiring the treasure of getting sea otters, hunters kill many and build a house of their skins (ibid:44). (In this context house and skin are equated as coverings). Before there were boxes the dead were wrapped in mats (Boas and Hunt

1905:57). Blankets fall from the red cedar bark neck ring (a primary source of supernatural power), and if a man's rival should stand in the way he would drown in it (Boas 1966:191). When tribes are given blankets it is known as "swallowing the tribes"; property that is distributed is said to be vomited out (ibid:192–193). A chief is a great mountain down which wealth rolls (Boas 1897:350).

Masks. There are two classes, the ancestral dress when the ancestor first appeared, and the gifts of supernatural beings worn in ceremonial dances. "When the ancestor becomes a human being he generally sends his mask dress back to the place of his former residence . . . the dress itself is conceived of as being alive" (Boas 1935b:78). Myth people do not always use their own masks, but borrow freely from others (ibid:79). The bird mask taken off by a man flies back again into the sky world (Boas 1935a:65). The Grizzly Bear masks and skin return home by themselves (ibid:79). Seals are surprised and seen as men before they have time to put on their masks (ibid:207). Wolves put on their wolf masks, which are their treasure masks (Boas 1930:49). The severed head of wolf child is worn as a mask (ibid:81). Born to be Sun (Mink) reveals his supernatural power and wears a mask on his forehead (Boas 1910:139). Sun gives his mask to Mink (ibid:125). Thunderbird, asked to become a man, opens his Thunderbird mask and becomes a clan founder (ibid:83–85). On Owl masks: "Owls are men, for we all have owl masks." The dead go toward their owl masks and fly about as owls. "The owl names the name of the owner of the owl mask" (Boas 1930:257). Masks become excited behind their curtain at the sounds of beating and yelling at a ceremony (ibid:171). The Grizzly Bear mask is a food obtaining mask (ibid:188). Masks are kept in boxes (Boas 1910:37, 399).

Boxes. In the Winter Ceremonial, boxes are represented as alive. Cedar bark boxes have character as ritual beings (Boas 1930:92). They put on eagle down (ibid:96), and they become Sparrows (ibid:99). At the beginning of the winter dances the people bring boxes for their chief (Boas 1910:483). Boxes contain masks and names (ibid:305) and they fill themselves with food (ibid:357). When Scab gets a box from

Dzonoqwa he cannot lift it, and discovers that it contains the water of life (ibid:59). Boxes given as a marriage gift are found to contain the Qweqsotenox tribe (Boas 1935a:182). Tiny whales are taken out of a box and then grow to full size (Boas 1910:257). When a slave steals boxes and carvings from his master the boxes turn to stone (Boas 1935a:133). Boxes are included in marriage exchanges (ibid:53, 87, 182). Boxes are commonly inexhaustible cornucopias (see, e.g., Boas 1935b:108–109). Burials are often in boxes set in trees (Boas 1897:441).

Poles.   The "potlatch" pole *(maxpeq)* is known as a "wealth bringer" that will make "property swell in the house" (Boas 1935b:108). It is a gift of Thunderbird, and is given by supernatural beings to people; it is a marriage gift (Boas 1935b:75). It rises from the water (ibid:108). It is regarded as the "thick root and the thick tree of the tribes" (Boas 1921:1290). The Post of Heaven stands in water and holds up the upper world. At the foot of the post are sea lions, seals, whales, and killer whales, that look like the house dishes (Boas 1935a:215–216). A child grows up and erects a pole upon which his ancestor sits. He then becomes a chief (Boas 1910:95). The *hamatsa* dancers are sent into the woods to bring back a cannibal pole. If they make a mistake, life will be made short by the supernatural power of the cannibal pole. They say to the pole: "put into the house your ceremonial body" (Boas 1930:106). To obtain a Man Eater dance a youth climbs a cannibal pole and swallows a person whole. The pole is a series of mouths which he enters and from which he emerges (Boas 1910:425–431). The cannibal pole is the supernatural gift of the Man Eater spirit. He gives it to a youth by plaiting a small piece of hemlock at the nape of his neck (ibid:35). The cannibal pole made of cedar is called Life Shortener, but also Healing Woman, and Long Life Maker (Boas 1930:105). A princess pole with an eagle perched on top is set in front of the house of Oldest One in the World (Boas 1910:267). Only One obtains as part of his house two speaking posts that greet visitors, one saying: "Go at those who come into your house"; and the other "take pity on them "(Boas 1935a:49). A louse pole is set in front of a house, and huge lice crawl down it into the house and devour all the men in it (ibid:75). Qanekelak causes many men to come out of the posts of his house, and they become his tribe (Boas 1935b:43). Men are created from alder trees (Boas 1910:377). Raven makes a whale from poles (ibid:241).

Houses. The house of Sentlae, Son of Abalone in the World, a sky deity, has painted front boards with Sun on the right wall, Moon on the left, and Thunderbird over the door. The main posts are men, the cross beam is Sisiutl, a rear post is Thunderbird. The house is 10 steps deep. Abalone of the World gives the house as a wedding gift to his daughter-in-law (Boas and Hunt 1905:45–53). Cause of Weeping Woman (a death bringer) has the name which she gives away: Pulling Off Roof Boards (ibid:108). Houses are brought down from the sky (see Head Winter Dancer) (ibid:185). Houses are often given in marriage (Boas 1935a:129). Roof boards are given away at conclusion of first menstruation of a princess, at investiture of a chief, at the death of the heir (Boas 1921:709; Boas 1925:235). The crown of the head is the doorway of the soul (Boas 1930:8) (and hence an analogy with roof boards). The dance house of the Winter Ceremonial is referred to as the house of Healing Woman (ibid:121). The house hungers to devour the tribes. It is said to carry the tribes in one hand (Boas 1921:1279). The door of the house is often described as the mouth of an animal or monster (Boas 1935b:2). The house is often bestowed on an ancestor who had an encounter with a supernatural being (ibid:50).

Canoes. In myth, canoes are often self-paddling and made of copper (Boas 1910:165, 229); they are also folding (ibid:217, 227, 229, 245). Canoes that are broken deliberately become whole again. But if a menstruant sits in a canoe it cannot become whole again (ibid:351). When the canoe has been brought ceremonially it goes to the ghosts, who then return it (ibid:253). The Spirit of War travels about the world in a canoe (Boas 1897:394); brides are always brought home by canoe. Capsizing a canoe is a ritualized means of invoking ritual shame and fomenting a distribution of property (Boas 1925:133). The whale form of an ancestor is a canoe (Boas 1921:836). The Sisiutl is worn as a belt, and the belt is also a canoe (Boas 1935b:147).

Grease. (Grease is clear rendered oil of *oulachen* or candlefish or whale oil.) Blankets are given for the weight of a man's name, oil for the weight of a woman's name (Boas 1921:963). Boxes of grease are part of the purchase price of a copper (Boas 1910:93). If a woman carries on her back a basket containing grease she will have twins (Boas 1932a:238). Raven Sound in House eats so much grease from a perpetually self-filling dish that it comes out through his anus and floods the house (Boas 1910:265). The theme of grease flooding the house appears in ritual feasts as well (see Boas 1895:169). A boy vomits grease and his parents discover he has obtained a great treasure from the ravens, who had filled his head with blubber and connected him to the place where whales go ashore (Boas 1935a:112). Crane gives grease that cannot be all consumed. It is a supernatural gift (Boas 1930:100). Hadaho gives a grease feast for his ancestors (Boas 1910:367–369). Sexual intercourse is forbidden during *oulachen* fishing season. Menstruants and, for a period of four years, widows and widowers avoid contact with *oulachen* fish (Boas 1932a:238). The oil feast is the greatest (Boas 1921:755). Vomiter beam is a carved human image from whose mouth oil spouts (Boas 1921:812).

Crabapples. Qomogwa eats the eyes of men in the way people eat crabapples (Boas 1935b:130). The crabapples of many supernatural beings are human eyes (ibid:106). When War Leader is *hamatsa* he is caught, tamed, and given crabapples and other food (Boas 1935a:104). As a curing technique copper plates are driven into a crabapple tree (see Copper). The copper driven into the crabapple tree is then eaten by Healing Woman (Boas 1930:238–239). Tribes take crabapples from the house of a dead Dzonoqwa (Boas 1910:121). Oil and crabapple feasts are angry feasts (Boas 1895:169). The power of the Sisiutl is in its eyeballs (Boas 1935a:5). Skin Dresser Woman's bear husband asks his two sisters to pick crabapples for food. The bears then excrete cleaned crabapples and eat them. The woman who eats them becomes rooted to the ground (Boas 1935a:221–222).

Berries. Berries are "long life makers" (Boas 1930:193). They are supernatural ones (ibid:203). Birds give a berry feast to restore harmony after a contest in which they defeat Thunderbird. Thunderbird is eager for berries (Boas and Hunt 1905:298). Thrush Woman gives a feast with berries that are magically ripened. Mink tries to do the same but fails (Boas 1910:151).

Food (General). Water Ousel gives a feast with magically produced salmon eggs. Mink tries the same, but fails (Boas 1910:155). Hawk gives a salmon feast, and Mink tries the same but fails (ibid:155–157). Dzonoq-was give a child tallow to eat (ibid:119). Salmon roasts his own children (ibid:173). Using a death bringer, a youth acquires food and slaves (ibid:155). When Hadaho reveals the secret of his magical food supply it disappears (ibid:365–369). Crane gives food that is inexhaustible, providing the gift is kept secret (ibid:361). Hada Woman has a self-filling grease dish (ibid:265). When she is deserted by her people for greedily eating sea eggs, she regains all by marrying Raven, the son of Qomogwa, who gives her the treasure of limitless food. Then she turns him out because he eats greedily from his grease dish (Boas 1935a:16–17). Greedy Child eats all the food of Crabapple Woman (Boas 1910:213). A Dzonoqwa steals salmon, but is followed home, and the Dzonoqwa store of food and bearskins is taken away from them (ibid:443–444). A woman hides food from her blind husband and eats it all herself (ibid:448). Mink's pretense for refusing to give sea eggs to Otter is that warriors do not share their food (ibid:495). A boy given a supernatural harpoon by his father brings back a great quantity of food and feasts his tribe (ibid:452). A whale washed up on the beach is given in feast to the tribes (Boas 1930:264–269). A special ceremony for a firstborn daughter is to make her adept in food gathering (ibid:284). Copper-Maker's house is filled with seals and other animals, and he allows a guest to club his sea otters (Boas 1935a:216–217). When the *hamatsa* dancer is caught he is feasted on dry salmon, crabapples, viburnum berries, and dry berry cakes (ibid:104). The feast-giving name is distinct from the blanket-giving name (Boas 1925:99). Not to own the privilege of giving a feast is equivalent to being dead. Spirits of the dead are always poor and hungry (Boas 1966:165). A change of name is most appropriate at a feast (Boas 1921:1021). It is ritually proper to kill a guest at a feast as a demonstration of warrior arrogance (Curtis 1915:154).

Sea Mammals.   Killer Whale is a shaman maker (Boas 1930:10). Seals who are invited to a Winter Ceremonial put on eagle down (ibid:96) and then become Sparrows of the Winter Ceremonial (ibid:99). Sea lions attend the Winter Ceremonial as a group (ibid:154). Sea lions appear as humans, and seals as their dogs (Boas 1935a:84). Seals are the dogs of Copper-Maker (ibid:216). A man carves an otter of wood which then dives under and pulls his rival out to sea (ibid:152).

Siwit, a youth, goes through a series of transformations from one sea mammal after another and ends as a bird. Having been beaten in various tests of strength and agility by his playmates he is taken underwater and given supernatural powers to kill creatures freely, which he does. He then becomes successively Sea Otter, Whale, Dolphin, Seal. He brings up the house of Qomogwa and then turns into a bird (ibid:179–182).

The sleeping place of seals is called Place of Wealth. They hold their winter dances there, and that is why there are so few seals in winter. The place is on a mountaintop where they can be easily killed (ibid:201–206). Hunters of sea otters, hair seals, and fur seals are rivals, one called Day Hunter and the other Night Hunter (ibid:212). Because of their rivalries, in the course of which one tries to kill the other, they both gain supernatural power (see ibid:212–219, Night Hunter and Day Hunter). The sea mammals are gathered at the base of the Post of the World (ibid:216). Seal hunters and twins (children of salmon) are sacred (Boas 1927:388). The house of Rich One (Qomogwa) has sea lions as vomiter beams (Boas 1910:81). A bird ancestor seated on a pole reveals his power by holding a whale by the tail in his claws (ibid:93). Whale is a curing shaman (ibid:115); Wolf claims to be a sea otter (1935a:140–142). Sea Otters are exchanged for supernatural feathers (Boas 1910:103). A young seal invites the myth people to a feast (ibid:237). Raven enters the body of a whale he has made of wood (ibid:243). Sea mammals are among the properties owned by Dzonoqwa woman (ibid:444). Deer obtains fire from Sea Otter, who carries it on his tail (ibid:494). Killer whales are fond of mountain goat tallow (1930:188). People treated with mountain goat tallow become fearless, and great mountain goat hunters (ibid:285). The souls of sea mammal hunters go to the killer whales (ibid:257). A woman's excrement becomes whales that wash up on the beach (ibid:265).

Wolves. Wolf dung can destroy a man's supernatural power (Boas 1910:466). Wolves eat corpses (ibid:139), steal salmon (ibid:147); they give the death bringer (ibid:183); they are the antagonists of the deer and Thunderbird (ibid:243). They are antagonists of Mink (Boas 1897:478). They are warriors (Boas 1910:161); they are founders of the Winter Ceremonial (Boas 1935b:154). They are chiefs of the myth people (ibid:154). They are makers of shamans (1930:41ff). Wolves take off their masks and create land on the water with their skins (Boas

1935a:65). Land hunters' souls go to the wolves (Boas 1930:257). Wolves devour men and them vomit them out in a resurrection motif (Boas 1935a:156). In their ceremonial house the wolves take off their skins and appear as humans. They are donors of supernatural powers and of the *nontlem* ceremony. "It sounded as though the world was breaking to pieces when the wolves came down" (Boas 1935a:142–143).

Grizzly Bear. Grizzly Bear is ancestor of Walibaye *numema* (Boas 1930:177). Grizzly bears live in the house of Qomogwa, "the place of wealth" (Boas 1935a:185, 206). The following supernatural powers are obtained from him: the ability to get property easily; his wildness; his lack of respect for anything. A hunter who kills the grizzly bear takes all these powers from him (Boas 1930:194–196). Grizzly bears are allied with wolves in killing Thunderbird (Boas 1910:243). Grizzly bears tear a man to pieces and then revive him by gathering together his bones (ibid:111). Grizzly Bear swallows Wren, who emerges from his rectum and then kills him saying: "Although I am a small man you cannot overcome me" (Boas 1935a:21). Dzonoqwa owns grizzly bear skins (Boas 1910:456), and the four corner posts of her house which had a snapping door were grizzly bears (ibid:456). Grizzly bear is tricked into cutting off his own testicles and dies (ibid:215).

Mountain Goat. Mountain goats invite guests to a Winter Ceremonial where they appear as Sparrows (Boas 1930:62). The one-horned mountain goat is a feared killer. It is later found dead and its tallow is a great supernatural treasure that increases in size (Boas 1910:27). House of Mountain Goat has white smoke issuing from smoke hole (ibid:385). Mountain goats appear as human in their ceremonial house, having taken off their skins. They give their skins as a supernatural treasure that will catch other mountain goats.

Salmon. Spring Salmon is the keeper of all the salmon masks (Boas and Hunt 1905:302). By donning the masks, an entire tribe converts itself into salmon (ibid:32). Salmon are associated with Thunderbird who is a salmon fisherman (ibid). Salmon must be avoided by widows, widowers, dying persons, twins, and menstruants (Boas 1932a:238). Salmon is a healer who takes illness back to his own country (Boas 1930:184). Salmon are eaten by those who have purified themselves after the Winter Ceremonial (ibid:137). Salmon is known as "Swimmer," and is greatly respected. To club a salmon twice is to kill its soul (ibid:205–206). Salmon is identified with copper, which comes to salmon traps to be fed (ibid:185); dried salmon is fed to the copper (ibid:186–188). The Sisiutl is a salmon (ibid:75). Twins come from the salmon, and their souls go back to Salmon-Maker (ibid:257). Salmon are the givers of heavy weight (ibid:205). The daughter of Killer Whale is able to create salmon (note that devourer of salmon is creator of salmon) (Boas 1935b:158). The daughter of Salmon Chief is the wife of Killer Whale (ibid:159). Salmon revive when their bones are thrown back into the water (ibid).

Dzonoqwa   The Dzonoqwas, usually rendered by Hunt as Wild Woman of the Woods, are actually a tribe of inland-dwelling wild beings. But the female is usually their representative (Boas 1935b:144). Dzonoqwa and Sisiutl are paired as aggressive monsters (Boas and Hunt 1905:204). In antagonistic distribution Dzonoqwa is the patron of chiefly terror (see Boas 1921:1286–1288). Dzonoqwa is one of the devouring supernatural beings, the bottom figure of a cannibal pole, from whose mouth an initiate emerges (see Boas 1910:433–437 passim). Even an infant that has been abducted kills the Dzonoqwa woman (ibid:117ff). A girl discovering Dzonoqwa woman stealing salmon kills her with arrows in her breasts, strikes her children dead, and then uses the mother Dzonoqwa's skull as a bath for strengthening her own child (ibid). The Dzonoqwa's breasts hang to the ground. When encountered by boys she gives them supernatural treasures—a self-paddling canoe, the water of life, and death bringer (ibid:490). Scab marries a Dzonoqwa daughter who then revives his dead father (Boas 1935a:160ff). She fights like a shaman throwing her powers into an opponent. Scab, who kills a Dzonoqwa, cures her by pulling the arrows out of her breasts and is rewarded with her daughter as a wife (ibid). Dzonoqwa is a giant who steals salmon and prevents people from fishing; also a war maker who seeks to enslave the chiefs (Boas and Hunt 1905:203). Male Dzonoqwa is the warrior of his brother Man Eater, and acquires wives and wealth (ibid:209). Dzonoqwa woman gives ornaments to a pubescent girl to strengthen her. Her kin then kill Dzonoqwa and seize her nightmare-bringer nest mask (ibid:92). The Dzonoqwa cry "ho!" dazes all people who do not have real power (ibid:206), kills them (ibid:209), and sets a house afire (ibid:228).

Qomogwa   Qomogwa is known as Wealthy, as Copper-Maker, and as Chief of the Ocean (Boas 1935b:68, 128–131). His house made of copper is west of the ocean, apparently a death destination since it is beyond the places to which charcoal, sand, driftwood, and toilet sticks go (ibid). It is at the entrance to the underworld (ibid:129). He marries a dead woman whose body has been thrown into the sea and sends her back alive. He is associated with the Sisiutl, with the Thunderbird, with birds, and with all sea mammals (ibid). He is the owner of copper, but has no cedarwood, which he must get from a human son-in-law (ibid:130). He eats human eyes (ibid). There is an apparent Sedna analogue in the motif that his many hands have to be cut off to kill him (ibid). He is a donor of wealth and houses as well as of the usual supernatural treasures. His house, which has several names, is given as a gift, and it arises from the sea. He is the owner of the herrings (ibid:131).

Sisiutl.   The double-headed serpent is a fish figure, usually a salmon (Boas 1935b:146–148). Those who see it faint or become contorted. Canoes that come within its sight turn to stone. Its clotted blood rubbed on skin causes that skin to turn to stone. It is the food of Thunderbird, but poisonous to others. Worn as a magical belt, its skin kills monsters. It appears as a death-dealing canoe, and its scales and intestines become a river. It is associated with Qomogwa and with Dzonoqwa (ibid). It can be overcome or rendered harmless by spitting blood from the tongue on it. Mink uses it as a weapon to contort people (Boas 1930:88, 92). Qanekelak uses Sisiutl eyeballs in a sling to kill whales (Boas 1935a:8). A man faints from observing the brightness of the Sisiutl. It is also a giver of the treasure of wealth (ibid:131). A child rubbed with clotted Sisiutl blood becomes a Dzonoqwa (Boas and Hunt 1905:199).

Thunderbird.   He is the chief of the village of the birds of the upper world, all of whom are mythical creatures, such as Hoxhoq, Raven of the Middle of the Sky, and Crooked Beak; and he is at war with the land animals led by Raven who defeat him after constructing an artifical whale. Sometimes it is Woodpecker who leads the animals against him. He has a salmon weir, and eats the double-headed serpent as though it were a salmon. It thunders whenever he moves from the winter side of his house to the summer side, or vice versa. He lives on earth near Crooked Beach, and in the sky. When Thunderbirds and their children are killed by the animals, the infant survivor goes back into the sky to live in shame (Boas 1935b:157). In the upper world he is known as Too Large, in the lower world as Head Winter Dancer. He duels inconclusively with Qanekelak (Boas and Hunt 1905:167). He lives in a copper house with Hoxhoq, Thunderbird, Sisiutl, Moon, and Sun crests (ibid:186). Thunderbird shows he is human beneath his mask (ibid:166). His child is born after a four month pregnancy and becomes a full man after only four more months (ibid:179). His second child is a man-eater (Baxbakwalanukwe—not the Man Eater at the North End of the World) (ibid:180). He calls down his original copper house from heaven in the presence of a third son, Real Chief, who must cover his face while that happens (ibid:185). The masks of Head Winter Dancer are Sun, Dawn, and Copper (Potlatch Giver) (ibid:187). His wife cohabits with a Dzonoqwa and bears a child who becomes a stone-hard Dzonoqwa after being rubbed with Sisiutl blood (ibid:199). The ankle straps placed on children 10 moons old are Thunderbird emblems (Boas 1932a:201). The eagles are the lice of Qolos, the brother of Thunderbird (ibid:250).

NOTES

Chapter 1

1. "Powers may also be obtained by killing the supernatural beings. Then the murderer takes their place and their powers" (Boas 1935b:92).

Chapter 2

1. Edward S. Curtis, whose principal informant was George Hunt, discusses ritualized forms of fraternal and intertribal rivalries. The head of the tribe was the Eagle, and the head of the second ranking lineage—an equivalent to, if not an actual younger brother—was its rival or *upsikyis*. Curtis comments on the constant rivalry between these two in all forms of distributions and destructions of property and in giving of winter dances, and compares this rivalry with that between paired tribes. Curtis was fully aware that such rivalries involved no personal animosity, no matter how insulting the speeches appeared to be (see 1915:141).

   At the same time, Hunt also suggests that the formal antagonisms between rival chiefs, as in copper breaking, may transcend formal hierarchy. Speaking of Kwakiutl and Mamaleleqala rival chiefs, he remarks, "Therefore their rank was of equal value" (Boas 1925:89).

   The family histories bring out several actual examples of fraternal rivalries. Qatenats, jealous of his elder brother who is a great shaman, acquires powers of his own by curing a sick sisiutl. In a rage his elder brother tears out his internal organs, killing him (Boas and Hunt 1908:22–27). Also in a rage, a man kills his elder brother who has an overbearing attendant (ibid:257).

   A more cosmological form of fratricide is described among wolves. When the wolves take off their masks to become human, the elder bites his younger brother's throat, and then tears his body to pieces. Gathering the torn flesh together into a ball he tosses it into the air. It is transformed into eagle down and scatters about the earth, giving rise to the tribes (ibid:256ff). This legend is the most powerful example of fraternal antagonism as a source of transformation and development.

2. In genealogical succession, the Gwascla marriages were with the following tribes: Qomoyaye, Walas Kwakiutl, Nakwaxdax, Lalasikwala, Mamaleleqala, Dzawadenox, Haxuamis, Gwawenak, Tlawitsis, Nakwaxdax, Heiltsuq, Gwasela, Heiltsuq, Lalasik-wala, Nakwaxdax, Nakwaxdax, Nakumgilisela, Gwasela, Nakwaxdax.

3. Hunt lists the tally of names for two tribes and their lineages (by rank order): (ms Vol.1:1719)

Gwetela		Qomoyaye	
Maamtagila	11	Kwakweakem	6
Loyalatlawa	5	Haenatlena	8
Gexsem	9	Yaexagemaye	6
Kwakwakwem	8	Haeyalekawe	5
Sentlem	10	Laxsa	2
Laalaxsendayo	3	Gigelgem	7
Elgunwe	2		

4. Curtis stresses the norm of patrilineal descent, observing that if a chief has a daughter his seat goes to her eldest son, or in trust for an expected son (1915:138–139).

5. A woman may, however, give a firstborn name from her father's lineage to her own child (Boas 1925:107). This is equivalent to placing the child into her own lineage.

Chapter 3

1. A generic term for the entire class of chiefs, that is, for a nobility, is *naxsala* (Boas 1921:1416), a term whose root is apparently *naqe*, meaning the mind. Its nearest cognates are *naxsatla* ("without sense"), and *naqade* ("song leader"). The references would seem to be to the religious state of ecstasy. Thus *naxsala* seems to point up the shamanic character of the nobility.

2. The opposition of chiefs to illegitimate efforts to exercise chiefly prerogatives is illustrated by the case of Hawaselatl of the Wiwomasgem lineage of Mamaleleqala. He had as a "sweetheart" a woman of another lineage of his tribe, who came to him with three pretty daughters. The woman proposed they all go to Victoria where she and her three daughters would be prostitutes. After one winter they returned with a great deal of money and bought the expensive copper, Dry-Mouth-Maker-Cause-of-Shame. Shortly thereafter all three daughters died, and it was said they had been bewitched. The narrator observes: "[Hawaselatl] . . . was only a common man and the real chiefs do not allow a common man to buy expensive coppers." When Hawaselatl also fell ill he decided to give up the copper to a chief who had befriended him. In this postcontact narrative the common man, Hawaselatl, had a seat and a name in his lineage, but not, as the narrator observes, "the office of giving away property to his numaym, the [Wiwomasgem], for he was only a common man" (Boas 1925:93–95).

   The case of Teqwap, another common man but a more successful interloper, comes to the same sad conclusion. Teqwap was the younger brother of Hawaselatl's sweetheart. The narrator describes him as "clever in his ways for he had much property." He never married, but he distributed property and gave feasts to the tribes. He possessed a feast name and a name for the giving away of blankets, which was Wamis. The narrative says, "Now [Wamis] was also hated by the chiefs of the [Mamaleleqala], for when one of the chiefs gave away property, then [Wamis] also gave away blankets, just as if he were making fun of the chief in doing so . . . . Then [Wamis] became afraid of the chiefs of his tribe for they kept on threatening to kill him." He therefore invited his Mamaleleqala tribe to his house and informed them he was giving away his copper and his seat to the same noble who was the beneficiary of Hawaselatl. Then he said, "Now, tribe, now I am dead, according to your wish, tribe" (ibid:97–99).

3. Boas distinguishes head chiefs *(xamagame gigame)* from all others, who are known

as "lower chiefs" or "new chiefs," and addressed by courtesy as chiefs. The wife of a head chief, he explains, also had an official position as *modzitl* ("lifting the dress in the house") a reference to her role as hostess at feasts. The women of lower rank are *oma*, a term rendered as "lady." The chief's oldest son and prospective successor is *tlewelgame*, or "prince" (Boas 1966:51).

4. The mourning songs document the necessary ritual accomplishment of chiefs. In one text (Boas 1925:77) these accomplishments are listed as the number of times the chief had: (1) invited the tribes; (2) given grease feasts; (3) given away property; (4) given away canoes; (5) given potlatches to his own tribe; (6) broken coppers.

In the same text (ibid:79) the ritual accomplishments are listed as dances. Each dance in the sequence mentioned is named as follows: giving away canoes, feast-giving, property-destroying, copper-breaking, throwing into the water, giving away roof boards, striking to kill, marriage debt paying, paying for princess, canoe-breaking, giving away bad things (that is, the return marriage gift). In the context of a dance, which is always accompanied by a song, each of these accomplishments is a spirit impersonation.

5. An incident that occurred at a grease feast at Fort Rupert in 1864 illustrates the Kwakiutl capacity to fuse a political reality (murder) with myth and ritual. Chief Nukapnkyim shot one of his guests in cold blood and then cried out: "That will be one of them in my song." He then sang, "that blood on the floor horrifies everybody in the house of the double-faced chief" (Curtis 1915:154). In a similar vein, Boas observed, from his review of mythological themes, that "Warriors commit murder on unoffending guests, only to show their disregard for human life, and these acts seem to be accepted as proof of their prowess" (1935b:75).

6. Under certain conditions a commoner may give a feast to chiefs, but his name will not be called out (Boas 1921:792). That is, he may give a feast that does not invoke the ancestral or mythological spirits, which, of course, he does not possess.

7. All human beings and indeed all forms of life, animal and vegetal, have souls, which are called by various terms. The generic term is *bexune* (cognate with *begwanem*, "person") (Boas 1932a:211). Other terms for soul apply especially to mankind. These are *bexwenaye* ("man on the body"), *bekwaye* ("man strength"), *begwanemgemtl* ("man's mask"), *tsekwa* ("bird of man"), and *qwalayu* ("life keeper") (Boas 1921:727). The souls of men are egalitarian in the sense that all are associated with the owl. The owl is a sacred bird and is referred to therefore as "owl mask." The Kwakiutl say that every man has an owl belonging to him. If it should be killed he would die. The screech owl is special. It is said to be the soul of a deceased person (see Boas 1932a:221).

Another set of beliefs brings out the special character of souls. The human soul may be generically a bird (ibid:22), but it is also said that the souls of sea hunters go immediately into their killer whale masks, and they go hunting seals (Boas 1921:715). Or, all souls return after death to the ancestor of the clans, or all go to the country farthest inland; or they go to a country like the present and continue to be what they have been on earth (Boas 1932a:216).

8. Bearing most directly on the idea of name as a soul is the apparent identity between the terms for the top of the head, *xlä*, and one of the terms for a name (see Boas 1947:374).

9. *Keso*, the basic term for "crest," also has reference to the seat of rank *(kwas)*, to a title owner *(kwanux)*, to a hereditary owner *(keso nokwa)*, to the expression "fine and beautiful" *(kaso)*, and to "real" *(kas)*. (See, respectively, Hunt ms 14:3458, 3460, 2265, 2276; Boas 1947:356).

10. Thunderbird, also known as Head Winter Dancer, brings down from the sky his great house to give to his son (Boas and Hunt 1905:186). This house, which would seem to be a celestial representation, is copper-covered, and contains within it the Hoxhoq crane, Thunderbirds, Sisiutl, Moon, and Sun. The concept of house as a container that is transported intact from one domain to another bears out the suggestion that it is a form soul. We would then assume that the contents of houses are conceptually linked.

Chapter 4

1. Kwakiutl traditions bring out the opposite side as well. The Dzawadenox tale of Hethlamas, for example, tells of daughters who marry a sky being and acquire from him great treasures, including the Winter Ceremonial (Boas and Hunt 1905:45ff). The theme of supernatural acquisitions from the female side is not common, however, and the tales may simply demonstrate a Kwakiutl desire to deal with the unusual case.

2. The feast name and the Winter Ceremonial privileges have a certain equivalence on the scale of supernatural values. Hunt refers to the feast name as the most important name received in marriage from the father-in-law. It is a great shame, he comments, for a chief not to have a feast name (Boas 1921:786). To lack the name is to lack the right to give a feast. On the analogy of the animal who is a primary donor of his flesh, the feast giver is a secondary donor of life to the tribes, and is himself therefore a center of vitality. Consequently, one who cannot give feasts for lack of a name is as dead. It is understood, of course, that he is dead only in the sense that he lacks the attributes of duality, of not representing an ancestral or mythological being.

3. The *qotexa* is commonly delivered in a box to the son-in-law. His younger brother, his face smeared with charcoal (the warrior insignia), breaks the box, a mode of "sinking" the canoe that has delivered the marriage debt payment. Since *qotexa* means "bad things," or as Hunt has explained, great things that provoke ecstatic madness (see ms. 4:3285), this destruction suggests a parallel to the breaking of a copper, with its implication of a resurrection.

4. Boas wrote that the marriage was annulled after the *qotexa* had been paid (1897:358). Since there are no references to such a custom in the traditional texts, I assume Boas was reporting a postcontact and, perhaps, an unusual event. He may have had in mind the example of a pregnant woman who left her husband because, as Hunt explains, her father had already paid the marriage debt (Boas 1921:348). In another example given by Hunt, a man and his wife deliberately enter into a sham quarrel and separate and come together again so that the original marriage exchanges could be given again. A man who does not pay *qotexa* is, of course, insulting his son-in-law. But, as Hunt explains, it is only in recent days that chiefs do not make the return payment promptly (ibid:295).

5. A black and white design on a ceremonial curtain from Fort Rupert or Kingcome Inlet (Chapter design from Hawthorn 1967:71) depicts at least one symbolic context within which Kwakiutl visualize the copper. A copper is the centerpiece of the design, which also includes the double-headed serpent (sisiutl), a pair of flying ravens, and a rainbow made from two salmon arching downward from the head of the copper. The salmon heads rest against the two heads of the sisiutl who forms the base of the design. The bottom or body part of the copper rests upon the human head

which is always the center of the sisiutl. The two ravens flying upward are placed symmetrically above the arched bodies of the rainbow-salmon. The rainbow is arched over the sisiutl, and the copper is its centerpost, so to speak. It is reasonable to assume, especially from all else we know about the meanings of the elements that their spatial relationships are contrived to record symbolic meanings. I decipher these meanings as follows:

The Sisiutl, commonly thought of as a canoe, is the conveyor of the rainbow, the salmon, and the copper. That is to say, he is a bringer of light of the sky and of wealth of the sea. All the five elements of the design have, at the same time, a common significance as modalities of light. The copper which supports the rainbow is in many associations (see Analytical Index) a shaft of light from the sky. The salmon who are here depicted as the organic components of the rainbow, are commonly associated with copper as a red light. The sisiutl is often depicted as a blazing salmon and as a lightning bolt that paralyzes and contorts people. The raven is the culture hero who first obtained the daylight, fire, the waters of the rivers, the tides, and salmon. He is also a primary antagonist of the Thunderbird (see Boas 1935b:152). As the focus of the entire design the copper is made to appear as the central image of light, and of the unity through light of all the cosmic realms, earth, sky, sea. Perhaps the underworld is implied through the associations of raven with fire, and of fire with access to the lower reaches of ghosts.

Another dimension of meaning is suggested by the treatment of forms as though they had been split down the middle in the plane of mouth to tail. Boas depicted various forms of such split representation in Northwest Coast art and explained them as a transition of the animal form from sculpture to a flat surface that allows the entire animal to be shown (Boas 1951:221ff). In the aforementioned design the theme of split representation is suggested by the absoluteness of symmetry that shows the forms as double. The rainbow is formed by two salmon that might have been split from the tail end to produce two heads. The same treatment is suggested by the theme of the double-headed serpent. The two ravens are in absolute symmetry. As for the copper, the characteristic T-bar that splits the lower and body part is at the precise center at which the entire design could be folded back on itself in such a way as to produce a single raven, a single salmon, and a sisiutl with one serpent head at one end and one human head at the other.

I interpret the meaning of split representation differently from Boas in that I see the artist's aim in depicting the whole animal form as religious rather than technical. In all the examples Boas has shown, the split animal is wrapped around the object it is ornamenting—around a dish, a hat, a bracelet, the circular opening of a house, on blankets and aprons (ibid). The theme of a wrap-around through split representation is in keeping with the idea of the form as a container on the analogy of the animal skin as a covering. From this analogy we have a possible explanation of the use of sisiutl, the mythical being who is permanently shown in split representation, as a magical belt that grants its wearer impregnability. For Kwakiutl the canoe form is also a container. Following out the logic of this line of reasoning one would say then that the entire design as an illustration of the modalities of light conveys the additional theme of light as a comprehensive envelope. For still a different interpretation of the meaning of split representation see Lévi-Strauss (1963b).

Chapter 5

1. *Laxsa* is also a common expression for dying, in the phrase, "he has gone through" (Boas 1932a:212).

2. When initiates return, it is said, "What in the world can vanquish us. Even Baxbakual-anuxsiwae is unable to overcome us" (Boas 1966:218).

Chapter 6

1. The distinction between curing shaman and Winter Ceremonial shaman is genuine, but not absolute. A person "disappearing" in the course of the Winter Ceremonial may sicken and then receive real shamanistic power (see Boas 1921:733–742 for a case history).

2. The myth of Mink and the Wolves (Boas 1930:57–86) sets the Winter Ceremonial among animals prior to the existence of human beings. Thus the animals are granted priority as well as parity. The Laalaxsendayo lineage of Gwetela takes this tradition of wolves as the first Winter Ceremonial performers to be the source of their own rites. The sons of Head Wolf "disappear" as initiates, but are, in fact, ambushed in the woods by Mink and Deer, who kill them. The wolves then use their supernatural powers to try to restore the wolf youths to life, but are thwarted by Mink who has the powers of Sisiutl. In shame at their failure to overcome Mink and his powers, the wolves slink away into the woods to remain forever animals. When the Laalaxsendayo took over the rites from the wolves they added the *hamshamtses* dance. Among wolves there is no Man Eater, and no overt theme of devouring. They are in their natural element. Head Wolf sponsors a Winter Ceremonial because he is downcast at the coming of winter. The tale implies that the animals are primary sources of Winter Ceremonial powers. Deer, a warrior chief among animals, is the first Fool dancer. Deer, Mink, and Raven (Great Inventor) are the constant antagonists of wolves. Raven, who had secretly witnessed the ceremony, passes on his knowledge to the first ancestor of the Laalaxsendayo.

3. The man-eater powers are said to be greater when seized in war than when received in marriage (Boas 1921:1,017)

4. Chief Tlawages meets Cause of Weeping Woman in a stream. Both faint. But he recovers and embraces her until she gives him four treasures, the property obtainer, the property accumulator, the water of life, and the apron that burns everything. She gives him also the name Pulling off Roof Boards (a reference to death). After copulating with her he meets Man Eater who gives him two of his names, Man Eater and Swallowing Everything, the dance of being vomited out by Raven, and another set of powers that include red cedar bark, the fire bringer, the death bringer, the water of life, and the unfailing harpoon (Boas 1921:107–111).

5. "There is no doubt that the winter ceremonial is essentially religious, but it is so intimately associated with nonreligious activities, such as feasts and potlatches, that it is difficult to assess its religious value. It is my impression that its essential religious element lies in the belief in the presence of a supernatural power in and around the village which sanctions all activities." (Boas 1966:172).

Chapter 7

1. In the Soul Catcher dance, property and the human soul are equated. Property is said to symbolize the soul. When the dancer catches a soul he takes a quantity of property from the owner and distributes it among the guests (Boas 1966:195).

2. Woolen blankets are distinct as *pelxelasgeme* (Hunt ms. 14:1463). As for *naenxwa*, it

is to be considered with *naenxsagila,* which means, "half-done, high tide" (Boas 1947:248).

3. They say of the chief who has property to distribute: "Now he have a power" *(tlaxweno-kowa)* [Hunt ms. 14:1725].

4. Blankets are kept in boxes, as were the scalps of enemies (Boas 1921:829).

5. The source of the word "potlatch" is uncertain. *The Oxford English Dictionary* derives it from Nootkan while *Webster's Third New International Dictionary* derives it, by way of the Chinook language, from Chinook jargon—a trade patois of the region. In the early Nootkan vocabularies of Cook (Beaglehole 1967:327) and of Moziño (Moziño 1970:108) *pa'chatle, pa'cheetle,* and *pachitle* are listed as meaning "to give." On the other hand, Sapir and Swadesh (1939:261), acknowledged authorities on the Nootkan language, list "potlatch" as an intrusion from Chinook jargon, and *nahi* as the Nootkan word for "give." Even though the fur trade did not fully develop along the Northwest Coast until after Cook's visit in 1788, native trade may have been active before European contact (see Drucker 1965:169–70). In any case, the Spanish expedition of Pérez and La Bodefa y Quadra of 1774–1775 coming up from the south and crossing Chinook territory, had already preceded Cook.

6. 1. *yaq, yak, yax*

yaq, "to lie dead" (Boas 1947:434)
yaq, "dead body" (ibid:333)
yaqudzas, "place of lying dead on ground" (ibid:472)
yaqawe, "to be beaten" or "to lie dead" (see Boas 1911:459; Hunt 1906:116)
yak, "bad" (Boas 1947:499)
yaxsamex, "bad (angry) words" (Hunt ms. 14:4686)
yaqwas, "give away" (ibid:4690)
yaq, "to distribute" (Boas 1947:508)
yaqwas laxa pesa, "giver of the giver away property" (Hunt ms. 14:2277)
yaxwede, "give away property" (ibid 1:1722)
yaqolas, "place of obtaining property" (Boas 1921:825)
yakwa, "giving away" [to the tribes] (Hunt ms R35:879)
yaextlana, "property" (ibid:1285)

2. *max, maq, mak*

maxotl, "the dead" (Boas 1911:485)
max, "to pursue secretly" (ibid)
maxenox, "killer whale, the one who pursues secretly" (ibid)
maxtsa, "to be ashamed" (Boas 1921:1404)
maxtsolem, "cause of shame" (Boas 1897:344)
mux, "to potlatch" (Boas 1911:504)
maxwa, "property giver" (Boas 1921:1404); "to carry property" (ibid)
amaxagila, "lots of property giver" (Hunt ms. 14:4674)
maxwinox, "potlatch giver" (Boas 1911:504)

3. *pesa, pasa*

pes, "to flatten" (ibid:487)
peseda, "give away property" (Hunt ms. 14:1511)
pesa, "give away" (ibid)
paselatl, "give away property dancer" (ibid:4674); "potlatch dancer" (Boas 1921:898)
peku, "one to whom potlatch is given" (Boas 1911:487)

4. Other Terms

tso, "to give" (Boas 1911:555)
tsasa, "to give" [one pair blankets] (Hunt ms. 14:2253)
tsexede, "thrower away of property" [name] (ibid R35:846–847)

qadzetla, "to walk into house with property" (ibid 1:2290)
qadzelelela, "to go to marry" (Boas 1947:351)
qotexa, "to return bride price" (ibid:217)
kwitl, "to feast in house" (Boas 1911:486).

7. Hunt explains that one who is purely a woman (i.e., has no man's name) does not take part in property distributions. Those who do are known as "men-women" (ms. 14:4135–4136). The woman who takes on a man's name turns into a man, he adds. She blackens her face with charcoal and wears a black headdress and a black head band. Since only half her name is involved she is a man on one side of her body and gives away property to women with her woman's side. In other words, the distribution of property by women among women would seem to be among men-women.

8. Hunt gives an example of distributions by rank: one slave to the first seats in the lineage; one canoe to the first seats in the lineage; 80 sewed blankets to the second rank chiefs; 240 cedar blankets to the commoners (1921:1025ff).

9. Hunt describes the participation of the lineage in a distribution *(pasa)* to the tribes that is planned by their chief (Boas 1921:1340–1344). The chief assembles his lineage, informs them of the number of blankets he owns, and asks them to contribute either an equal amount or more. He says to them:

you will treat me as your chief, and you will give me your property for the potlatch, great numaym, for it will not be in my name. It will be in your name, and you will become famous among the tribes, when it is said that you had given your property for a potlatch, that I may invite the tribes. (ibid:1342)

The lineage mate next in rank replies:

Now rise numaym, let us open our boxes to give property for the potlatch to our chief; for will it be in our chief's name what we shall do? It will be in our name what we shall do. (ibid)

The next in rank may be angry—an appropriate mode of ritual rivalry—and propose excessive giving to the chief. He says:

I am annoyed by our chief, because he asks us too often for property for his potlatch. I shall try to make him ashamed. Therefore, I shall give him one hundred blankets, that we may bury his name under our property. (ibid:1343)

The text concludes with Hunt's observation: "the numaym fellows do not expect the chief to return what is given for his potlatch" (ibid:1344).

Chapter 8

1. In essence the giver reverses himself at the point of distribution by displaying that side of himself that was the awesome killer-devourer. In parallel fashion the receiver

reverses himself to act the role of the originally killed-devoured. Reversals, in this case a necessary double reversal, are in keeping with the ritual objective of sustaining the continuity of life-death reversals. It is a ritual phenomenon similar to shamanistic transvestism. In that instance, the reversal of the sexual poles is in the service of the mystical mechanics of reversing the life-death poles. The "Contrary Ones" of the Plains are in the same ritual tradition. In the Kwakiutl case the setting of the Winter Ceremonial is itself a reversal whereby men return to the original animal condition as Sparrows and Seals.

2. When chiefs are angry with each other, Hunt writes, "they put out the madness of the fire with this thousand blankets" (ms. 14:4691). I take this statement to mean that the antagonism of rival chiefs is the setting for overcoming the voraciousness of fire, which like Man Eater devours property within the cycle of death and resurrection.

3. That rivals are antagonists but not enemies is demonstrated by their ritual interdependence. For example, it is the rival who does the honors of washing the corpse and painting its head with red ochre (Boas 1932a:212). A person's head is painted twice, once after the age of 10 months (the pregnancy period) and again at death. Hence it is a rebirth insignia, and the rival is then the source of resurrection.

Chapter 9

1. The term for wealth is *qoma* (as in Qomogwa), and refers to the blanket worn over the regular skin robe (Boas 1921:1429). Thus there is in the concept an implication of excess.

2. Among the many transformations he brings about, Qanakelak grinds down the teeth in the vagina of Death-Bringing woman after he marries her. In the Kwakiutl context the familiar *vagina dentata* theme concerns the necessary differentiation between the two openings, vagina and mouth. Having two mouths she is the true Death-Bringing Woman. Having been properly differentiated she assumes a requisite dual character of devourer and life-giver.

3. The theme of devouring is sometimes portrayed in Kwakiutl traditions with crystal clarity. The tale of Yaxstatl, for example, depicts a sequence of passages down the figures mounted above each other on a cannibal pole, going in one mouth and out the other. At the same time, it depicts other passages through the alimentary tracts of other beings, that is, in the mouth and out by way of the anus (see Boas 1910:415–442). Mouth to mouth passages are evidently on the analogy of vomiting, portrayals of death and resurrection through rebirth, for reasons already given. The mouth-anal analogy is evidently asexual, demonstrating rather, as Mouse Woman explains, that one can pass through the great Man Eater and come out whole and alive. The patent unity of both themes, in the same narrative, suggests their linked and complementary relationship. The paradigm of the reliable continuity of the life cycle is completed in this tale when the human hero, Yaxstatl, and Man Eater pass orally-anally through one another, achieving in this manner a near identity between eater and eaten, and between donor and seeker of supernatural powers.

In this tale, Mouse Woman (perhaps a counterpoint to rooted woman) instructs a young *hamatsa* initiate on how to deal with Man Eater so as to obtain his dance. She brings him to a spruce tree, which is like the cannibal pole of Man Eater, and remarks:

Now watch me really! for when I come down I shall take you and swallow you whole, and you will go through me, and you will remain alive; and that will be the way done to you by Cannibal-at-North-End-of-World when he will show you this; and you will also do the same to me when you go up. (ibid:429)

After her demonstration, Man Eater arrives to repeat the performance on his true Cannibal pole. He climbs to the top:

and he turned down the Cannibal pole with his face downward, he uttered the Cannibal cry, and entered the mouth of the man on top of the Cannibal pole; and he came out at the mouth of the raven in the middle; and when his body was out of the raven in the middle he uttered the Cannibal cry and entered again the mouth of the man under the raven, and he came out of the mouth of the [Dzonoqwa] at the bottom of the cannibal pole, and he uttered the Cannibal cry when he came out of it. (ibid:433).

The same ascents and descents are repeated by Man Eater and Yaxstatl but with the difference that now Man Eater and Yakstatl swallow men whole at the top. As each comes down he is swallowed by the other and is passed out through the anus: "As soon as his [Yaxstatl] body came out, he took Cannibal-at-North-End-of-World and swallowed him whole, and he also went right through (and came out) at his anus" (ibid:437).

4. The so-called "totem" pole is known as *tsaoxsaye*, which means the "growing pole" or the "stretching pole." The man-eater pole has the same meaning (see Hunt ms. R35:856–857, and Boas 1921:857).

5. The song of Salmon (Boas 1897:475) in honor of guests arriving establishes mythological and symbolic meanings: The present salmon who are guests drawn by the chief arrive in company with the "true salmon," who are the original and mythical proto-salmon. They come to dance for the chief who is hailed as the Post in the Middle of Heaven. They come from the salmon country to dance at the "righthand side of the world," and they tower over, surpass, and outshine all. They are the "true salmon that were." The general meaning is clear. The guests invoke the primordial past and so are accorded high honor, as is the chief to whom they have been attracted. The myth beings are honored as surpassing all. The reference to "outshining" is to the image of salmon as light. Since salmon are also metaphysically fused with copper, so are guests, by extension of the image. Thus, the breaking (killing) of a copper comes to mean the breaking and killing of the tribes who are invited (see also Hymes 1965:331).

BIBLIOGRAPHY

Adam, Eduard Leonhard, 1922, "Potlatch," in *Festschrift Eduard Seler,* pp. 27–45, Stuttgart, Verlag von Strecker und Schröder.

———, 1936, "North-west American Indian Art and Its Early Chinese Parallels," *Man* **36**:8–11.

Bancroft, Hubert Howe, 1887, *History of the Pacific States of North America,* Vol. 27, San Francisco, The History Company.

Barnett, Homer G., 1938, "The Nature of the Potlatch," *American Anthropologist* **40**:349–358.

Beaglehole, J. C. (ed.), 1967, *The Journals of Captain James Cook on His Voyages of Discovery. The Voyage of the "Resolution" and "Discovery" 1776—1780,* 2 volumes, Published for the Hakluyt Society, University Press, Cambridge, Hakluyt Society Extra Series XXXVI.

Benedict, Ruth Fulton, 1932, "Configurations of Culture in North America," *American Anthropologist* **34**:1–27.

———, 1934, *Patterns of Culture,* Boston, Houghton Mifflin.

Birket-Smith, Kaj, 1964, "An Analysis of the Potlatch Institution of North America," *Folk* **6**:5–13.

———, 1967, *Studies in CircumPacific Culture Relations,* Vol. 1, *Potlatch and Feasts of Merit,* Det Kongelige Danske Videnskabernes Selskab Historisk-Filosofiske Meddelelser **42,** 3, Copenhagen.

Boas, Franz, 1887, "Census and Reservations of the Kwakiutl Nation," *Journal of the American Geographical Society,* (New York) **19**:225–232.

———, 1888, "The Houses of the Kwakiutl Indians: British Columbia," *United States National Museum, Proceedings* **11**:197–212.

———, 1891, "The Indians of British Columbia: Lku´ugen, Nootka, Kwakiutl, Shuswap," Sixth Report on the Northwestern Tribes of Canada 1890. *Report of the British Association for the Advancement of Science,* 1891:553–715.

———, 1893, "Vocabulary of the Kwakiutl Language," *American Philosophical Society, Proceedings* (Philadelphia) **31**:34–82.

———, 1895, "Indianische Sagen von der NordPacifischen Kuste Amerikas," in *Verhandlung der Berliner Gesellschaft für Anthropologie, Ethnologie, und Urgeschichte,* Berlin, A. Asher.

———, 1896, "The Growth of Indian Mythologies," *Journal of American Folklore* **9**:1–11. Also in Boas 1940.

———, 1897, *The Social Organization and Secret Societies of the Kwakiutl,* United States National Museum, Report for 1895:311–738.

———, 1909, *The Kwakiutl of Vancouver Island,* American Museum of Natural History, Memoirs Vol. 8, Pt. 2:301–522.

————, 1910, *Kwakiutl Tales,* Columbia University Contributions to Anthropology Vol. 2, New York, Columbia University Press.

————, 1911, "Kwakiutl," see Boas (ed.), *Handbook of American Indian Languages.*

————, 1920, "The Social Organization of the Kwakiutl," *American Anthropologist* **22**:111–126.

————, 1921, *Ethnology of the Kwakiutl,* Bureau of American Ethnology, Thirty Fifth Annual Report, Pts. 1, 2, Washington, D.C., U.S. Government Printing Office.

————, 1924, "The Social Organization of the Tribes of the North Pacific Coast," *American Anthropologist* **26**:323–332.

————, 1925, *Contributions to the Ethnology of the Kwakiutl,* Columbia University Contributions to Anthropology Vol. 3, New York, Columbia University Press.

————, 1927, "Die Ausdrücke fur Einige Religiose Begriffe der Kwakiutl Indianer," *Festschrift Meinhof,* Hamburg, pp. 386–392.

————, 1930, *The Religion of the Kwakiutl Indians,* Columbia University Contributions to Anthropology Vol. 10, New York, Columbia University Press.

————, 1932a, "Current Beliefs of the Kwakiutl Indians," *Journal of American Folklore* **45**:177–260.

————, 1932b, *Bella Bella Tales,* American Folklore Society Memoirs Vol. 25, New York, G. E. Stechert.

————, 1933, "Review of Locher's 'Serpent in Kwakiutl Religion,' " *Journal of American Folklore* **46**:418–421.

————, 1935a, *Kwakiutl Tales, New Series,* Columbia University Contributions to Anthropology Vol. 26, New York, Columbia University Press.

————, 1935b, *Kwakiutl Culture as Reflected in Mythology,* American Folklore Society, Memoirs Vol. 28, New York, G. E. Stechert.

————, 1940, *Race, Language and Culture,* New York, Macmillan.

————, 1947, "Kwakiutl Grammar with a Glossary of the Suffixes," Helene Boas Yampolsky with Zelig S. Harris (eds.), *Transactions of the American Philosophical Society,* (Philadelphia), New Series, Pt. 3:203–377.

————, 1951, *Primitive Art,* New York, Capitol Publishing.

————, 1966, *Kwakiutl Ethnography,* Helen Codere (ed), Chicago, University of Chicago Press.

Boas, Franz (ed.), 1911, *Handbook of American Indian Languages,* Bureau of American Ethnology, Bulletin 40, Pt. 1, Washington, D.C., U.S. Government Printing Office.

Boas, Franz and George Hunt, 1905, *Kwakiutl Texts,* Memoir of the American Museum of Natural History Vol. 5, Publication of the Jesup North Pacific Expedition Vol. 3.

————, 1908, *Kwakiutl Texts, Second Series,* Memoir of the American Museum of Natural History Vol. 10, Publication of the Jesup North Pacific Expedition.

————, no date, *Manuscript in the Language of the Kwakiutl Indians of Vancouver Island,* 14 vols. Special Collections, Columbia University Libraries.

Borden, Charles, 1951, "Facts and Problems of Northwest Coast Prehistory," *Anthropology in British Columbia,* British Columbia Provincial Museum, Victoria, B.C.

————, 1953–54, "Some Aspects of Prehistoric Coastal–Interior Relations in the Pacific Northwest," *Anthropology in British Columbia,* No. 4:26–32.

———, 1962, "West Coast Cross Ties with Alaska," *Arctic Institute of North America* (Montreal), Technical Paper No. 11:949.

Chard, Chester S., 1956, "Northwest Coast–Northeast Asiatic Similarities: A New Hypothesis," *Selected Papers of the Fifth International Congress of Anthropological and Ethnological Sciences,* (Philadelphia), pp. 235–239.

Codere, Helen, 1950, *Fighting with Property,* Monographs of the American Ethnological Society Vol. 28, New York.

———, 1956, "The Amiable Side of Kwakiutl Life: The Potlatch and Play Potlatch," *American Anthropologist* **58**:334–351.

———, 1957, "Kwakiutl Society: Rank Without Class," *American Anthropologist* **59**:473–486.

———, 1959, "The Understanding of the Kwakiutl," in *The Anthropology of Franz Boas,* Walter Goldschmidt (ed.), Memoir No. 89, American Anthropological Association Vol. 61, Pt. 2, pp. 61–75.

Curtis, Edward S., 1915, *The North American Indian,* Vol. 10, New York, Johnson Reprint.

Davy, George, 1922, *La foi jurée,* Paris, Alcan.

Dawson, George M., 1887, "Notes and Observations on the Kwakool People of the Northern Part of Vancouver Island . . .," *Proceedings and Transactions, Royal Society of Canada,* Vol. 5, Sect. 2.

Drucker, Philip, 1939, "Rank, Wealth and Kinship in Northwest Coast Society," *American Anthropologist* **41**:55–65.

———, 1940, "Kwakiutl Dancing Societies," *University of California Anthropological Records* Vol. 2, No. 6:201–230, Berkeley, University of California Press.

———, 1945, "The Antiquity of the Northwest Coast Totem Pole," *Journal of the Washington Academy of Sciences* **12**:389–397.

———, 1951, *The Northern and Central Nootkan Tribes,* Bureau of American Ethnology, Bull. 144, Washington, D.C., Smithsonian Institution, U.S. Government Printing Office.

———, 1955, "Sources of Northwest Coast Culture, New Interpretations of Aboriginal American Culture History," *75th Anniversary Volume of the Anthropological Society of Washington,* pp. 59–81, Washington, D.C.

———, 1965, *Cultures of the North Pacific Coast,* San Francisco, Chandler Publishing Company.

Drucker, Philip and Robert F. Heizer, 1967, *To Make My Name Good: A Reexamination of the Southern Kwakiutl Potlatch,* Berkeley, University of California Press.

Duff, Wilson, 1964, "The Contributions of Marius Barbeau to West Coast Ethnology," *Anthropologica,* n.s. **6**, No. 1:63–96, Ottawa.

Durkheim, Emile, 1947, *The Elementary Forms of the Religious Life,* Joseph Ward Swain (trans.), Glencoe, Ill., The Free Press.

Eliade, Mircea, 1964, *Shamanism, Archaic Techniques of Ecstasy,* Willard R. Trask (trans.) Bollingen 77, New York, Pantheon.

Evans-Pritchard, E. E., 1940, *The Nuer: A Description of the Modes of Livelihood and Political Institutions of a Nilotic People,* Oxford, Clarendon Press.

Ford, Clellan S., 1941, *Smoke from Their Fires,* New Haven, Yale University Press.

Fortes, Meyer, 1953, "The Structure of Unilineal Descent Groups," *American Anthropologist* **55**:17–41.

BIBLIOGRAPHY

Goldman, Irving, 1937, "The Kwakiutl of Vancouver Island," in Margaret Mead (ed.), *Cooperation and Competition Among Primitive Peoples,* pp. 180–209, New York, McGraw-Hill.

———, 1940, "The Alkatcho Carrier of British Columbia," in Ralph Linton (ed.), *Acculturation in Seven American Indian Tribes,* pp. 333–386, New York, Appleton-Century.

———, 1941, "The Alkatcho Carrier: Historical Background of Crest Prerogatives," *American Anthropologist* **43**:396–418.

———, 1970, *Ancient Polynesian Society,* Chicago, University of Chicago Press.

Goldschmidt, Walter (ed.), 1959, *The Anthropology of Franz Boas,* Memoir No. 89, American Anthropological Association Vol. 61, No. 5, Pt. 2.

Gunther, Erna, 1972, *Indian Life on the Northwest Coast of North America,* Chicago, University of Chicago Press.

Hawthorn, Audrey, 1956, *People of the Potlatch: Native Arts and Culture of the Pacific Northwest Coast,* Vancouver, British Columbia Art Gallery.

———, 1967, *Art of the Kwakiutl and Other Northwest Coast Tribes,* Seattle, University of Washington Press.

Hazlitt, William Carew, 1858, *British Columbia and Vancouver Island,* New York, G. Routledge.

Heyerdahl, Thor, 1952, *American Indians in the Pacific: The Theory Behind the Kon Tiki Expedition,* London, Allen and Unwin.

Hoffman, W. J., 1886, *The Midewiwin or "Grand Medicine" Society of the Ojibwa,* Seventh Annual Report, Bureau of American Ethnology, pp. 143–300, Washington, D.C., U.S. Government Printing Office.

Holm, Bill, 1965, *Northwest Coast Indian Art,* Seattle, University of Washington Press.

Hunt, George, 1906, "The Rival Chiefs," in *Boas Anniversary Volume, Anthropological Papers,* pp. 108–136, New York, G. Stechert.

———, no date, see Boas and Hunt, *Manuscript in the Language of the Kwakiutl Indians of Vancouver Island.*

Hymes, Dell, 1965, "Some North Pacific Coast Poems: Problems in Anthropological Philology," *American Anthropologist* **67**:316–341.

Josselin de Jong, J. P. B. de, 1929, "De Oorsprong van den Goddelijken Bedrieger," *Mededeelingen der Koninklijken Akademie der Wetenstrapen* 68, Vol. 1.

Kroeber, A. L., 1923, "American Culture and the Northwest Coast," *American Anthropologist* **25**:1–20.

Lenoir, Raymond, 1924, "Sur l'institution du potlatch," *Revue Philosophique de la France et de l'Etranger* **97**:233–267, Paris, Alcan.

Lévi-Strauss, Claude, 1963a, *Structural Anthropology,* Claire Jacobsen and Brooke Grundfest Schoepf (trans.), New York, Basic Books.

———, 1963b, "Split Representation in the Art of Asia and America," see Lévi-Strauss, *Structural Anthropology,* pp. 245–268.

———, 1963c, *Totemism,* Rodney Needham (trans.) Boston, Beacon Press.

———, 1969, *The Elementary Structures of Kinship,* James Haile Bell, John Richard von Sturmer, and Rodney Needham (trans.) Boston, Beacon Press.

Locher, G. W., 1932, *The Serpent in Kwakiutl Religion, A Study in Primitive Culture,* Leyden, E. O. Brill, Ltd.

Mauss, Marcel, 1954, *The Gift,* Ian Cunnison (trans.), London, Cohen and West. (Translation of *Essai sur le don,* 1925).

[252]

BIBLIOGRAPHY

McClellan, Catherine, 1954, "The Interrelations of Social Structure with Northern Tlingit Ceremonialism," *Southwestern Journal of Anthropology* **10**:75–96.

McFeat, Tom, 1966, *Indians of the North Pacific Coast*, Toronto, McClennand and Stewart.

Moziño, José Mariano, 1970, *Noticias de Nutka, An Account of Nootka Sound in 1792*, Iris Higbie Wilson (trans.), Seattle, University of Washington Press.

Müller, Werner, 1955, *Weltbild und Kult der Kwakiutl Indianer*, Studien zur Kulturkunde 15, Wiesbaden, Franz Steiner Verlag.

Niblack, Albert P., USN, 1890, "The Coast Indians of Southern Alaska and Northern British Columbia," *U.S. National Museum Report for the Year Ending June 30, 1888*, pp. 225–386, Washington, D.C., U.S. Government Printing Office.

Olson, Ronald L., 1940, "The Social Organization of the Haisla of British Columbia," *Anthropological Records* Vol. 2, No. 5:169–200, Berkeley, University of California Press.

———, 1954, "Social Life of the Owikeno Kwakiutl," *Anthropological Records* Vol. 4, No. 3:213–259, Berkeley, University of California Press.

Parker, Seymour, 1964, "The Kwakiutl Indians: 'Amiable' and 'Atrocious,' "*Anthropologica* n.s. **6**:131–158.

Piddocke, Stuart, 1965, "The Potlatch System of the Southern Kwakiutl: A New Perspective," *Southwestern Journal of Anthropology* **21**:244–264.

Quimby, George I., 1948, "Culture Contact on the Northwest Coast, 1785–1795," *American Anthropologist* **50**:247–255.

Rassmussen, Knud, 1931, *The Netsilik Eskimos*, Report of the Fifth Thule Expedition Vol. 8, Nos. 1–2.

Rohner, Ronald P. (ed.), 1969, *The Ethnography of Franz Boas*, Chicago, University of Chicago Press.

Rosman, Abraham and Paula Rubel, 1971, *Feasting with Mine Enemy*, New York, Columbia University Press.

Ruyle, Eugene E., 1973, "Slavery, Surplus, and Stratification on the Northwest Coast: The Ethnoenergetics of an Incipient Stratification System," *Current Anthropology* **14**:603–631.

Sapir, Edward, 1911, "Some Aspects of Nootka Language and Culture," *American Anthropologist* **13**:15–28.

———, 1915, "The Social Organization of the West Coast Tribes," *Proceedings and Transactions of the Royal Society of Canada*, Section 2, Series 3, **9**:355–374.

Sapir, Edward and Morris Swadesh, 1939, *Nootka Texts, Tales and Ethnological Narratives*, Linguistic Society of America, Philadelphia, University of Pennsylvania Press.

Scammon, Charles M., 1968, *The Marine Mammals of the Northwestern Coast of North America*, New York, Dover.

Smith, Marion, 1952, "Culture Area and Culture Depth: With Data from the Northwest Coast," see Tax (ed.), *Indian Tribes of Aboriginal America*, pp. 80–96.

Spencer, Robert F., Jesse D. Jennings, et al., 1965, *The Native Americans*, New York, Harper & Row.

Spradley, James P. (ed.), 1969, *Guests Never Leave Hungry: The Autobiography of James Sewid, A Kwakiutl Indian*, New Haven, Yale University Press.

Tax, Sol (ed.), 1952, *Indian Tribes of Aboriginal America*, Selected Papers of the 29th International Congress of Americanists, Chicago, University of Chicago Press.

Vayda, Andrew P., 1961, "A Re-examination of Northwest Coast Economic Systems," *Transactions, New York Academy of Sciences*, Series II, Vol. 25, No. 7:618–624.

BIBLIOGRAPHY

Waterman, T. T., 1923, "Some Conundrums in Northwest Coast Art," *American Anthropologist* **25**:435–451.

White, Leslie, 1963, *The Ethnography and Ethnology of Franz Boas,* Memorial Museum Bulletin No. 6, Austin, University of Texas Press.

Wike, Joyce, 1952, "The Role of the Dead in Northwest Coast Culture," see Tax (ed.), *Indian Tribes of Aboriginal America,* pp. 97–103.

———, 1957, "More Puzzles on the Northwest Coast," *American Anthropologist* **59**:301–317.

Willey, Gordon R., 1966, *An Introduction to American Archaeology,* Vol. 1, Englewood Cliffs, Prentice-Hall.

KWAKIUTL NAMES AND TERMS

[255]

INDEX